Robert Hess

BR 115
.E3N22

NATIONAL COUNCIL OF THE CHURC[...]   IN THE
UNITED STATES OF AMERICA.   [...]MATION
CENTER.

CHURCH INVE$TMENT$ CORPORATION$ & $OUTHERN AFRICA

G
INDIANA-
PURDUE
LIBRARY
WITHDRAWN
FORT WAYNE

Published for the
Corporate Information Center
Office of the General Secretary
National Council of Churches
475 Riverside Drive
New York, New York 10027
(212) 870-2295

by Friendship Press, New York

© 1973 Corporate Information Center, National Council of Churches.
Produced in cooperation with the Programme to Combat Racism of
the World Council of Churches.

Printed in the United States of America

RELATED RESOURCES

From the Programme to Combat Racism of the World Council of Churches

Time to Withdraw, a booklet which sets forth the persuasive arguments convincing the Central Committee of the WCC to sell the Council's investments in Southern Africa. Churches, financial institutions and individual investors are confronted with the question: where do you stand? (75¢)

Portugal and the EEC, written in cooperation with the Angola Committee of the Netherlands, tells the little known story of the non-effect of Portugal's colonial wars with Angola, Mozambique and Guinea-Bissau on the conclusion of the European Economic Community's free agreement with her. (75¢)

(WCC items are available from World Council of Churches, Room 439, at 475 Riverside Drive, New York 10027.)

Publications from the Corporate Information Center

The Corporate Examiner, monthly newsletter examining actions and policies of major U.S. corporations in the areas of consumerism, environment, foreign investment, labor and minority policies, military production, and corporate responsibility. Includes news of church and other institutional investor actions as well as a "CIC Brief" on a specific company or issue. Church rate: $10.00 per year
Non-church rate: $17.50 per year

Books	Corporate Responsibility and Religious Institutions	$2.95
	Church Investments, Technological Warfare and the Military Industrial Complex	2.00
	The Philippines: American Corporations, Martial Law and Underdevelopment	2.95

CIC Briefs   .60 each
Recent case studies include: (1) The Western Coal Rush: Power, Profits, and Pollution (2) Corporate Social Responsibility Challenges - Spring 1973 (3) An Analysis of the Multinational Corporation (4) Social Criteria in Investment - National Council of Churches Guidelines (5) An Analysis of American Metal Climax and the Environment (6) The Withdrawal Debate: U. S. Corporations and South Africa (7) The Frankfurt Documents: Secret Bank Loans to the South African Government (8) Fall Corporate Challenge: Northern States Power Co. (9) Nuclear Power: The Angel of Death

Other case studies are available on corporations and military contracting and companies with operations in Southern Africa. Write for detailed publications list. Corporate Information Center, Room 846, 475 Riverside Drive, New York 10027.

INDIANA PURDUE LIBRARY JUN 1975 FORT WAYNE

CONTENTS

Page

I. PREFACE

More than a year in the making, <u>Church Investments, Corporations, and Southern Africa</u> is the most extensive study undertaken to date by the Corporate Information Center. We hope that it will be one of the most useful.

We have attempted to look at the issues in detail from three points of view, presenting background on Southern Africa itself, a thorough examination of the corporations invested there, including in-depth profiles on 15 companies, and a listing of church investments in 53 major corporations. Action and resource sections are also included for those wishing more information or desiring to bring about change. To our knowledge, this document is the most complete survey available to church investors on this topic.

We are indebted to many groups, especially those that have been engaged in Southern African studies such as the American Committee on Africa and the Church Project on U.S. Investments in Southern Africa for assistance in compiling this information. The study would not have been possible without the valuable contributions of the Southern Africa Committee South; Tami Hultman and Reed Kramer wrote major portions of the introduction to Southern Africa and the profiles of the 15 largest U.S. corporations.

The cooperation of denominational treasurers was also vital. To them and to all others, including the corporations that participated, we are grateful.

Corporate Information Center
October 1973

II. INTRODUCTION TO SOUTHERN AFRICA

It is possible to select vignettes from any time and place that reflect misery, poverty, and fear. But the stories from Southern Africa that depict suffering and oppression are not selective. Rather, they reflect ordinary, day-to-day reality for millions. Their misery is a product of an authoritarian economic system that exploits workers in urban factories and peasants in semi-feudal rural areas, a system imposed by the rigid racial domination of 5 million whites over 38 million African, Asian, and Coloured people.

South Africa is the financial hub of a subcontinental network comprising five white-ruled nations and three sovereign but economically dependent former British protectorates. These former protectorates - Botswana, Lesotho, and Swaziland - attempt to chart an autonomous path in domestic policy and international relations, but they share a common currency with South Africa and are land-locked hostages of surrounding territory governed by whites.

While having in common non-democratic minority regimes, the five white-ruled nations are not alike. Angola and Mozambique, along with Guinea (Bissau) on the continent's West Coast, are colonies of Portugal, against whom the African people are waging wars of independence. In Zimbabwe, where white settlers in this British colony called Rhodesia illegally declared their independence in 1965, resistance has taken the form of both political protest and sporadic armed conflict. In Namibia, the former German colony of South-West Africa, South Africa is violating United Nations and World Court rulings in its occupation and administration of that country.

The United States already has extensive economic and strategic interests in all the countries of Southern Africa. As struggles against the white-minority rulers intensify, so will the pressure for more direct U.S. intervention. The course of events in the area therefore has implications not only for the people of Southern Africa but for millions of Americans as well.

SOUTH AFRICA

Within South Africa's 471,000 square miles of astonishing physical beauty and diversity, 5 million white descendants of eighteenth-century European settlers enjoy the highest standard of living in the world at the expense of a black population numbering over 15 million. Whites, when they attempt to justify their dominance historically, argue that their ancestors landed in South Africa and spread northward at about the same time that Africans were moving south from East and Central Africa. However, the Oxford History of South Africa cites archeological evidence for habitation of the area prior to the coming of the whites. Remains of the Acheulian or hand-ax culture, for example, dating as far back as 40,000 years, have been found in the Transvaal area.[1]

The first Europeans at the Cape were Dutch settlers, who were supplied with meat by San hunters and herders of the highly disciplined Khoi society, known to whites as Bushmen and Hottentots. In 1664 a Khoi woman called Eva was married to Pieter van Meerhoff, explorer and chief surgeon for the house of Dutch commander Jan van Riebeck. In a chapter of history painful to today's white nation, which reveres van Riebeck as the founder of the country, the commander gave his aide a full military wedding and generous nuptial gifts.[2] From such early liaisons began the Coloured people (now numbering 2 million), who pose an embarrassing problem to the current South African government; no marriage or sexual relations between white and African, Asian, or Coloured are permitted today.

The Question of Land: "Bantustans"

Disintegration of the Khoi society began when it lost its land to the more aggressive foreigners, and land continued to be the major point of friction with local inhabitants as whites expanded their hegemony north from the coastal settlements. Today, land is still a critical South African issue. Under a policy known as "apartheid" or "separate development," the government has reserved for whites 87 percent of the country, which encompasses nearly all arable land, mineral wealth, ports, harbors, and industrial areas. The remaining 13 percent of the land has been assigned to the Africans.

The lands assigned to Africans by the government are called Bantustans, stemming from the practice of miscalling all African peoples "Bantu," a name that correctly applies only to specific linguistic groupings. Bantustans are theoretically "Homelands," the only areas in the republic where Africans can hope to obtain political rights. Only whites may vote or hold office in Parliament. Eight Bantustans -- Zulu, Xhosa, North Sotho, South Sotho, Tswana, Swazi, Tsonga (Shangaan), and Venda -- are designated to receive eventual independence, meaning that certain local matters will be decided by a tribal authority whose head is a South African government appointee. However, all political, security, military, legislative, foreign, and banking affairs would continue under the white regime, and no law may take effect unless it receives the approval of the South African state president.

Hundreds and thousands of Africans, however, are urbanites who have never seen their desginated "homelands." Despite government "influx control" measures (efforts to diminish the number of blacks in white areas by allowing only economically active Africans to stay), a smaller percentage of blacks actually lives in the Bantustans each year.

In addition, Bantustan leaders, under pressure from their people, have not become the docile spokesmen for official policy they were intended to be. Pointing to the impoverishment of the land, and its inability to support adequately even its present population, they are demanding more territory as a precondition of advancement toward independence under apartheid. The existence of Coloured and Asian (primarily Indian) communities creates a special problem for the government. As products of contact between black and white, or as descendants of immigrants, Coloureds cannot plausibly be assigned an ancestral "homeland," yet whites are unwilling to share either power or land with them.

LAND DISTRIBUTION IN SOUTH AFRICA[3]

	% of Population	% of Land Reserved
White	17.6	87
African	70.2	13
Asian	2.8	None
Coloured	9.4	None

Restrictive Legislation

The ultimate political power of the white minority is wielded in terms of restrictive legislation. This legislation also has the effect of controlling economic opportunities of Africans, Asians, and Coloureds.

EXAMPLES OF RESTRICTIVE LEGISLATION IN SOUTH AFRICA
Act, Date, and Repressive Effects

<u>Bantu Administration Act</u>, 1927 Makes it an offense for any African to address a meeting of more than ten other Africans without written approval to do so. Also allows the state president to control the movement of Africans from one black area to another.

<u>Suppression of Communism Act</u>, 1950 The state president may declare an organization unlawful if he is satisfied that it is engaged in activities calculated to further any of the aims of Communism. (Communism is defined very broadly.) Leaders can be banned from attending gatherings and forbidden to write or be quoted even after death.

<u>Bantu Consolidation Act</u>, 1945 Empowers labor officers to issue and terminate working permits of Africans.

<u>Population Registration Act</u>, 1950 Compels persons to obtain a racial classification and be registered accordingly.

<u>Native Act</u>, 1952 Requires persons to possess and carry reference books containing identity, tax receipts, etc., but it is applied mainly to Africans and with severe penalties, often leading to deportation to the homelands.

<u>Bantu Labour Act</u>, 1953 This act prohibits strikes of any sort by Africans, including work slowdowns or joint resignations intended to "induce or compel" an employer to accept certain proposals, change conditions of employment, or hire/fire another employee.

<u>Industrial Conciliation Act</u>, 1956 This law prohibits Africans from being members of registered trade unions and allows the Minister of Labour to regulate the racial composition of employment in certain industries and/or occupations. This policy of job reservation allots the most highly skilled and best paying jobs to whites.

<u>Immorality Act</u>, 1957 Converts into a criminal act sexual intercourse between persons of different races.

<u>Prisons Act</u>, 1959 This act restricts the publication of information on prison conditions and prisoners, including treatment of political and other inmates.

<u>Unlawful Organizations Act</u>, 1960 The state president may declare that any existing organization is an <u>already</u> unlawful organization and its members will be liable to prosecution. Similar powers of dissolution are vested in the state president if in his opinion a new movement has been founded to advance the aims of, or if it is furthering the aims of, any banned organization.

<u>Sabotage Act</u>, 1962 Though ostensibly concerned with the suppression of sabotage, it defines sabotage so broadly as to cover the commission of or intent to commit damage to any property with a political aim. It provides for trial without jury and death sentences even for juveniles. Minimum penalty is five years imprisonment and the burden of proof that the offense was not committed with political intent is on the accused rather than the state.

<u>Publications and Entertainment Act</u>, 1963 Specifies as a criminal offense the freedom of the press where a newspaper strongly criticizes apartheid as unjust.

<u>"90 Day Law"</u>, 1963 Any commissioned police officer may arrest <u>without</u> <u>warrant</u> any-one he suspects of having committed or intending to commit a political offense, or who is in possession of information relating to such an offense. Such person may be detained for interrogation at any place he sees fit until he has answered questions to the police commissioner's satisfaction. Detainment is limited to 90 days, but detainees may be redetained for successive 90-day periods. No court may order the release of a person so detained.

<u>Group Areas Amendment Act</u>, 1965 Gives the Minister of Planning the right to proclaim non-African areas for occupation by whites, Coloureds, or Asians. Out of 57,439 families resettled under this act by 1970, only 1,196 were white.

<u>"180 Day Law"</u>, 1965 The Attorney-General may detain any person when in his opinion there is danger of intimidation (or of absconding) of a person likely to give material evidence for the state in criminal proceedings. The person is detained until the criminal proceedings are concluded or for a period of six months after his arrest. No person other than an officer of the state has access to the detainee. While ostensibly aimed at protecting witnesses or preventing them from absconding, this clause is used by the police for entirely different purposes.

<u>Group Areas Act</u>, 1966 This act allows Asians, Coloureds, and Africans to be employed in "white areas" but restricts their employment opportunities to menial jobs.

<u>The Terrorism Act</u>, 1967 Any police officer from the rank of lieutenant colonel upwards may detain any person in solitary confinement <u>indefinitely</u> if he has reason to believe the person is a terrorist or is withholding information about terrorists from the police. It also provides that no court of law may pronounce upon the validity of any action taken under this section or order the release of any detainees. In addition, it eliminates the defense of double jeopardy. Among the definitions of "terrorist" is any person who cooperates with any international organization to achieve economic, political, or social change.

<u>"Influx Control"</u> (including Pass Laws) Although millions of Africans are still allowed to work in the cities, there is an elaborate system of control over their movements based on the checking and stamping of pass books. With minor exceptions, <u>all</u> Africans working in the cities are treated as temporary migrant laborers. For example, no African residing in a town by virtue of a work permit issued to him is entitled to have his wife and children living with him unless he renounces all rights to live anyplace other than where the government sends him. No friend is entitled to visit him for more than 72 hours. If he loses his job and cannot find another, he must go back to the reserve set aside for his tribe,   even though he may never have been there and may have no relatives there. A further method of depriving Africans residence in urban areas has been the recent reduction or elimination of building schemes for family housing in urban African townships. Bachelor compounds are encouraged, thereby forfeiting all urban rights. Women without husbands are not accepted on housing waiting lists. Widows are not allowed to remain in their houses as tenants when their husbands die - they can only become subtenants or be resettled.

Source: Derived from "Apartheid in Operation," <u>Basic Facts on the Republic of</u>
         <u>South Africa and the Policy of Apartheid</u>, United Nations Unit on Apar-
         theid, ST/PSCA/SER A./12, 1972, pp. 18-26

Economics of White Control

Class divisions in South Africa are almost entirely along racial or ethnic lines. Whites, comprising less than one-fifth the population, supply nearly all managerial, administrative, and skilled personnel. Africans, Asians, and Coloureds form the bulk of the industrial work force and the rural peasantry.

The South African system of "forced" labor enables white mining, industrial, and manufacturing concerns to keep labor costs at a bare minimum. Every black person in South Africa is taxed and is compelled to leave his "homeland" to return to the white urban areas and work in order to pay taxes to a government in which he is unable to participate. The African works under restrictions (see laws above) of migratory labor, the Job Reservation Act, pass laws, restricted trade unions, and the illegality of strikes. "Job reservation" is the practice by which all skilled work is kept for whites. Because of the shortage of white workers, however, blacks are being moved into positions formerly filled by whites. By "fragmentation," which breaks complex jobs down into their simpler component parts, and by "downgrading," which reclassifies jobs into levels of lesser skill, low black wages are maintained even though the skill level of black employees is increasing.

Another aspect of economic control is the government's establishment of "border industrial areas" on the edge of African "homelands" to decrease the flow of Africans to the cities. Besides a supply of cheap and plentiful labor, industrialists are offered tax incentives by the government to establish factories in these areas. Those facilities located in urban areas are prevented from increasing the size of their African work force without special exemptions. The control over black wages and income levels exercised by the whites is reflected in the following charts. Not only are wages paid blacks far below those paid to whites, but also the ratio between white and black income continues to widen:

AVERAGE MONTHLY PAY IN SOUTH AFRICA [4]

	1971	1972
Manufacturing		
African	$ 69	$ 84
White	419	493
Mining		
African	25	29
White	453	505
Construction		
African	65	84
White	433	517

7

WAGES: RATIO OF WHITE TO AFRICAN [5]

	1960	1966	1971	1972
Mining	16.6:1	17.5:1	20.3:1	17.2:1
Manufacturing	5.2:1	5.1:1	5.7:1	5.9:1

Decades of Protest

For more than two hundred years, black resistance to white incursion took the form of armed struggle. In 1906, with the decisive military defeat of the Zulus the conflict entered a new phase. The next half-century was a time of gradually building opposition to minority rule. Large numbers of African, Asian, and Coloured people participated in nonviolent actions designed to gain political rights. As each tactic developed into an effective weapon, however, it was crushed by increasingly harsh repressive measures.

Massive nonviolent resistance peaked with the Defiance Campaign in the early 1950's, when hundreds of thousands of black South Africans, along with some whites, refused to comply with discriminatory legislation. More than 8,000 were jailed during the protests. This second phase ended with overt violence by the authorities. The last nonviolent demonstrations were in March 1960 at local police stations. In the townships of Sharpeville and Langa police fired on the gathered crowds. Sixty-nine were killed and hundreds more injured.

During the 1960's, a policy of armed resistance was formally pursued by the major black political organizations, the African National Congress, the Pan Africanist Congress, and the Unity Movement. Leaders of all three went into exile, while underground organizing continued inside the country. Overt political activity by blacks is once more on the rise in South Africa. During the last two years, there have been bus boycotts, bread boycotts, strikes, and militant speech making. Activists in the movement are jailed, banned, or banished to rural reserves, but others replace them. In many case s Africans, Asians, and Coloureds are acting together in solidarity as "Blacks," despite strenuous government efforts to force wedges among them.

The United States and Southern Africa

United States economic and strategic interests in Southern Africa have important implications for the region. Partly because United States pressure in Southern Africa has been small in comparison to some other areas, such as in Latin America, most Americans are unaware of the steady growth of U.S. involvement there. During the Eisenhower administration, U.S. investment in South Africa alone doubled, and during the Kennedy and Johnson years, it tripled.[6] It has been the presidency of Richard Nixon, however, that has seen not only an accelerated pace of economic investments but also of diplomatic overtures to the minority white regimes.

The Nixon administration is quietly pursuing a policy of deliberately expanded contacts and communication with the white

governments of Southern Africa. . . . In practical terms the
policy has resulted in a number of concrete developments,
ranging from major new economic undertakings, such as the recent Azores agreement with Portugal, to the authorization of
previously forbidden sales of jet aircraft to Portugal and
South Africa.[7]

The above was stated by Robert Smith, Deputy Assistant Secretary of
State for African Affairs. The Azores pact and airplane sales he mentions are
elements of an emerging pattern of increasing concern for the security of U.S.
interests on the continent and in its surrounding waters.

A second focus for U.S. military interest in Southern Africa is the Cape
Sea Route and the region's strategic location at the junction between the Indian
and Atlantic oceans. Oil fields around the Persian Gulf have heavy U.S. investment and supply half the oil imported by Western Europe, 90 percent of Japan's
intake, and 65 percent of Australia's.[8] With the Suez Canal closed, all of the
oil shipped from the gulf to Europe (except for small amounts carried by pipeline)
must pass around South Africa's Cape of Good Hope; and the canal, even if opened,
will not accommodate some of the newest supertankers. White South Africans have
long argued that this fact, plus their own commitment to "Western civilization,"
makes their country a vital link in the defense against Communism.[9]

U.S. Investments Expanding Rapidly

The South African Information Service, a New York-based South African government organization, makes frequent appeals to American businessmen, both through
its own publications and through large advertisements in major financial periodi-
cals. Proclaiming that the republic "offers the richest return on American capital invested abroad except for foreign oilfields," the propaganda emphasizes that
South Africa has the "Western free-enterprise system with political stability."[10]

American corporations do not need to be told. Sales by U.S. companies to the
area began in the mid-1800's. And, as Fortune magazine has observed, businessmen
have long looked with favor on conditions there:

> The Republic of South Africa has always been regarded by
> foreign investors as a gold mine, one of those rare and re-
> freshing places where profits are great and problems small.
> Capital is not threatened by political instability or nation-
> alization. Labor is cheap, the market booming, the currency
> hard and convertible. Such are the market's attractions that
> 292 American corporations have established subsidiaries or
> affiliates there. Their combined direct investment is close
> to $900 million, and their returns on that investment have
> been romping home at something like 19 percent a year, after
> taxes.[11]

South Africa is no exception to the worldwide pattern of expanding U.S. investments in the postwar era. In 1943, the total book value of U.S. capital in
South Africa was $50 million. It increased to $140 million by 1950, $284 million
by 1960, and $800 million in 1970.[12] Actual value is considerably higher than the
book value.

Much of this investment has come from undistributed profits of South African subsidiaries, although significant capital flow from the United States to South Africa has occurred during the past decade despite the fact that in 1962, the United Nations General Assembly called upon member countries to enact sanctions against South Africa. From 1950 to 1969, new capital totaled $215 million and reinvested earnings reached $452 million. All but $8 million of the new investment has come since 1960. [13]

The nature of this economic involvement has changed significantly as U.S. business has helped white South Africa develop an industrialized economy. In 1950, 27 percent of U.S. capital was invested in mining, while 31 percent was in manufacturing. Presently, mining accounts for about 12 percent. Current U.S. investment in manufacturing, about 50 percent of all U.S. capital in South Africa, is nearly twice as high as total investment was in 1960. [14]

NAMIBIA [15]

History

Namibians have been victims of colonial white domination for almost 100 years. The country was colonized by Germany in the 1880's, during the scramble for Africa by the European powers. Settlement by white farmers began in 1891, and the familiar pattern of white seizure of land and the establishment of "native reserves" - or labor reservoirs, as they really were - was soon established. By 1962 the 73,200 whites occupied 48.26 percent of the total land area, while the 431,000 Africans were allocated 25.05 percent of the land in reserves. The remaining percentage was divided between town area, game reserves, government lands and prohibited diamond-mining territory.*

Namibia and South African Control

When World War I began, a South African army occupied Namibia in the name of the Allies. In 1919 South Africa was granted the League of Nations Mandate for the former German colony, on condition that it would "promote to the utmost the material and moral well-being and the social progress of the inhabitants of the Territory." The United Nations acquired the legal responsibilities for Namibia from the League of Nations, and there is ample evidence that South Africa has not fulfilled its obligations to the area. In fact, this is the only case where a power has refused to relinquish the mandate to the U.N. and eventual independence. In 1966, the General Assembly of the United Nations passed a resolution stripping South Africa of the mandate and taking over responsibility for the administration of Namibia in order to prepare for independence. South Africa refuses to recognize U.N. jurisdiction or to allow the U.N. Council on Namibia, the transitional authority, to visit the territory; Namibians began guerrilla warfare in the north in the same year.

In 1968 and 1969, South Africa passed legislation that divided tribal areas into Bantustans and in effect made the country a South African province, extending the domain of apartheid measures. In 1970, the U.N. Security Council passed resolutions declaring South Africa's actions illegal and asking member states to refrain from any relationship that would imply recognition of South African authority over Namibia. Member states were also called on to ensure that their corporations had no dealings with Namibia. Finally, in June, 1971, the World Court ruled that, "The continued presence of South Africa in South West Africa being illegal, South Africa is under the obligation to withdraw its administration from Namibia immediately and thus put an end to its occupation of the territory." [16]

*Ruth First, as quoted in Namibia: U.S. Corporate Involvement.

Economics of South African Control and U.S. Investment

Namibia has been split into two zones - the "police zone" in the south, which includes the cities and the white farming areas, and the northern zone, which includes most of the reserves or Bantustans, where the land is typically infertile and unproductive. Between 55 and 60 percent of the African population is forced to live in this northern zone. In order to produce the required supply of black labor, taxes have been imposed on the Africans; since the land cannot support the population and there is little wage work in the reserves, men are driven to seek work in the white police zone under contract labor.

Book value of U.S. capital in Namibia is listed as $50 million. However, actual investment in the largest U.S.-owned firm, the Tsumeb Coporation, a subsidiary of American Metal Climax and Newmont Mining, alone totals about $75 million. See corporate profiles for a description of the Tsumeb Corporation. [17]

A Workers' Action and Current Resistance

The largest ethnic group in the north are the Ovambos, whose assigned homeland occupies the far northern sector of the territory, stretching to the Angolan border. A strike led by Ovambo workers in Windhoek erupted in December 1971 in widely separated places. It was disciplined, nonviolent, and well organized. Before it ended in February 1972, the strike had involved 30,000 workers in mines, fisheries, and manufacturing plants, as well as agricultural laborers on white-owned farms.

While settlement of the strike did not resolve most of the important complaints of the workers, who wanted not simply improved conditions but the right to make decisions for themselves, it marked the first time that the South African government had ever made concessions to striking blacks.

The tradition of resistance to foreign incursion is being maintained steadily, though not always in such dramatic fashion as the strike. Especially outspoken is the elected chief of the Herero people, leader of the second-largest ethnic group in the country. Chief Clemens Kapuuo has received international attention in pleading for an end to South African rule as well as to the operation of foreign mining firms. Kapuuo elequently explains the African's case:

> This country, which is our country, is being exploited by greedy
> entrepreneurs, robbed of its wealth, and rendered barren for
> the future. One fear is that when freedom finally comes to this
> land, it will be returned to us with no minerals left. [18]

Internal protests are supported by the South West African Peoples Organization of Namibia (SWAPO), which in 1966 launched an armed struggle in the northern area of the country, including the jutting finger of land called the Caprivi Strip, which is nearly surrounded by Angola, Zambia, and Botswana and is therefore an easy access to the territory.

South Africa maintains heavy security in the strip, and land mine explosions and skirmishes are frequent. As SWAPO grows and becomes stronger, the fighting is likely to intensify. The regime is not likely to give in easily, for at stake is not only Namibian mineral wealth but the security of South Africa itself. A united, independent Namibia would provide a 1,000-mile-long desert border that might be used as a staging ground by South African revolutionaries for an attack on the most powerful white stronghold in Africa.

THE PORTUGUESE COLONIES

History

Angola, Mozambique, and Guinea (Bissau) are remnants of the world's last major colonial empire. In four centuries of what Portugal has regarded as its Christian mission of civilizing Africa, Portuguese rule has produced a literacy rate of 3 percent in Angola, 2 percent in Mozambique, and 1 percent in Guinea.[19] It has failed to diminish the predominance of preventable diseases, such as malaria, smallpox, typhoid, and yellow fever. And for ten years it has fought against the escalating independence struggles which could eventually draw the United States into a new "Vietnam" on the African continent.

The Economic Base

Since 1951, the three African territories have been promoted by Portugal from the status of colonies to "overseas provinces" and then to "states." The new stature, however, has not altered the fundamentally exploitative nature of the relationship between them.

In Angola, for example, 88.7 percent of the economically active population is employed in agriculture.[20] One crop - coffee - provides nearly half of Angola's exports to Portugal and the rest of the world. Diamonds and coffee together account for two-thirds of Angola's exports.[21] Thus, the nation's economy rests on one agricultural crop whose fluctuating value is determined by a board dominated by "purchaser" nations and several extractive industries including oil and iron, as well as diamonds which are monopolized by South Africa's De Beers Company.

Portugal is the major exporter to all three African territories, and the terms are to the advantage of the Portuguese. Because Portugal is such a poor country itself, its major exports are items that could easily be produced in the colonies: wines, textiles, olive oil, and canned fish.

The case of cotton illustrates the value to Portugal of its colonies. In 1926 Portugal needed 17,000 tons of raw cotton annually, only 800 tons of which were imported from Africa. The following year, the government decided to solve its problems by relying on the colonies. Areas were designated for obligatory cotton production, prices were established, and a quota for export to Portugal was imposed. At the same time, restrictions were placed on the local manufacture of textiles. By 1960 the manufacture of cotton thread and cloth was one of Portugal's most important industries, and 87 percent of the raw cotton being used came from the colonies.[22]

Forced Labor

In the areas remaining under Portuguese control, semi-feudal structures are still the dominant economic form. When a peasant lives in an area where cultivation of a cash export crop is required, the produce is sold to the Portuguese at controlled low prices. Subsistence foodstuffs must then be bought at high cost on the market. Where large settler or foreign-owned plantations produce export crops, African farmers are driven there to seek work in order to pay their taxes assessed by "head" rather than income.

12

In Angola and Mozambique, many men are made migrant laborers. Through agreements between the South African and Portuguese governments, 100,000 men each year travel south from Mozambique to work in the Repbulic of South Africa's gold mines.[23] The arrangement aids both administrations. Repatriated earnings of the miners give Portugal foreign exchange, and South Africa is guaranteed a steady supply of cheap labor without the political problems posed by a domestic work force.

Wars of National Liberation

Only in this century, after more than 300 years of conquest, did Portugal manage to quell the armed resistance to its colonization and consolidate its rule beyond coastal settlements. For a while resistance continued in mostly nonviolent forms which were met with harsh repression. Educated Africans who attempted to work through channels of the Portuguese administration for change found their efforts blocked.

Time after time, peaceful demonstrations became bloody massacres. Villages of protesting Angolan workers were bombed in 1961. The year before in Mozambique, people who had gathered for a mass meeting with the Portuguese governor of the territory at Mueda were shot by army troops. In 1959, police and troops had shot and killed more than 50 striking dock workers at Pidgiguiti in Guinea. Everywhere, political activity was banned and African leaders were detained or exiled. [24]

By 1964, armed struggle had been launched by the people of all three African colonies. Most progress has been made in Guinea (Bissau) where the Party for the Indpendence of Guinea-Bissau and Cape Verde (PAIGC) now controls two-thirds of the countryside. In Angola and Mozambique, liberation forces hold between one-fifth and one-third of the land area. [25]

In the liberated zones an infrastructure of schools, medical clinics, and village governments is gradually being built. Agricultural production has shifted from the cash export crops grown at Portuguese insistence to food crops needed for self-sufficiency.

While the African populations did not decide lightly to begin what they knew would be a protracted guerrilla war involving much suffering and sacrifice, their leaders emphasize the positive aspects of a development they felt was necessary and inevitable. Through common effort, remnants of tribalism and ethnic rivalry are being replaced by a national culture. Sexual division of production is breaking down and discriminatory practices, such as child marriage for women, are being eradicated. People are practicing skills and learning confidence and self-reliance.

There is no question in the minds of the African people that they will win their fight against Portuguese colonialism - and, if necessary, against Portugal's allies as well. But they know that the more active the support of Portugal from other countries, the longer the wars will drag on. A major factor in the resolution of the conflicts, therefore, is the stance of the United States and other Western powers toward Portugal's colonial policies.

The Question of Security: Portugal's Colonies

The United States government officially supports self-determination for Angola, Mozambique, Guinea-Bissau, and Cape Verde Islands, though opposing violence as a means to achieve it. Yet, between 1950 and 1970, 2,175 Portuguese mil-

itary personnel received American training. In 1969, the present commander of
Portugal's army in Mozambique made a two-week visit to the United States hosted
by the State Department. [26]

U.S. strategic aid to Portugal has also been important. Although military
aid received through the North Atlantic Treaty Organization (NATO) is formally restricted from use in Africa, reports of violations have been numerous. Two examples illustrate the accusations. On January 12, 1968, the Christian Science Moni-
ter, not a supporter of the liberation struggles, carried this report:

> Napalm and phosphorous bombs marked "Made in USA" have been
> dropped in African villages not far from here, according to
> numerous eyewitness reports and photograhps which appear to
> be genuine. The villages are part of Portuguese Guinean
> territory wrestled from Portuguese control by nationalist
> forces.

A 1972 United Nations document refers to reports that the Portuguese are using
T-6G aircraft in Guinea-Bissau. The U.S.-built plane is "reportedly considered
to be one of the most effective anti-insurgency weapons available." [27]

Portuguese strategy in the colonies forms a familiar pattern - creation of
strategic hamlets, pacification programs, heavy dependence on air war and use of
herbicides and defoliants to destroy the food and shelter which support the population. Herbicides ("for agricultural use only") are one of the major U.S. exports to Portugal.   U.S. exports of herbicides to Portugal rose from $57,330
in 1969 to $227,320 for the first 11 months of 1970. [28]

The Nixon administration authorized the sale of Boeing 707's, 727's and 747's
to Portugal. These planes are now used for the transport of Portuguese troops to
Africa, and the sale of Bell helicopters for use in Mozambique was authorized. [29]

The most impressive illustration of U.S. support for Portugal is the Azores
agreement. During his series of summit meetings in 1971-72, President Nixon held
discussions with French President Pompidou in the Azores. He also consulted with
Portuguese Premier Caetano, and together they announced a new agreement which extended the U.S. right to utilize the Lajes base. The U.S. made $436.5 million in
credit available to Portugal, including $400 million through the Export-Import Bank.
This amount is eight times more than Portugal had received in the previous twenty-
five years and more than the total of bank loans to the whole of Africa since 1946.
The agreement does not include any regulations prohibiting goods furnished from
being used in Africa in support of Portuguese forces. [30]

U.S. Investment

Gulf Oil Corporation's Cabinda (Angola) operation, valued at more than $200
million, is the largest U.S. investment in any of the Portuguese colonies (see
corporate profile on Gulf in Angola). Other capital in Angola totals about $50
million, while the total for Mozambique is about $10 million. [31]

In Portugal itself U.S. direct investment more than doubled between 1969
and 1971, from $6 million to $13.6 million. [32]

ZIMBABWE

History

In the fourteenth and fifteenth centuries in central Southern Africa there
flourished a wealthy kingdom whose major city was known as Zimbabwe. To display
and protect their wealth the kings of Zimbabwe had huge elliptical stone fort-
resses constructed. Archeological evidence shows that the builders were ancestors of the Shona people, who still live in the area, and indicates that mining was
done by Sothos (who later migrated to South Africa) as early as 900 A.D. [33]

When explorer Cecil Rhodes spread his economic domain north from South Africa's
gold fields in the late nineteenth century, he claimed the land of Zimbabwe, and
Britain and its settlers have since that time called it Rhodesia.

Whites have occupied Zimbabwe (Rhodesia) less than eighty years. In the 1890's
there were several uprisings by blacks which were severely crushed by whites. Over
the years, the whites in Zimbabwe have entrenched themselves by force and by legislation to the point where presently a 5 percent (250,000) minority controls the
lives of 95 percent (5,000,000) of the people, even though for all this time Britain has considered Zimbabwe a crown colony.

Unilateral Declaration of Independence (U.D.I.)

The white-minority government had been pushing for independence since 1962,
and on November 11, 1965, the Smith government illegally proclaimed a Unilateral
Declaration of Independence. In 1970, following a referendum in which only 0.1
percent of the blacks were allowed to participate, Rhodesia declared itself a
republic, unrecognized by the world community.

A new constitution was drafted very similar to the apartheid structure in
South Africa. Under these laws, the education system is segregated, interracial
worship is illegal, and blacks have been apportioned about 50 percent of the land
(the most underdeveloped sections). The franchise covers only a few blacks - those
with financial and educational qualifications nearly impossible for blacks to achieve
under existing laws and practices. About 80 percent of the blacks live below the
Poverty Datum Line, the barest minimum existence. [34]

Sanctions

In 1966, the United Nations Security Council imposed mandatory sanctions on
Rhodesia and in 1968 widened these sanctions to a total trade boycott. As a result, Rhodesia's economy has suffered, even though consumer goods continue to be
available. One example of the effect of sanctions is seen in the deterioration of
Rhodesian Railways, a crucial artery of commercial intercourse. Thirty-three percent of the estimated development expenditure of the country in 1971 went to hold
together the railroad, whose stagnation had hindered economic prosperity in all
sectors. According to one estimate, if sanctions were ended immediately, almost
all of the nation's foreign exchange for the next three years would be required to
rebuild the railways to handle present needs, which would still represent a three-
year lag between need and capacity. [35]

Industry has suffered the same problems in replacing equipment and obtaining new machinery. The long-term implications are a depressed rate of growth, spiraling inflation, and rising unemployment. The longer sanctions are maintained, the more severe will become the problems.

It is against this background that the position of the United States with respect to sanctions is critical. For in December 1971, under strong pressure from lobbyists on behalf of Union Carbide and Foote Mineral Company, Congress passed the Byrd amendment. This legislation had the effect of lifting sanctions on certain materials on the premise that these materials were "strategically necessary" for the U.S. Thus, the U.S. broke sanctions and allowed these companies to begin the importation of chrome and other metals. The U.S. is 100 percent dependent on foreign sources for chromium. The net effect is to contribute to Rhodesia's illegal white regime.

Opposition

Opposition to the Smith regime has been both consistent and courageous. Numerous black political leaders have been banned, jailed, and placed in detention camps. After a black political organization was banned and 1,400 persons were arrested in 1959, many Africans felt their only recourse was armed struggle against the white government.

During this decade, both violent and nonviolent forms of resistance have become important factors in the Rhodesian equation. The government has been forced to declare a state of emergency in northern and eastern areas, where liberation forces have been successful in winning the sympathy and cooperation of the local population. Confrontations between guerrillas and security troops have become frequent, and several whites have been killed or injured in attacks on their farms. Many Africans have been detained and tortured by the government in an attempt to solicit information about liberation movement activity.[36]

Nonviolent protests have been focussed on negotiations between the British and Rhodesian governments. A tentative settlement was reached in November 1971, subject to the approval of the African majority. A British parliamentary committee, the Pearce Commission, was sent to ascertain African opinion on the proposal, which would have provided for gradual black enfranchisement corresponding to economic and educational requirements but would have deferred majority rule indefinitely. A new black political organization, the African National Council, headed by Methodist Bishop Abel Muzorewa, led the fight against settlement. Despite the argument of settlement supporters that it represented a last opportunity for blacks to be guaranteed a part in the political process, the Pearce Commission was met with a strong, nearly unanimous "No" from Zimbabwe's blacks. Neither intimidation nor persuasion shook their stand of "No settlement without majority rule."

In the United States, legislation was recently introduced in both the Senate (S. 1868) and House (H.R. 8005) to reinstate sanctions against Rhodesia. The legislation would amend the U.N. Participation Act of 1945 so as to reinstate U.S. adherence to United Nations sanctions, thereby halting the imports of chrome ore and other materials from Rhodesia. The Senate Bill was introduced by Senator Hubert Humphrey, Chairman of the Senate Subcommittee on Africa, with Senators McGee, Kennedy, Brooke, Javits, and Case as principle co-sponsors, and 18 additional Senators sponsoring the legislation. The primary sponsors of the House Bill are Representatives DonaldFraser and Charles Diggs, joined by 51 other co-sponsors.

THE WITHDRAWAL DEBATE

For more than a decade the question of foreign investment has been a central issue with respect to apartheid and white-minority rule in Southern Africa. In the United States, Europe, and Africa corporations have been scored for their investment and economic support in countries that carry out oppressive racial and economic policies. Based primarily in Britain, the United States, and some European countries, including France, Germany, and Switzerland, such firms have been called on to withdraw their investments in order to weaken white rule and make possible the realization of black economic and political self-determination. On the other hand, companies and their spokesmen have argued that investment, spurring economic growth, will eventually break down racial economic and political barriers. Some supporters of continued investment have also proposed adopting reform measures in their hiring and training policies, wages, and other benefits provided blacks as the answer to the racial situation in Southern Africa.

The debate on withdrawal has included analysis of U.S. firms and others trading with Rhodesia despite United Nations economic sanctions; the Portuguese colonial territories of Angola, Mozambique, and Guinea-Bissau; and Namibia, whose occupation by South Africa has been declared illegal by the United Nations and the World Court. Discussion over the role of foreign investment in Southern Africa has, however, focused on South Africa because that country has not only the largest foreign investment but is also in the most advanced stage of racial oppression. South Africa has a strong economy with far-reaching effects on the surrounding territories.

The debate over foreign investment and the racially oppressive system of apartheid in South Africa has concentrated on the following three primary arguments:

1. <u>Argument for Increased Investment</u> To promote increased investment and accelerated infusions of technological expertise, in the belief that the economic growth thus stimulated will inevitably alter the economic conditions and social structure and ultimately lead to the involvement of blacks (African, Coloured, and Indian South Africans) in the political process;

2. <u>Argument for Reform</u> To press business interests to raise black wages, offer training and better promotion opportunities for black workers, and plow back a portion of their profits into educational and other benefits for the black community;

3. <u>Argument for Withdrawal</u> To stop providing direct economic and material support to the white-minority regime and advocate the withdrawal of investment and the severing of economic links as the consistent moral alternative which at the same time offers solid support to Southern Africans committed to winning their freedom.

Significance of Foreign Investment in South Africa

Foreign investment has played an important role in the overall support of the South African government, making it possible for the regime to carry out its apartheid policies. The issue of apartheid and foreign investment in South Africa was first seriously dramatized after the tragic shooting of peaceful demonstrators at Sharpeville in March 1960. At this juncture in the Republic (then "Union") of South Africa's effort to administer apartheid policies (enactment of the "Pass

Laws," over which 69 peaceful demonstrators were killed and hundreds more wounded by South African police), international attention exploded over South Africa's apartheid system. Foreign investors, having had historic involvements in South Africa's gold and other mineral industry and since World War Two having played a crucial role in the transformation of the country into a modern industrial economy, were seen as contributing vital support to the racially oppressive regime. In 1960, recognizing the threat to international peace in the turmoil following Sharpeville, the United Nations passed a resolution calling on the South African government to bring about "racial harmony ... and to abandon its policies of apartheid and racial discrimination."[37]

In the aftermath of Sharpeville, the relationship between foreign investment and the internal policies of the white-minority regime became apparent. As foreign capital invested principally in the stock market fled rapidly, depleting the country's foreign exchange by nearly 50 percent by 1961, international confidence in the financial stability of the country diminished. Merton Dagut wrote in his study The South African Economy Through the Sixties that

> The economy hinged on a sharp decline in confidence, as growing unrest in the country and the changing colours on the political map of Africa seemed to presage a large-scale internal conflict of wills, the flow of foreign as well as domestic investment became more hesitant. These uncertainties were clearly reflected in a net outflow of private capital of about R194 ($271) million during 1960. Of the R176 ($207) million was a repatriation of foreign indirect investment via sales of listed securities, and R28 ($39) million was previously South African resident capital being placed abroad. A further net R45 ($63) million of foreign capital left the country during the first half of 1961.[38]

The South African government carried out repressive measures against active African political parties, banning them all, and thousands were arrested and imprisoned. Within a few years after Sharpeville the regime had proven to the international investment community that whites could maintain the order. During the crucial years subsequent to Sharpeville, foreign firms directly invested in South Africa in manufacturing facilities continued providing capital inflow to the shaky regime and economy (between 1961 and 1966, British direct investment averaged over $67 million a year, and U.S. investment over the same period averaged over $33 million a year). In 1965 over $307 million flowed into the country, reversing the preceding year's net outflow of some $50 million.[39] Charles Englehard of Englehard Minerals and Chemicals, holding major mining interests in South Africa, initiated the American South African Corporation to attract American capital back into the country, and other American firms ran advertisements indicating their confidence in the white regime's ability to maintain a suitable investment climate. The South African government also drew on a $40 million revolving credit arrangement provided by a consortium of ten major American banks and received similar credit from European banks as well as the World Bank.[40]

By 1970, ten years after Sharpeville, South Africa's foreign reserves had quadrupled. From 1961 to 1969 British investment, at an estimated 60 percent the largest in South Africa, had increased nearly 700 percent, while investment from the United States increased 400 percent.[41] In 1970, when South Africa faced its largest trade deficit in history, the Financial Gazette noted that "the trade gap has very fortunately been covered by a substantial inflow of capital so that gold and foreign exchange reserves have emerged relatively unscathed."[42] In 1970 the United States sent a record $98.4 million into South Africa.[43]

The historic role of foreign capital in undergirding the South African economy has thus led critics to assert that foreign capital has been an essential support system for South Africa's continued minority rule and racial oppression. "At each stage of the country's industrial development since the Second World War especially," writes journalist Ruth First, "foreign investment has provided the capital equipment and the technological skills which have enabled South Africa to build new sectors of its economy."[44] In recently obtained confidential documents, American and European banks are discovered to have negotiated over $215 million in credit to South African government agencies organized by the European-American Banking Corporation in New York. Directed in part to the steel and electricity development agencies of South Africa, the credit arrangement testifies to the ongoing commitment of foreign capital to South Africa's basic growth and industrial capability.[45]

With an increasing investment stake in South Africa, foreign firms are wedded to the economic and political future of South Africa. Sharing in a growth rate of 8 or 9 percent a year, and with a rate of return on investment one of the highest in the foreign arena (between 17 and 25 percent annually, more than twice the domestic rate), U.S. firms and other foreigners have joined their capital and technology to the overall development objectives of the regime.[46] Thus, investment over the past decade shifted appreciably from emphasis on mining to the manufacturing sector, increasing South Africa's industrial capability to produce locally rather than rely on imports for goods and assembly (see company discussions).

In conjuction with South African public corporations, such as ESCOM (electricity), ISCOR (iron and steel), and SASOL (petroleum), American and other foreign firms are advancing the industrial base and self-sufficiency of the economy in the search for oil, oil refining, petrochemicals, steel, nuclear energy, computers, and other advanced technology.[47] Consistent with the growth in foreign investment has been the Western nations', especially French, supply of arms in building a strong military for the South African government.[48] Although the U.S. and Britain have an official arms embargo against South Africa, the country's military/industrial capability has also developed through foreign investment, especially in metallurgical enterprises, vehicle and chemical plants, and petroleum refineries, and the country has become self-sufficient in production of some weapons, including munitions and rockets (see company discussions). The U.S. government has also recently permitted the sale of "light jet aircraft," technically classified as non-military but which forms a basic component to anti-guerrilla actions.[49]

Through its expanding economic and military power, South Africa today stands stronger not only internally but also externally in its influence over Namibia and support for Portuguese colonialism and Rhodesian white-minority rule. The arguments for investment - reform or withdrawal from South Africa - must be viewed within a military context. South Africa has stated repeatedly that it will assist its white allies militarily to oppose African guerrilla movements fighting for independence and majority rule. Therefore, to strengthen South Africa militarily is to strengthen the military power of all of white Southern Africa.

Argument for Investment

Corporations have been among the foremost advocates of increasing investment in Southern Africa in order to promote progressive change. They argue that through economic progress the apartheid system ultimately will yield to the demands of a dynamic industrial economy. They further maintain that since they comprise a small percentage of the population, whites increasingly are unable to rely solely on themselves for vital skilled labor and management jobs required by a burgeoning economy. In time, they conclude, apartheid restrictions, such as the Job Reservation Act, which states certain jobs must be reserved for whites only, will collapse. Through the gradual economic improvement of the African, Asian, and Coloured populations, living standards will rise, education will become more widespread, and as blacks become acclamated to the Western style of living they will assume political responsibility.

As early as 1967, Chase Manhattan Bank, under criticism for its involvement in the bank consortium and other direct banking activities in South Africa, stated that "U.S. and other foreign investments in South Africa have created a widening range of jobs, training and educational opportunities. These opportunities have helped give the black people of South Africa a higher standard of living than that of the black people anywhere else on the African continent."[50]

In 1970 General Motors' South African managing director echoed this theme, noting with optimism the prospects for industrialization. "The greatest growth (in the U.S.) has followed from industrial development. The same thing is happening here. It is industry almost more than anything else that is and will continue to provide this vehicle for the development of non-white people, because unless there are jobs for them ... there will be no useful opportunities for them."[51]

South Africa's business community shares the "progress through growth" view. Thus, Financial Mail, South Africa's influential business weekly, argues that every new investment "is another ray of hope for those trapped on the dark side of apartheid" and postulates that "economic development will bring change that will loosen chains, just as it did in the Middle Ages in Europe."[52]

Perhaps the most elaborate defense of this position appears in "The Stages of Growth and the Future of South Africa," by M. C. O'Dowd, an officer of the giant South African-owned Anglo-American Corporation.[53] Basing his treatise on The Stages of Economic Growth by American economist Walt Rostow, O'Dowd believes there is historical precedent in Western Europe, Japan, the USSR, and the U.S. for the view that industrial growth and economic expansion bring in their wake successive stages of well-being for all.

The Policy of Reform

A variation of this view argues that reform in employment policies and benefits for African, Asian, and Coloured workers is the necessary course for continued investment. Though some corporations holding this view accept the notion that investment itself will not ultimately challenge the apartheid system, these corporations increasingly consider themselves responsible for and measured by their provision of "reform" programs. Thus, Mobil, IBM, ITT, GM, and other corporations, in response to public questioning of their conduct in South Africa, now make readily available reports showing the improvements they have offered blacks in employment, wage scales, training, promotion, and other benefits.[54]

In July 1972, Time magazine Nairobi-based bureau chief for Africa, John Blashill, articulated the position of change through progressive employment policies in a Fortune article.[55]

In "The Proper Role of Corporations in South Africa," Blashill is critical of those corporations that are not aware of the fundamental changes going on in South Africa, a growing industrial society which, he says, is making apartheid an anachronism. He quotes Harry Oppenheimer, chairman of the large mining firm Anglo-American Corporation: "A country that refuses to allow something like 80 percent of its labor force to do the best work of which they are capable cannot hope to progress as it should or hold its place in the world." He draws two principal conclusions from his extensive research and interviewing. First, he claims that the time for change is "ripe" and only a few companies through their progressive employment practices could be considered in the forefront of change. Second, he notes that withdrawal by U.S. firms, besides creating unemployment for at least 100,000 Africans, "would serve no useful purpose at all.... The withdrawal of American investment would not bring down the apartheid system. More likely, the system would almost certainly cause a violent reaction among South Africa's whites. In fact, American withdrawal might be the only thing that could save apartheid in the long run."

As a result of extensively advertising its efforts, Polaroid Corporation may be the best-known advocate of using investment as a tool of reform. On January 13, 1971, the company announced its response to the Polaroid Revolutionary Workers Movement in Cambridge, Massachusetts, which demanded that the company withdraw from South Africa. With full-page advertisements in seven major U.S. dailies and twenty black newspapers, the company reported it would undertake a one-year "experiment" of dramatically upgrading wages and benefits for black employees and contributing to black education. Polaroid said, "Since we are doing business in South Africa and since we have looked closely at that troubled country, we feel we can continue only by opposing the apartheid system." While recognizing that it is only a small economic force in that country, Polaroid stated it hoped other American businesses could have a "large effect" there.[56]

Since January 1971, according to many U.S. investors, reform has become the key to change in South Africa. In July 1972 Mobil Oil Corporation disclosed its employment picture in South Africa at the request of the United Church Board for World Ministries of the United Church of Christ, noting the advances blacks had made since 1962. Mobil said, "What is needed for the continued improvement of the material well-being of non-whites in South Africa is not disinvestment but greater investment."[57]

Other corporations stressing the same theme have made disclosures of information about their South African operations at the request of religious groups. Ford stated in its 1973 "Special Informational Report to Stockholders" that "the industrialization of South Africa is bringing social and economic changes that will increasingly benefit all groups in that nation.... The presence of American-owned companies in South Africa is a positive factor in encouraging economic progress and equal opportunity."[58]

Similarly, ITT noted in its presentation to church representatives in January 1973, "ITT in South Africa," that productivity and enlightened employment policies are the proper course for companies operating in South Africa. The company proposed to stay and "work for the day of racial equality in South Africa."[59]

Revising its earlier view on investment, Chase Manhattan Bank now states that foreign investors "have both a chance and an obligation to work within these nations (of Southern Africa) to bring about improvements in the education, training, and opportunities available to the non-white populations. American investors, in particular, should bring to bear all of the energy and imagination that have characterized their socially-oriented activities at home. By their policies and examples, they have the occasion to expand the broad and promising horizons of southern Africa for all the inhabitants of those lands."[60] Official U.S. government policy on investment favors the reformers and calls for "enlightened employment practices within the laws of South Africa."[61]

Some well-known South Africans are among the advocates of reform, including writer Alan Paton, who lauded Polaroid for its efforts in South Africa in a 1971 commencement address given at Harvard.[62] Perhaps the most prominent African to champion the view that foreign companies should remain in South Africa and improve conditions, particularly in the "homeland" areas, where 13 percent of the land is designated for tribal settlement, is Chief Gatsha Buthelezi of the Zulu Bantustan. Speaking at the ceremony laying the cornerstone for a $65,000 student center at Inanda Seminary, a church-supported secondary school for African women, Buthelezi praised Mobil Oil Corporation, which is financing the construction. Other black leaders of the homelands have also expressed hope in the potential for economic development of their territories.[63]

Argument for Withdrawal

The view that investment and reform will undermine the apartheid system is opposed by proponents for withdrawal on primarily two grounds. One is that the white regime in South Africa has become more powerful through Western European and United States investment and military assistance, all of which has made possible South Africa's domination of blacks throughout the republic. The other is that the conditions in housing, health, education, employment, and income under which 18 million blacks are forced to live have deteriorated or improved only marginally for a few. Over the past two decades and especially in the 1960's, when foreign investment increased rapidly, white supremacy has continued under the guise of an official government policy of "separate development." The government has established "Bantustans" (homelands), where millions of Africans daily face unemployment, disease, malnutrition, starvation, and death. The migrant labor system draws able-bodied blacks to white urban areas, breaking up families, since only the employable are allowed to live in these areas. Workers are deprived of the right to organize and bargain collectively. Attempting to reduce the number of blacks in white areas, the regime's "Borderland" industrial program attracts industry through use of tax credits and other incentives to establish facilities adjacent to the homelands, where they can draw on an even cheaper black labor supply than the one in white urban areas. The homelands consist of 260 separate land areas encompassing less than 14 percent of the country but supporting 70 percent of the population. Between 1960 and 1968 the government created employment for over 100,000 blacks, but within the homelands fewer than 1,000 jobs developed out of government programs.[64]

In a 1971 African Affairs journal article, "Is Economic Growth Disintegrating Apartheid?" English economist Rick Johnston concluded, "The government is not in fact attempting to literally implement its official ideology of total separate development. The actual goal of apartheid policies is the pragmatic development of an economically powerful white supremacy."[65]

In addition, the thesis that a thriving economy is demanding more black skilled labor and will thus challenge basic white supremacy is simply not true. Protectionist white trade unions have maintained the discriminatory wage and labor structure and will continue to do so. Jobs usually reserved for whites only are often downgraded or fragmented (divided into several parts) when they are occupied by blacks. Moreover, the best jobs are always reserved for whites.

Analyses by economists and sociologists using various statistical data and trends published by South African government, business, and private agencies show that foreign investment has brought no substantial improvement in the standard of living for blacks and in fact has contributed to the worsening of their condition. Analyzing statistics covering the period 1958-70, John Sackur, in a March 1971 London Times article, showed that while white incomes more than doubled in that period, incomes for blacks in white urban areas remained static. The average per capita gain in income for blacks, increasing 65 percent during the twelve-year period, in real terms remained static because of the rise in the cost of living and the population growth. Between 1967 and 1971, the cost of living for blacks rose 31 percent but less than 18 percent for whites. If Africans living in the homelands, primarily dependent on income from fathers and husbands working in the white urban areas and representing nearly half of the over 15 million black population, are considered, African real income has dropped 30 percent since the mid-1950's. Therefore, it is evident that black wages have declined during the last decade, when foreign investment has been most rapid.[66]

Statistics further suggest that as foreign investment has increased, the income gap between blacks and whites has widened. Representing 19 percent of the population, whites have 74 percent of the income. On the average, whites earn at least 13 times more than blacks.[67] South African economist Francis Wilson wrote in Labour in the South African Gold Mines, 1911-1969 that in the mining industry, employing 13 percent of the black labor force in 1970, "black cash earnings in 1969 were no higher and possibly even lower than they had been in 1911." Real cash earnings for whites increased 70 percent during that period. In addition, the gap between white and black earnings has consistently widened, from 11.7:1 in 1911 to 17.0:1 in 1961 and 20.1:1 in 1969.[68] In agriculture, which employed 35 percent of the black labor force in 1970, a similar picutre emerges, with African real income no higher than it was 80 years ago.[69]

In the manufacturing and construction industries, employing 20 percent of the black labor force in 1970, black employment and wages increased during the previous decade. During the same period, white wages rose faster than black wages, thereby increasing the wage gap from 5.1:1 in 1966 to 5.7:1 in 1971. According to recent estimates, future pay increases for blacks would have to be 5½ times greater than for whites simply to prevent the gap from widening.[70]

While American firms propose that investment provides jobs and is helping to uplift blacks, they give no attention to the sheer magnitude of misery and poverty blacks suffer in South Africa. For example, in the Soweto township outside of Johannesburg, the most economically active area in the country, nearly 70 percent of the more than 600,000 blacks live below the Poverty Datum Line (PDL). This subsistence level, $115 a month, is established by the Johannesburg City Council and considers only bare essentials - food, fuel, and transportation - needed for an average African family to survive. The incidence of poverty in other townships is greater. In 1972, the Productivity and Wage Association noted that 80 percent of Africans live below the PDL.[71]

Another income level, the Minimum Effective Level (MEL), established by the Institute of Race Relations in Johannesburg, is higher than the PDL - $170 a month - and includes a number of other essentials considered necessary for subsistence. Using the MEL, at least 85 percent of the blacks in South Africa live below this level.

The Basic Minimal Level - $196 a month - is a new level now considered by some sociologists and doctors in South Africa to be the basic income necessary to begin to alleviate poverty and deficient nutrition among the blacks. Few corporations, American or otherwise, pay their black workers this wage (see company profiles). Ninety-five percent of all blacks in South Africa receive incomes below this level.[72]

Education and Health

The presence of foreign investment has not contributed to the health or educational advancement of blacks. The vast majority of Africans receive only a rudimentary education, a situation which has not changed since 1953 when the government established the Bantu Education Act. Government expenditures remained relatively constant between 1950 and 1963, and in 1963 it was 0.57 percent of net national income. By 1966, however, the percentage fell to 0.396, and presently per capita spending for black education is below the 1950 level. Blacks are provided inadequate elementary and secondary schooling, for which they are taxed, though not compelled to attend, while whites are afforded a free (and compulsory) education. Further, few blacks can enter higher education and are restricted from vocational and technical training schools because of regulations of white trade unions.[73]

Professor J. V. O. Reid of the Natal Medical School has noted that in 1970 the death rate for children in the homelands was 25 times that for white children. Of every 1,000 African children born in South Africa, it is estimated that 530 die before reaching the age of five. The number of cases of tuberculosis, ten times as common among blacks as whites and linked to malnutrition, continues to rise. Medical reports on conditions in the Bantustans show widespread malnutrition, infections, and other diseases due to the lack of meat, milk, and other nutritional foods and access to medical facilities. The 1970 South African census reported that whites have one doctor for every 455 persons, one of the best doctor-patient ratios in the world. The black doctor-patient ratio, however, is 1 to 100,000, and in rural areas the ratio is even lower.[74]

Call for Withdrawal

In light of the evidence that black poverty has become increasingly pervasive in South Africa during the period that foreign investment has increased rapidly, it is difficult to subscribe to the view that foreign investors' reformist measures are significantly helping blacks. Therefore, many individuals and groups within and outside Southern Africa have called for withdrawal of investment.

Espousing a preference for corporate withdrawal is a far more hazardous route for South Africans than remaining silent or opting for reform. Withdrawal of investment is a type of sanction against the present regime, and to advocate action hostile to South Africa is a treasonable offense, punishable by death. The late Chief Albert Luthuli of the African National Congress, exiled from South Africa, is an oft-quoted advocate of withdrawal. In the early 1960's he said,

> The economic boycott of South Africa will entail undoubted hardship for Africans. We do not doubt that. But if it is a method which shortens the day of bloodshed, the suffering to us will be a price we are willing to pay. In any case, we suffer already. [75]

The South African Students Organization, a four-year-old union of African, Asian and Coloured students, is forthright in its condemnation of foreign investment, seeing it as giving stability to the exploitative regime. The Coloured Labour Party, an anti-government political party, supports withdrawal. In 1972, its leader Sonny Leon said on a trip to the United States that investment strengthens the economy, thus enabling the government "to continue with measures that discriminate against the majority of the people."[76] Certainly among the groups most committed to withdrawal and to black political and economic freedom are the liberation movements in Southern Africa. They include FRELIMO in Mozambique, PAIGC in Guinea-Bissau and Cape Verde, MPLA in Angola, SWAPO in Namibia, and the African National Congress of South Africa, which is underground.[77]

In reports on their South African business, corporations give little attention to these organizations' activities. It is clear that U.S. and European corporate and government interests are increasing their stake in preserving the status quo. The possibility of a full-scale race war, with the U.S. siding with the white regimes, is all the more reason that foreign financial and political forces should recognize the injustice to which they are presently contributing. Even from within South Africa itself, the prospects of a race war are discussed. In a recent report issued by the Study Project on Christianity and Apartheid Society, sponsored by the South African Council of Churches and the Christian Institute of South Africa, leading academics concluded that unless "structural changes" took place in South Africa, the country faced "grave dangers" of war. The report noted that "a long-run danger that the entire subcontinent may be engulfed in a race war whose possibilities of escalation are incalculable."[78] As noted earlier in this report, war is already raging in the northern territories of Southern Africa.

Some business leaders have found investment in South Africa contrary to their sense of ethics. Neil Wates, head of Britain's leading construction company, refused to do business in South Africa after conducting a fact-finding mission. The London Observer ran a digest of his report in which Wates concluded that,

> . . . the parallel between Hitler's treatment of the Jews. . . and South Africa's treatment of the blacks today. . . was brought home most vividly to me when I saw blacks being literally herded like cattle through the Bantu Administration Courts. Just as I think with hindsight it would have been totally wrong to do anything to connive at Nazism in those days, so also do I think we should do nothing that would help to perpetuate apartheid.[79]

Church groups have been among the most vocal in endorsing the principle of withdrawal. In November 1971, an ecumenical church team of fourteen visited South Africa to report on U.S. involvement in that society and concluded that,

> Apartheid is wrong.
> It imposes inferior status on some of God's people solely on the basis of their race. It promotes the domination of a large number of these people by a much smaller number of white people. It is dehumanizing and it is undemocratic.
> Based on our understanding of the Scriptures and our first-hand knowledge of the situation in South Africa, we are convinced that any cooperation with or strengthening of apartheid is contrary to the fundamentals of Christianity.
> Some of the participants in this Consultation believe that if American corporations adopted vigorous new policies they might, over a period of many years, make a contribution to improving

the lot of the "non-white" worker.

Most of us believe that American corporations should totally disengage from southern Africa; that the presence of American corporations in which we are shareholders undergirds the system of racism, colonialism and apartheid which prevails in southern Africa.[80]

In Europe, the Central Committee of the World Council of Churches adopted a resolution on August 22, 1972, instructing its finance department to sell holdings in corporations directly involved in white-ruled Southern Africa and urged member churches "to use all their influence, including stockholder action and disinvestment, to press corporations to withdraw investments from and cease trading with these countries."[81]

The British Council of Churches has passed a resolution to set up a committee to develop policy vis-a-vis the World Council of Churches decision. The General Synod of the Anglican Church of Canada has called on member churches to boycott South African goods. The National Council of Churches in the U.S. has called on corporations to withdraw from Southern Africa.[82]

Summary of Withdrawal Argument

The growth of the white-controlled economy in no way ensures economic benefits for the majority of South Africa's black population. The myth that growth automatically benefits all of a country's people has been brought into question with respect to foreign investment and Third World development.[83] The problem in South Africa is compounded by the fact that the regime's policy of apartheid gives no evidence that blacks can even hope for a decent standard of living. As foreign investment works within this system, strengthening both the economy and military capability of the regime, the only moral alternative for the economic and political future of the blacks is withdrawal of support to the white regime.

In light of this, the position of the advocates of withdrawal can be summarized in the following ways:

1. The whole of Southern Africa is in the beginning stages of a major racial war. Africans have been fighting for independence from Portugal in Angola, Guinea-Bissau and Mozambique for over a decade now, and fighting has recently been renewed in Rhodesia. South Africa has stated repeatedly that it would intervene on behalf of its white allies to stop the threat, and has increased its defense budget for 1973-74 by 30 percent to $691.6 million.[84]

Through taxes and sale of products to the military, U.S. companies are bolstering this white military might. That support, critics argue, should cease.

2. The long-range economic programs of the South African government are planned with the clear intention of keeping whites in power. U.S. investors inevitably advance those goals, as evidenced by the history of foreign capital's role in supporting the white regime. In South Africa, Portugal or elsewhere, U.S. taxes paid respective governments, or products supplied, can be used to perpetuate the military capability of the whites to maintain the "order," and a suitable place to do business. Thus, the self-interests of U.S. firms are closely tied to the self-interests and policies of the white regimes.

26

3. The $1 billion of U.S. investment in South Africa is an important factor in U.S. foreign policy calculations. The conflict of interest between U.S. investors and the economic and political self-determination of blacks must be dissolved if justice is to be realized in Southern Africa. Withdrawal of U.S. firms would remove the vested interest in the status quo, apartheid and white-minority rule.

4. Since South Africa is substantially dependent on investment and trade relations with Western countries, withdrawal of U.S. investment from South Africa would signify the dedication of the United States to self-determination and majority rule. Presently, both United Nations and other diplomatic criticism of South Africa has no effect as long as "business as usual" can occur.

Foreign investment does not act as a stimulus for change. Rather, it undergirds the South African economy and the will of the white-minority regime to pursue apartheid policies. Withdrawal by U.S. firms would promote an end to such policies, white supremacy, and the oppression of blacks.

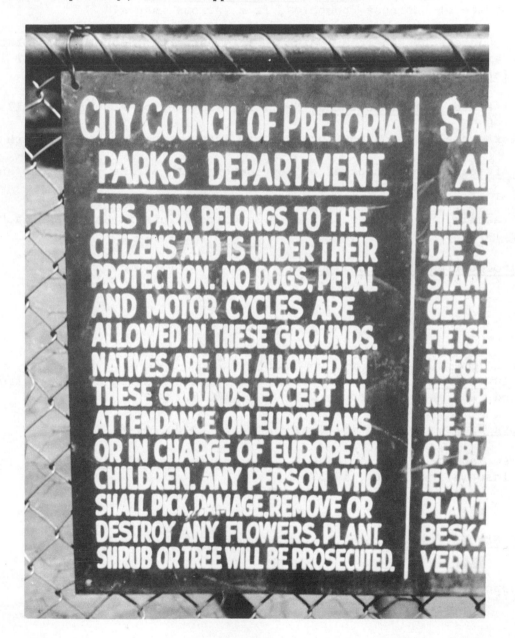

FOOTNOTES

1. Monica Wilson and Leonard Thompson, eds., Oxford History of South Africa, London, Oxford University Press, 1970, Vol. I, pp. 2-14.

2. Ibid., p. 66.

3. A Survey of Race Relations 1971, South African Institute of Race Relations, p. 59; and Muriel Herrell, The African Reserves of South Africa, p. 15.

4. A Survey of Race Relations 1972, pp. 269, 290, 298.

5. Ibid., 1960, p. 217; 1966, pp. 216, 218; 1971, pp. 208, 221; and 1972, pp. 269, 290.

6. Compiled from figures in Survey of Current Business, U.S. Department of Commerce, Office of Business Economics, from various issues.

7. From an address by Robert S. Smith, Deputy Assistant Secretary of State for African Affairs, before the American Society of International Law, April 10, 1972, quoted in Intercom #70, Center for War/Peace Studies, p. 25.

8. Michael Klare, War Without End, New York, Vintage Books, 1972, p. 317.

9. See, for example, Focus on South Africa, Information Service of South Africa.

10. South African Scope, Information Service of South Africa, September and October, 1971.

11. John Blashill, "The Proper Role of U.S. Corporations in South Africa," Fortune, July 1972, p. 49.

12. Survey of Current Business, op. cit.

13. Ibid.

14. Ibid.

15. This and other material for this section were taken from Namibia: U.S. Corporate Involvement, Winifred Courtney and Jennifer Davis, available from the Africa Fund, 164 Madison Avenue, N.Y., N.Y. 10016.

16. New York Times, June 22, 1971, as quoted in Ibid., p. 6.

17. See also Tsumeb: A Profile of U.S. Contribution to Underdevelopment in Namibia, Corporate Information Center, 1973.

18. Ibid.

19. UNESCO Statistical Yearbook, United Nations, 1965.

20. Americo Boavida, Angola: Five Centuries of Portuguese Exploitation, Liberation Support Movement, 1972, p. 41.

21. Ibid., p. 43.

22. Ruth First, Portugal's Wars in Africa, London, 1971, p. 10.

23. Francis Wilson, Migrant Labour in South Africa, Cambridge, Univesity Press, 1972.

24. First, op. cit., p. 15.

25. Profile on FRELIMO, World Council of Churches Programme to Combat Racism, Geneva; Basil Davidson, The Eye of the Storm, London, 1972.

26. The U.S. Military Apparatus, North American Congress on Latin America, New York, August, 1972, p. 44; and William Minter, "Allies in Empire," Africa Today, July-August, 1970, p. 32.

27. United Nations Document A/8723 (Part IV), September 11, 1972, pp. 19-20.

28. U.S. Exports and Foreign Trade, U.S. Department of Commerce, FT410, November 1970.

29. The Faces of Africa: Diversity and Progress; Repression and Struggle, Report of Congressional Study Mission to Africa, Committee on Foreign Affairs, Charles C. Diggs, Jr., Michigan, Chairman, February 7-March 7, 1971, August 5-September 8, 1971, January 7-25, 1972, available from the U.S. Government Printing Office, Washington, D.C., p. 5.

30. Ibid., pp. 189-91.

31. Gulf figures from the corporation. Investment figures from U.S. Business Involvement in Southern Africa, Hearings before the House Subcommittee on Africa, 1971, Part I, p. 269.

32. Ibid.

33. Elspeth Jack, Africa -- An Early History, London, 1970, pp. 60-61.

34. Productivity and Wages Association Survey of 1972, Johannesburg, South Africa.

35. Carl Keyter, Financial Mail correspondent in Rhodesia, interviewed by Tami Hultman and Reed Kramer, Salisbury, September 1971; and the South African Financial Gazette, March 12, 1972.

36. Charles Mohr, "Whites' Fear of Black Rebels Spreading in Rhodesia," New York Times, May 13, 1971, p. 1; see also weekly articles in the Airmail Star, Johannesburg.

37. "Security Council Resolutions on Apartheid," United Nations Unit on Apartheid, No. 24/70, October 1970.

38. Merton Dagut, "The South African Economy through the Sixties," Optima, Johannesburg, September, 1969.

39.   Jim Hoagland, <u>South Africa, Civilizations in Conflict</u>, Boston, Houghton Mif-
flin Company, 1972, pp. 132 ff., 338 ff.; and "Foreign Investment in Apartheid/
South Africa," <u>Objective: Justice</u>, United Nations Unit on Apartheid, Vol. 5,
No. 2, April/May/June 1973, pp. 24-25.

40.   Timothy H. Smith, "The American Corporation in South Africa, An Analysis,"
Council for Christian Social Action, United Church of Christ, Winter, 1971, p. 11
ff.; also, Harold Chesnin and William Lane, Jr., "The Silent Citizen," unpublished
M.A. thesis, 1972, pp. 121 ff.

41.   "Foreign Investment in the Republic of South Africa," United Nations Document
ST/PSCA/ Ser. A/11, p. 19.

42.   <u>Financial Gazette</u>, June 18, 1971.

43.   "Foreign Investment in Apartheid/South Africa," <u>op</u>. <u>cit</u>., p. 25.

44.   <u>Ibid</u>., p. 31.

45.   See the "Frankfurt Documents, Secret Bank Loans to South Africa," in <u>The
Corporate Examiner</u>, July, 1973, published by the Corporate Information Center.

46.   "Industrialization, foreign capital and forced labour in South Africa,"
United Nations Unit on Apartheid, ST/PSCA/Ser. A/10, 1970, Table C21.

47.   "Foreign Investment in Apartheid/South Africa," <u>op</u>. <u>cit</u>., pp. 26 ff.

48.   See, for example, "South Africa; A Southern Gibralter, Ignored by the West,"
<u>Armed Forces Journal International</u>, June 1973, pp. 21-35.
49.   <u>Fact Sheets</u>, American Committee on Africa, June 21, 1971.

50.   "The Silent Citizen," <u>op</u>. <u>cit</u>., Appendix III, p. 247.

51.   Interview with GM Managing Director, South Africa, 1970, by Timothy H.
Smith, investigating for the United Church of Christ.

52.   <u>Financial Mail</u>, September 11, 1970.

53.   Michael C. O'Dowd, "The Stages of Growth and the Future of South Africa,"
officer of the Anglo-American Corporation.

54.   See, for example, "Mobil in South Africa," July, 1972, published by Mobil
Oil Corporation, 150 East 42 Street, N.Y., N.Y., 10017; "Report to Stockholders,"
for 1972 and 1973, IBM, Armonk, New York; "1973 Report on Progress in Areas of
Public Concern," February 8, 1973, General Motors Corporation, Detroit, Michigan
48202;   "Ford and Public Concerns, A Special Informational Report to Stockholders,"
April 27, 1973, Ford Motor Company, Detroit, Michigan; and "ITT and South Africa,
A Presentation to Representatives of the United Presbyterian Church and the Nation-
al Council of Churches, New York, January 18, 1973, ITT World Headquarters, 320 Park
Avenue, N.Y., N.Y. 10022.

55.   John Blashill, "The Proper Role of Corporations in South Africa," <u>Fortune
Magazine</u>, July 1972.

56. "An Experiment in South Africa," New York Times, January 13, 1971.

57. "Mobil in South Africa," op. cit., p. 4.

58. "Ford and Public Concerns," op. cit., p. 21.

59. "ITT and South Africa," op. cit., p. 39.

60. Chase Manhattan Bank, in a reply to a questionnaire prepared by the Corporate Information Center, September 1972.

61. Testimony of David Newsom, Assistant Secretary of State for African Affairs, in U.S. Business Involvement in Southern Africa, op. cit.

62. Alan Paton reaffirmed this position in his article, "White South Africa's only hope for survival," New York Times Magazine, May 13, 1973.

63. The Natal Mercury, September 27, 1972.

64. Rick Johnston, "Is Economic Growth Disintegrating Apartheid?" African Affairs Journal, 1971.

65. Ibid.

66. John Sackur, "Casualties of the Economic Boom in South Africa," London Times, April 26, 1971.

67. Financial Mail, April 18, 1969.

68. Francis Wilson, Labour in the South African Gold Mines, 1911-1969, Cambridge, Mass., University Press, 1972, p. 46.

69. John Sakur, op. cit.

70. Francis Wilson, op. cit., p. 66-67, and Rick Johnston, op. cit.

71. Productivity and Wages Association Survey of 1972, Johannesburg, South Africa.

72. Donald Morton, "Wages in South Africa," Council for Christian Social Action, United Church of Christ, April 1973.

73. "Industrialization, foreign capital...," op. cit., pp. 32ff.

74. Survey of Race Relations 1970, pp. 255 ff.

75. Chief Albert J. Luthuli, Nobel Prize winner and president of the African National Congress.

76. SASO Policy Document, 1972; Address by Sonny Leon in the United States, October, 1972.

77. For more information on liberation movements and their views, see various issues of Southern Africa Magazine, published by the Southern Africa Committee, 244 West 27th Street, N.Y., N.Y., for 1972, and Richard Gibson, African Liberation

Movements, London, 1972.

78. "Whites Cautioned in South Africa," New York Times, June 10, 1973.

79. "A Businessman Looks at Apartheid," The Observer (London), August 8, 1970.

80. "Churchmen Report on U.S. Businesses in Southern Africa," Congressional Record, March 22, 1972, introduced by Charles C. Diggs, Jr., Michigan.

81. "Time To Withdraw, Investments in Southern Africa," World Council of Churches, Programme to Combat Racism, Geneva, January 1973, p. 1.

82. See "Investment in Southern Africa," Department of International Affairs of the British Council of Churches and the Conference of British Missionary Societies, April 1973, published by the British Council of Churches, 10 Eaton Gate, London, S.W.1.; "Being Black in South Africa," Bulletin 204, Anglican Church of Canada, December 1971, revised December 1972, Anglican Church of Canada, 600 Jarvis Street, Toronto, Ontario, Canada; and, National Council of Churches, General Assembly, Dallas, Texas, 1972, resolution on Southern Africa.

83. See, for example, Dr. Ronald Mueller's "The Multinational Corporation: Asset or Impediment to World Justice," presented at the 10th Annual Conference of the Catholic Inter-American Cooperation Program, Dallas, Texas, February 3, 1973.

84. Armed Forces Journal, June, 1973, p. 28.

III. CORPORATIONS IN SOUTHERN AFRICA

The following survey of U.S. corporate activity in Southern Africa is in three parts. The first contains profiles of the fifteen largest U.S.-owned corporations. The second summarizes in chart form the involvement of 37 other U.S. corporations, and part three is a full listing by country of corporations known to have operations in Southern Africa.

The fifteen companies discussed in the first section include the largest American investors in South Africa, Namibia (South-West Africa), Zimbabwe (Rhodesia), and the Portuguese colonies. Their importance in these countries includes not only the size of their investments but also the nature of their business. The firms on the list are all involved in strategically significant industries, such as automobiles, oil, tires, computers, electrical and communications equipment, mining, and earth-moving equipment. In addition, shares in all of the corporations are widely held by the church agencies surveyed in this study.

Twelve of the fifteen corporations supply about 70 percent of all U.S. capital invested in South Africa. (The South African investment of a thirteenth, Union Carbide, is not included because it is not known.) Cabinda Gulf Oil represents about three-fourths of U.S. investment in Angola, and U.S. investment in the other Portuguese colonies is negligible.[1] In Rhodesia, Union Carbide has 70 to 80 percent of total U.S. investment, while in Namibia the American-owned share of Tsumeb Corporation is over 80 percent of the total U.S. investment there. The following chart lists the fifteen corporations with the amounts of investment. Unless otherwise indicated, the amount of investment has been reported by the company. See footnotes for derivation of other figures.

15 LARGEST U.S. CORPORATIONS IN SOUTHERN AFRICA[2]

Name of Firm	U.S. Owner(s)	Approximate Investment ($ in millions)	Percent of Total ($900 million U.S. Investment in South Africa)
SOUTH AFRICA			
Caterpillar (Africa) & Barlow Caterpillar	Caterpillar	$ 6.4	.7
Chrysler South Africa	Chrysler	45.0	5.0
Firestone South Africa	Firestone	25 - 30[e]	3.0
Ford (South Africa)	Ford	80 - 100[e]	11.0
South African General Electric	GE	55*	6.1
General Motors South Africa	GM	125	14.1
Goodyear South Africa	Goodyear	15	1.7
IBM (South Africa)	IBM	8.4*	1.0
Standard Telephone & Cables (plus other companies)	ITT	50 - 70[e]	7.8
3M (South Africa)	3M	12[e]	1.3
Mobil Oil Southern Africa Mobil Refining Co. S.A.	Mobil	87.5	9.7
Caltex Oil (South Africa)	Texaco Standard Oil of California	103	11.4
	TOTAL	$613 - 657	68 - 73%

33

Name of Firm	U.S. Owner(s)	Approximate Investment ($ in millions)	Percent of Total
ANGOLA			
Cabinda Gulf Oil	Gulf	150* - 200^e	over 75% of total U.S. investment in Angola
ZIMBABWE (Rhodesia)			
Rhodesian Chrome Mines	Union Carbide	40 - 45*	70-80% of total
Union Carbide Rhomet	(also has invest-		U.S. investment
African Chrome Mines	ments in South		in Rhodesia
Mitimba Estates	Africa)		
NAMIBIA (South-West Africa)			
Tsumeb Corporation	American Metal Climax	70^e	80-90% of total U.S. investment
	Newmont Mining		in Namibia

* indicates that the figure was obtained from a source other than the company.
^{e} indicates that the figure has been estimated by CIC from available data.

Profiles on the fifteen companies listed above are introduced with general background on the corporation,* covering the corporation's general line of business, locations, importance of foreign operations, and other data providing a wider context for consideration of the corporation in Southern Africa. The premise is that corporations are increasingly looking to foreign fields for growth and earnings. All of these multinational firms are among those debated with respect to their accountabilities to the interests of domestic labor, the economy, and the economic and political authority of any one nation. An important question now being raised is whether multinational corporations can offer hope for economic development not only in South Africa but in the Third World as well.

Several criteria were used to select the thirty-seven additional corporations summarized in the second section:

(1) size of their Southern African involvement and significance of their business to the host country's economy;
(2) extent of stock ownership by and number of church agencies with investments in these firms;
(3) history of activity by church organizations regarding the company's Southern African involvement.

---

* SOURCES: Sources used to develop this introductory material were primarily corporate annual reports, prospectuses and other publications, and Standard and Poor's Corporation Descriptions for the current year. The Fortune 500 rankings are for 1971 and are taken from the May 1972 issue of the magazine. Department of Defense contractors' rankings are those reported for fiscal 1972. Standard references elsewhere in the profiles are (1) a Fortune article on South Africa by John Blashill, "The Proper Role of U.S. Corporations in South Africa," Fortune, July 1972, and (2) the company's response to the "Diggs questionnaire," sent out by Rep. Charles Diggs, Chairman of the Subcommittee on African Affairs, House Foreign Affairs Committee. The listing of responses appears as Appendix 20 of U.S. Business Involvement in Southern Africa, Hearings before the Subcommittee on Africa, 1971, Part I.

Points (1) and (2) were given more weight than (3), and in no instance did a company qualify solely on the basis of (3); most of the corporations that have been the object of church pressure appear in part one.

Every company that apparently had an investment exceeding approximately $500,000 or that had an active sales or mineral exploration effort in Southern Africa was included. When a company's involvement was relatively minor, it was only included when its stock was held by several church agencies in significant quantity. In every case where CIC deemed a company's involvement "significant," there was at least one church agency owning the stock.

The CIC study was undertaken primarily through a questionnaire. In August 1972 questionnaires were mailed to 204 corporations believed to have Southern African operations. Companies were selected from the Commerce Department's Trade List for South Africa, the list appearing in Africa Today (July-August 1970), a U.S. Consul list for Rhodesia, and several other sources. The questionnaire asked for information about the countries where the corporation is involved (South Africa, South-West Africa, Mozambique, Angola, Guinea-Bissau, and Rhodesia), names of subsidiaries, products, and customers. In addition, the questionnaires asked whether firms were involved in Rhodesia prior to the 1965 Unilateral Declaration of Independence and whether they presently have or in the future plan to have investments in South Africa's border areas adjacent to Bantustans. Companies were asked for any policy statements on Southern Africa, for details of benefits (including training programs, charitable contributions, etc.), financial statistics (sales, income, investment, taxes, percent of earnings reinvested and repatriated), and for detailed employment and earnings statistics for 1962, 1968, and 1972 by race and job category.

In October, a follow-up letter was sent to those firms that had not yet responded. Replies or acknowledgements were received from 63 of the 204. Some replies consisted only of brief letters refusing to reveal much of the requested information. The summary chart includes a rating of each firm's response.

Footnotes

1. U.S. Business Involvement in Southern Africa, Hearings Before the House Subcommittee on Africa, 1971, Part I, p. 237.

2. $900 million is the approximate preliminary Department of Commerce figure for 1971, indicating book value of total U.S. investment in South Africa. The investment figures for each corporation do not necessarily correspond exactly to the Commerce Department figures, since they may reflect book value for other years or estimated value of total share capital or other measurements not precisely the same as "book value." However, the figures are accurate enough to present a valid picture of the relative size of the listed firms.

In 1971 the Department of Commerce estimated total U.S. investment in Angola as $195 million. (From U.S. Business Involvement in Southern Africa, op. cit., p. 269.) Gulf's reported investment through 1970, $150 million, accounts for about 75 percent of the total. Currently Gulf's investment may approach $200 million (see text).

The Rhodesia Herald (September 18, 1970) reported that of $56 million invested by U.S. companies in Rhodesia, about $50 million was in chrome mines. Since Union Carbide accounts for about 80 percent of the country's chrome output, it appears that only a small portion of the $50 million is owned by Foote Mineral Company, the other U.S. firm involved in chrome mining in Rhodesia.

U.S. investment in Namibia has been placed at "roughly" $45 million by the Department of Commerce. Together, Newmont and American Metal Climax directly own about 58 percent of Tsumeb; and 58 percent of Tsumeb's value of $70 million is about $41 million, or over 90 percent of the total U.S. investment.

EXAMPLES OF DISCRIMINATORY ADVERTISING FROM SOUTH AFRICAN NEWSPAPERS

AVIS
are looking for a
COLOURED
MECHANIC
who is experienced, sober, married, bilingual and who is prepared and able to reflect the famed Avis 'We Try Harder' image.

If you are responsible and wish to get ahead, you can make a successful career with us.

Your salary will be negotiable and once we've said yes, we would prefer you to start right away.

CONTACT:
DISTRICT MANAGER,
EUGEEN VAN DE
MOORTELE,
51-3768.
(47019)

AVIS
We try harder

Argus 12/6/71

THE CALTEX
ORGANISATION
REQUIRES
CALTEX

COLOURED
LABORATORY TESTERS

for the Cape Town Refinery

Vacancies exist in our Laboratory for Coloureds possessing a Matriculation Certificate with Science as a subject or suitable higher technical education.

Duties involve routine chemical and physical laboratory testing of petroleum products, which would include petrol, diesels, asphalts, jet fuel, etc.

Salaries and employee benefits, which include cafeteria facilities, will be discussed with selected applicants during personal interviews.

Apply in writing to:

The Personnel Superintendent,
Cape Town Refinery,
P.O. Box 13,
MILNERTON,
or telephone 51-1341 (ext 232) to
arrange an interview.

(48977)

Argus 12/11/71

GROSVENORFORD, PAARDEN EILAND
require
EUROPEAN MECHANICS
and
APPRENTICES

Ring Mike Heath or Hew Brooke at 51-4101 or call in at our Marine Drive, Paarden Eiland, Workshops on Saturday morning and have a chat with us.

Grosvenor Ford
SOUTH AFRICA'S LARGEST FORD DEALER ORGANISATION
MARINE DRIVE, PAARDEN EILAND
x (47015)

Argus 12/6/71

Mobil Oil Southern Africa
(Pty) Ltd
have a vacancy for a
YOUNG
EUROPEAN MAN

seeking a career in the exciting field of MARKETING OPERATIONS

Applicants must be bilingual, between the age of 23 and 30 and preferably have had experience in the field of Transport.

Salary will be commensurate with experience, and in addition the Company offers excellent pension, an annual bonus and generous annual and long leave.

Applications to:
THE SUPERINTENDENT
P.O. Box 827
PORT ELIZABETH

Daily Dispatch 11/13/71

PROFILES OF 15 LARGEST U.S. CORPORATIONS IN SOUTHERN AFRICA

AMERICAN METAL CLIMAX
Ian MacGregor, Chairman of the Board
1270 Avenue of the Americas
New York, New York 10020

Founded in New York in 1887 as the American Metal Company, American Metal Climax (AMAX) adopted its present name in 1957 when it acquired Climax Molybdenum Company, making AMAX the principal supplier of molybdenum to the Western world. Ranking #162 on the Fortune 500 list in 1971, with $756.9 million in sales, AMAX is engaged in worldwide mining, smelting, refining, and marketing of minerals and metals. In 1972, sales of over $863 million reached an all-time high, with net earnings of $66 million. AMAX's molybdenum and iron ore operations accounted for over 50 percent of the company's net earnings in 1972, with the remainder accounted for by aluminum smelting and fabrication, fuels and chemicals (coal, carbon, potash, and petroleum), base and specialty metals (lead, zinc, copper, nickel, and others), and income from minority-owned companies. Major domestic mines and plants are located in such states as Colorado and Pennsylvania (molybdenum mining and processing), Arizona (copper mining in a joint venture with Anaconda), California, Washington and Chicago (aluminum smelting), Missouri and Oklahoma (lead-zinc mining and processing), New Jersey (metals refining), and New Mexico (potash). With the 1969 acquisition of Ayrshire Coal Company (now AMAX Coal Company), AMAX is a major strip-miner of coal, with properties principally in Illinois and Indiana and recently acquired interests in the Western coal fields of Montana and Wyoming.

AMAX's overseas operations have historically played a crucial role in the company's business and continue as areas for expansion of sources for raw materials, processing plants, and markets. In 1972, AMAX's foreign assets were located primarily in Europe, Canada, and Australia. In Australia, where some 55 percent of the company's foreign assets are concentrated, AMAX is active in iron ore mining (Mt. Newman Iron Ore Project), with a consortium of companies serving the Japanese steel industry. AMAX is also considering plans to mine bauxite and construct an aluminum smelter in Australia, along with the possibility of establishing an aluminum smelter in Puerto Rico, and is exploring for nickel. The company is engaged already in a joint venture with a French firm (Societe Miniere et Metallurgique de Penarroya, S.A.) to develop lateritic nickel deposits (strip-mining of nickel) in New Caledonia. The nickel will be refined at the company's Port Nickel, Braithwaite, Louisiana, plant beginning in 1974. In Canada, AMAX has a 75 percent interest in the Heath Steele Mines (lead-zinc-copper) in New Brunswick province and recently acquired interests for the mining of potash in Saskatchewan. In Europe AMAX operates a number of plants in Holland, Germany, Italy, and England (e.g., molybdenum processing and aluminum fabrication), including exploration activities for oil in the North Sea.

AMAX's minority investments, a principal source of income for the company over the years, have diminished since 1967 as a major contributor to the company's overall earnings from 25 percent to 14 percent. Nevertheless, the company maintains important investments in such countries as South Africa (O'Okiep Copper Company), Namibia (Tsumeb Corporations), Botswana (Botswana RST Limited), Zambia (RST International), and Canada (Canada Tungsten Mining Corporation). Investments in these and other companies increased by $20 million over 1971. AMAX carries out an active search for metals worldwide. In 1972, major explorations took place in Canada, Iran, Australia, the Fiji Islands, Indonesia, New Caledonia, Austria, Portugal, and the Republic of Ireland, as well as in the United States.

NEWMONT MINING CORPORATION
Plato Malozemoff, Chairman of the Board
300 Park Avenue
New York, New York 10022

Newmont Mining Corporation was incorporated in 1921 as a family-owned vehicle for managing the founder's oil and mining investments. After the stock market crash in 1929, the company began utilizing its portfolio to help finance new ventures into mining, principally in gold. Until 1939 the company's income was primarily accounted for by the Empire Star Mines Company, Ltd., of California and other gold-producing interests in Nevada and Canada. By 1939 the company was collecting more from investments in copper-mining firms (Hudson Bay of Canada, Rhodesian Anglo-American, Phelps Dodge, Kennecott, and Magma) than from its gold operations. From the Second World War to the present significant copper-lead-zinc mining operations in South Africa (O'Okiep) and Namibia (Tsumeb) contributed major earnings to the company. This "African" phase of Newmont's history allowed the company to consider projects much larger in scale than previously possible. Newmont is involved in the mining of copper, lead, zinc, gold, uranium, nickel, oil, and natural gas. Major mining subsidiaries (50 to 100 percent owned) in addition to those previously mentioned include Carlin Gold Mining Co. in Nevada; Idarado Mining Co. in Colorado; Dawn Mining Co. in Washington (uranium); Newmont Oil Co., which mines and markets oil and natural gas in North Slope of Alaska, Canada, and the U.S. and conducts exploration in Australia and other places; Resurrection Mining Co. in Colorado; Granduc Operating Co. in British Columbia, Canada; Atlantic Cement Co. in New York; and a number of minority investments, including in the Tsumeb Mine (Namibia), Palabora Mining Co. (South Africa), and Southern Peru Copper Corp. (Peru), among others.

For many years income derived from foreign operations have accounted for about 50 percent of Newmont's total income. Such "dependency" on foreign sources led the company in the early 1960's to expand domestic and Canadian interests in order to offset foreign income. In 1970 foreign operations accounted for about 32 percent of income, excluding Canada, and in 1971 22 percent, again excluding Canada. Newmont carries out an extensive exploration program, spending over $22 million in 1970 and 1971. Areas of exploration include Alaska, Arizona, California, Colorado, Montana, Nevada, Utah, and Wyoming in the United States and Canada, Australia, South Africa, Lesotho, Indonesia and the Philippines abroad. In Indonesia the company has a 15-percent interest in an Indonesian company that is planning to strip-mine nickel deposits.

Newmont and AMAX in Southern Africa

Newmont and AMAX each have several different types of Southern African investments. This study is focusing on one jointly-owned venture:
Tsumeb Corporation Ltd.
Tsumeb, Namibia (South-West Africa)

Newmont's other Southern African investments include:

O'Okiep Copper Company
Nababeep, Cape Province

Newmont owns 57.5 percent of the stock and is manager of O'Okiep, the second-largest copper producer in South Africa.

Palabora Mining Company
Palabora, Transvaal

Newmont owns 28.6 percent of Palabora, South Africa's largest copper operation, controlled and managed by Rio Tinto Zinc of the United Kingdom.

Maluti Holdings	Newmont manages and owns 50 percent of this dia-
Maseru, Lesotho	mond-exploration operation; U.S. Steel owns the
	other half.

Highveld Steel and	Newmont owns 14.5 percent of Highveld, which is
Vanadium Corporation	controlled by the giant South African mining firm,
	Anglo-American.

| Newmont South Africa Ltd. | A wholly-owned subsidiary involved in mineral explor- |
| | ation throughout South Africa and Namibia. |

Newmont owns 32.8 percent of the common and preferred stock of Foote Mineral Company, an American firm involved in chrome mining in Zimbabwe (Rhodesia). Newmont is also part of a consortium -- with U.S. Steel, International Nickel Company, and Tsumeb -- which is conducting base mineral and diamond exploration in Botswana.

AMAX's other Southern African investments include:

| O'Okiep Copper Company | An 18 percent stake. |

Botswana RST	AMAX manages and owns 30 percent of this firm,
	which is developing a nickel-copper property in
	Botswana.

Roan Consolidated Mines	AMAX owns 20 percent of this company, which is
	controlled by the Zambian government and operates
	that country's copper mines. Formerly, through
	Roan Selection Trust, AMAX owned a significant
	part of Zambia's copper industry.

Tsumeb Corporation is Namibia's largest producer of base metals, including refined lead, blister copper, and zinc concentrates, with by-products of silver, germanium, and cadmium. The corporation operates mines in Tsumeb and Kombat and a smelter at Tsumeb. A third mine, Matchless, was closed in 1972 but may be re-opened in the future.

A consortium of companies purchased the Tsumeb property in 1947 for about $4 million. It was formerly German-owned and had been inoperative for several years. Currently, Tsumeb Corporation represents an investment of more than $70 million.[1]

Newmont and AMAX have voting control of Tsumeb, and Newmont manages the company. There are ten other shareholders of record,[2] but over 90 percent of the stock is owned by six major companies, all registered outside Namibia.

OWNERSHIP OF TSUMEB CORPORATION LTD.[3]

Newmont Mining Corporation	(U.S.A.)	29.18%
American Metal Climax Corp.	(U.S.A.)	29.18
Selection Trust Ltd.	(U.K.)	14.25
O'Okiep Copper Company	(South Africa)	9.50
Union Corporation Ltd.	(South Africa)	9.00
South West Africa Co. Ltd.	(U.K.)	2.38
	TOTAL	93.49%

The Tsumeb investment has been profitable for Newmont and AMAX. Through 1971, Newmont received dividends totalling nearly $86 million, for an average annual rate of return of more than 300 percent on its original outlay of $1.2 million.[4] AMAX dividends have averaged 470 percent annual return on its original investment.

Tsumeb Exploration Company Ltd., in which Tsumeb Corporation owns 75 percent, is involved in exploration throughout Namibia. The South West Africa Company owns the other 25 percent. Tsumeb Corporation also holds a 20 percent interest in an exploration venture managed by Anglo-Transvaal Investment Company. The company is also reported to be involved in a consortium with Newmont, U.S. Steel, and International Nickel which is undertaking a major search for base metals and diamonds in Botswana.[5]

Relations to Government

Tsumeb's relationship with the South-West African administration and the South African government can be summarized under two headings: (1) participation in the government-run contract labor system; and (2) support for continued South African occupation of the territory, in defiance of the World Court and the United Nations.

Throughout its history, Tsumeb has obtained almost all of its African labor through the government's South-West African Native Labour Association (SWANLA). In 1971, over 11 percent of the contract labor force, 5,000 out of 43,000, was employed by Tsumeb. SWANLA handled workers like freight; each was assigned an order number and given a standard contract to sign. Workers had no bargaining rights under the contract, which spoke of the employer as "the said master" and employees as "the said servant."[6]

In a letter to the South African Prime Minister in late 1971, two Namibian church leaders described some of the system's ill effects: "There can be no doubt that the contract labor system breaks up a healthy family life because the prohibition of a person from living where he works hinders the cohabitation of families."

The contract labor system was the focus of a nationwide strike in Namibia during late 1971 and early 1972. Tsumeb, the largest employer of contract labor in Namibia, was seriously affected by the walkout of about 80 percent of its African work force. Without consultation with striking workers, the government, major employers, and African tribal leaders worked out a settlement that eliminated some of the harsher aspects but essentially left intact the contract labor system. SWANLA was replaced with a network of recruiting offices in African areas, the old contract was replaced by a written agreement between employer and employee, and workers were given the right to quit their jobs as well as some choice of employer.

Newmont vice-president David Pearce, who also serves as Tsumeb managing director based in New York, flew to Namibia during the strike to participate in negotiations. He did not meet with Tsumeb's dissident workers while there, although he and other employer representatives had a discussion with the Africans who make up the Ovamboland Council.[8] Forty-five percent of Namibia's population and most of the contract laborers live in the northern region called Ovamboland, which has been given limited self-rule by the South African government. All members of the council are appointed by the government.

After Pearce's return, Newmont expressed pleasure with the terms of the settlement, saying that the strike had "ended satisfactorily for employers, employees, and Governments" and that "most of the demands of the striking workers were granted."[9] In contrast, a South African reporter noted, "The contract system ... remains intact."[10] One strike leader, who in February urged workers to accept the agreement, charged five months later that the government and employers were not keeping their promises and that unrest remained high throughout the territory.[11]

Since its inception, Tsumeb Corporation has paid over $150 million in taxes to the South African government. Its 1970 taxes accounted for 8.6 percent of the territory's budget; its sales contributed over 15 percent of Namibia's gross domestic product.[12]

AMAX and Newmont have been accused of supporting South African occupation of Namibia not only through tax payments but also by the very fact of their presence in the territory. The International Conference on Namibia, meeting in Brussels during June 1972, resolved that investments by foreign companies gave economic and political encouragement to South African rule.[13] The United Nations Security Council has also called upon states to discourage private investment in Namibia.[14]

Tsumeb's continuing and intensive exploration efforts, aimed at ensuring future earnings, will also contribute indirectly to the ability of South Africa to remain in Namibia. This exploration, costing at least $1 million each year,[15] is directed toward not only extending the life of presently operating mines but also the discovery of new deposits.

Finally, to view Tsumeb's involvement from the perspective of the Namibian people, it is important to look at what is happening to the territory's natural wealth. Ninety percent of Namibia's mineral output comes from the mines owned by Tsumeb Corporation and the Consolidated Diamond Mines, and both companies expect to exhaust their major reserves in the next twelve to fifteen years.[16] Clemens Kapuuo, a well-known Namibian leader and head of the Herero people, has expressed the concern felt by many Namibians: "We ask for the immediate removal of foreign mining firms; we demand that the mineral rights of this nation be protected to prevent them from being totally removed before they can be applied to the building up of this country for the well-being of all its people."[17]

Wages and Benefits

During 1972, Tsumeb's African workers received wage increases ranging from 10 percent to 40 percent and averaging 25 percent. The smaller, 4 percent increase given white workers contributed little to the enormous differential between white and African wages. Management points out that African wages must be seen in the context of non-cash benefits (or wages in kind) offered by the company in the form of "free food, housing, medical care, recreation, and on-the-job training for blacks" and stresses that "any inflation in the cost of living in these major elements of cost is borne entirely by the company."[19] The most recent pay rates (August 1972) supplied by Newmont to CIC appear in the following chart.

MONTHLY WAGES AT TSUMEB CORPORATION [19]

August 1972   (R1=$1.33)

| AFRICANS | | | WHITES | | |
Minimum	Maximum	Average	Minimum	Maximum	Average
$24*	$146	$39 - cash	$300**	----	$490 - cash
$28		$43 - kind			***

*   The lower figure is the minimum for above-ground work; $28 is the minimum underground.
**   Estimated.
*** The company reports no figures on non-cash (kind) wages paid to whites.

Company statements never mention non-cash benefits for white workers, and officials have been unable to supply CIC with any figures. On occasion the company has denied that such benefits for whites exist, but Tsumeb advertisements for miners in South African newspapers enumerate many.[20]

Compare the following conditions: Africans receive a tiny bunk in a barracks; whites get a free house or a subsidized furnished apartment. Africans are given seven days' paid leave at the end of each six-month contract period; whites have thirty days' paid vacation, plus a large bonus after one year's employment. Although Africans receive free medical care (for themselves, not their families), Tsumeb's responsibility is only for a pre-employment check-up and matters not covered by Workmen's Compensation. The company has no obligation "where illness or injury is due to the employee's own misconduct or actions."[21] For white employees, the company pays for life insurance and subsidizes medical insurance (which also covers members of their families). The cost of bringing one white worker and family to Tsumeb (from South Africa, England, etc.) is certainly far greater than the expense of a return bus ride from Ovamboland to Tsumeb. And finally, the company's outlay on the long list of recreational facilities for whites (including golf, tennis, bowling, cricket, swimming, rugby, soccer, skittles, squash, horse riding, flying, and a modern cinema) must be considerably larger than for those provided Africans. In addition, at least some whites receive money for their children's educational expenses, a privilege not granted to African employees, whose children's schools are never free, often hard to reach, and vitally important for future opportunities.

Although Newmont management can supply no figure for the cost of "non-cash" wages paid to white employees, such remuneration is clearly quite high. And, therefore, to the company's frequent reminder that cash wages for Africans are only part of the story must be added the observation that the same is true for whites. The wage gap is wide, indeed.

Companies' Position on Investment in Southern Africa

In 1972, the Episcopal Churchmen for South Africa filed a shareholder resolution with both AMAX and Newmont asking for disclosure of information about Tsumeb's operations covering the company's history in the country and relations with workers and government. AMAX opposed the proposal by stating that although it owns 29.2 percent of Tsumeb Corporation, Limited, "the Company does not directly conduct any business in South Africa or South West Africa, and it has no officers or employees stationed in those countries." AMAX also asserted in the proxy statement, "In the opinion of Management the Annual Meeting of Shareholders is not the place for airing of grievances or the solicitation of general information about the politics of countries within which the Company has investments and the reactions of local companies to political factors in those countries."[22]

Newmont management, in recommending a vote against the proposal, stated the following:

> The proposal to request information is unprecedented in the massive volume of detailed operating data to be presented as well as in its quest for historical information and geopolitical analyses respecting South Africa and South West Africa. Such information, pertinent as some of it may be in some other contexts, is not clearly relevant to a stockholder's interest in arriving at an informed business judgment on the retention or the evaluation of the worth of mining properties, in some of which your Corporation has held an interest for well over a quarter of a century....[23]

Companies' Release of Information

Officials of AMAX and Newmont cooperated with CIC in preparation of a document on Tsumeb during 1972. They supplied almost all of the information requested and thus were not asked to complete the questionnaire.

History of Actions Against the Companies

During the Namibian strike in early 1972, AMAX and Newmont were the focus of U.S. concern and received inquiries and protests from various groups and individuals. The Episcopal Churchmen for South Africa, an organization of Episcopalians interested in Southern Africa, filed a shareholder resolution with both companies requesting "full disclosure" of the companies' activities in Namibia and South Africa.

Both firms opposed the resolutions. At the Newmont meeting Chairman Plato Malozemoff announced adjournment before the resolution had been discussed, but following a protest from Dr. Howard Schomer, representing about $2 million in shares owned by the United Church of Christ, Mr. Malozemoff reconvened the session. Speaking in support of the resolution at the AMAX meeting were the Rev. Dillard Robinson, on behalf of the Episcopal Church, Theo Ben Gurirab, from the South-West African People's Organization, and Julius Duru, a Nigerian student representing the Colorado Conference of the UCC. The resolutions received less than 3 percent of the shareholder vote from both companies.

Ian MacGregor, AMAX chairman, promised a full report on the information requested; as of October 1973 the document had not been issued. In 1973 the Episcopal Churchmen for South Africa filed shareholder resolutions with Newmont and AMAX urging the companies to withdraw from Namibia. Also in 1973, the Pension Boards and the Board for Homeland Ministries of the United Church of Christ filed a resolution with Newmont urging the corporation to adhere to "principles of fair employment" in international operations. Because of a late ruling by the Securities and Exchange Commission, however, the resolution did not appear on the company's proxy materials.

Footnotes

1. Much of the data about Tsumeb Corporation was learned or confirmed in conversations and correspondence with Newmont and AMAX officials during early and mid 1972. The figure on total investment in Tsumeb is computed from various figures released by the companies. A more detailed breakdown appears in "Tsumeb: A Profile of U.S. Contribution to Underdevelopment in Namibia," published by CIC, April 1973.

2. Erwin A. Weil, Vice President and Secretary of AMAX, in a memorandum to the Securities and Exchange Commission regarding the AMAX Proxy Statement, March 2, 1972.

3. Various annual reports of Newmont, AMAX, O'Okiep, Selection Trust, South West Africa Company, and Tsumeb Corporation.

4. Newmont annual reports, 1947-71; total dividend figure compiled from the reports by Terence Strom, Columbia University School of Business.

5. "South Africa: An Explosive Mining Potential," Engineering and Mining Journal, November 1972, p. 271.

6. "Employee Contract," South West Africa Native Labour Association (photocopy).

7. "Open Letter to His Honour The Prime Minister of South Africa," Bishop Dr. L. Auala, Chairman of the Church Board of the Ev. Luth. Ovambokavango Church, and Moderator Pastor P. Gowaseb, Chairman of the Church Board of the Ev. Luth. Church of S.W.A. (Rhenish Mission Church), (mimeo), June 30, 1971.

8. D. O. Pearce, in a telephone conversation with Reed Kramer, CIC, January 24, 1972.

9. "Statement of Newmont Mining Corporation," February 4, 1972, p. 12.

10. Observer, London, January 30, 1972, p. 6.

11. Windhoek Advertiser, July 7, 1972, p. 1; and The Star, Airmail Weekly edition, Johannesburg, July 22, 1972.

12. Advertisement in Wall Street Journal, September 5, 1969; Tsumeb Annual Report, 1970; and G. M. Leistner, "South West Africa's Economic Bonds with South Africa," in A. Lejeune (compiler), The Case for South West Africa, London, 1971, p. 223.

13. Resolutions of the International Namibian Conference (mimeo).

14. Security Council Resolution 283, 1970, para. 7.

15. J. P. Ratledge, General Manager of Tsumeb Corporation, interviewed by Tami Hultman and Reed Kramer, Tsumeb, Namibia, March 9, 1971.

16. Ibid.; and South West Africa Survey 1967, South African Department of Foreign Affairs, p. 71.

17. Clemens Kapuuo, in a letter and enclosure to London solicitors, September 3, 1971, reprinted in Leonard Lazar and Roger Murray, <u>Namibia: 'Ill Fares the Land . . .'</u>, The Africa Bureau, London, 1972; also reprinted as United Nations Document S/10356.

18. "Statement of Newmont Mining Corporation," <u>op</u>. <u>cit</u>., pp. 10-11.

19. Data supplied to CIC by Newmont Mining Corporation.

20. <u>Sunday Times</u>, Johannesburg, September 26, 1971, and July 9, 1972.

21. "Agreement of Employment," Tsumeb Corporation, Ltd., (photocopy supplied by Newmont officials).

22. Proxy Statement, American Metal Climax, Inc., April 6, 1972.

23. Proxy Statement for Annual Meeting of Stockholders, May 1, 1972, Newmont Mining Corporation.

CALTEX PETROLEUM CORPORATION
J. M. Voss, Chairman of the Board
380 Madison Avenue
New York, New York 10017

Caltex Petroleum Corporation was formed by Texaco and Standard Oil Co. of California (SoCal) in 1936 when the two companies arranged consolidation of certain of their foreign interests. Caltex is 50-percent owned each by Texaco and SoCal and is engaged in exploration, producing, transportation, refining, and marketing in the Eastern Hemisphere, principally east of Suez. It is also responsible for the major Southern African interests of the two companies. Brief descriptions of both corporations follow.

TEXACO INC.
Maurice F. Granville, Chairman of the Board
135 East 42nd St.
New York, New York 10017

Incorporated in Delaware in 1926, Texaco is the third-largest U.S. oil company and one of the leading integrated organizations in the petroleum industry. From crude oil and natural gas liquids, the company manufactures petroleum products including automotive, aviation, marine, home, and industrial fuel oils, asphalts, industrial lubricants and oils, gases and gas by-products, petrochemicals, oil burner equipment, lawn food products, and other related products. Texaco brand names include Sky Chief, Fire Chief, and Texaco gasoline and Green Chief lawn food. In 1971 the company ranked #8 on the Fortune 500 list, having over $7.5 billion in sales. Approximately two-thirds of the company's earnings come from operations in the Western Hemisphere, particularly the United States, Canada, and Libya. Of Texaco's total worldwide gross production of 4 million barrels a day, 907,000 barrels come from operations in the United States, having production second only to Saudi Arabia operations. Texaco is also a major military contractor, ranking #48 on the Department of Defense list in 1972, with over $24.7 million in contracts. Like other oil companies, Texaco is concerned about the domestic energy crisis. Its 1972 annual report stated, "We badly need an energy policy--especially an import policy--designed to encourage domestic refiners to expand refining capacity. The growing energy shortage also points to the urgent need to develop additional petroleum resources in this country. The tax laws should encourage production and assist in meeting the heavy financial burden of installing facilities to meet environmental standards."

Having 67 subsidiaries, Texaco has operations in 86 countries, including exploration, production, marketing, and research facilities and tanker routes and pipeline routes. The Middle East is Texaco's principal source of crude oil outside of the United States. However, the company has stated that as oil-producing countries in that region demand increasing concessions from foreign-based oil companies, new sources of oil must be found. Throughout 1972 the company carried on intensive negotiations with members of the Organization of Petroleum Exporting Countries (OPEC), made up of Arab oil-

producing countries. Agreement was reached with Persian Gulf countries in
response to OPEC for an ownership position in the oil-producing concessions.

Texaco hopes that significant production increases in Indonesia
will provide increasing flexibility in foreign crude oil supplies. The
company also has exploration activities in 43 countries, 9 in the Western
Hemisphere and 34 in the Eastern Hemisphere. Recent oil discoveries have
been made not only in Angola but also in Indonesia, Saudi Arabia, Dubai,
Nigeria, West Germany, Ecuador, and the United States. Texaco also is
exploring in the North Sea, has exploration rights in the Gulf of Thailand
and offshore Korea, and has contracted for exploration rights with the
Philippines. Texaco markets and manufactures in 135 countries, having
facilities both in developed countries and in developing nations such
as Brazil, Trinidad, South Vietnam, and the Philippines.

STANDARD OIL CO. OF CALIFORNIA
Otto Miller, Chairman of the Board
225 Bush Street
San Francisco, California 94104

Incorporated in Delaware in 1926, Standard Oil Co. of California
(SoCal) is the fifth-largest United States oil company, whose operations account
for more than 6 percent of the non-Communist world's petroleum production.
The company manufactures from natural gasoline and crude oil gasoline,
lubricating, fuel, and gas oil, greases, asphaltic emulsions, detergents,
agricultural sprays, napthas, solvents, and waxes. SoCal's brand names
include Standard, Chevron, and RPM for gas and oil products and by-products,
and Ortho, Chevron, and Oronite for chemical products. In 1971 the company
ranked #12 on the Fortune 500 list, having $5.1 billion in sales. The company
markets in 38 of the 50 states and bases 20 of its 57 refineries in the
United States. Its domestic production accounts for approximately 20 percent
of that worldwide. SoCal is also a major military contractor, ranking #39
on the Department of Defense list in 1972, with over $57.5 million in contracts.

The company was involved in a major environmental class action
suit in February 1971. Schoefeld et al. v. Standard Oil Co. of California
et al. included five classes claiming damage to personal property and to the
ecology of the San Francisco Bay region caused by a massive oil spill resulting from the collision of two SoCal tankers in the bay. The company has been
found guilty on a number of counts in the case but escaped with paying minor
damages.

SoCal has 92 subsidiaries and markets in approximately 75 countries.
Approximately half of its oil production is from Saudi Arabia, which is
seeking increasing control over its own oil supply. The company's 1971
annual report noted, "Preliminary discussion began in late January 1972,
concerning government 'participation' in oil operations, as expressed in
resolutions adopted by the Organization of Petroleum Exporting Countries.
Efforts are continuing in order to find a satisfactory solution to this
problem." Outside the United States the company's other major sources of
oil are Indonesia, Iran, Libya, and Canada. The company is exploring
in 32 locations and made recent discoveries in Canada, Ecuador, the North
Sea, Saudi Arabia, Libya, Australia, and Indonesia. Of the company's 57
refineries, 15 are in Europe and 15 are in the Far East.

Caltex in Southern Africa

Caltex Oil (South Africa) (Pty.) Ltd.
P. O. Box 714, Cape Town

Standard of California also has two wholly-owned U.S. incorporated subsidiaries: Chevron Oil Company of South Africa
Chevron Oil Company of South-West Africa.
Texaco also owns several Southern African subsidiaries:
Regent Petroleum South Africa, Ltd.,
Regent Petroleum South-West Africa,
Texaco Africa, Ltd., in Angola. (in a joint venture)
In Mozambique, the Caltex affiliate is Caltex Oil, Ltd.

Caltex (South Africa), established in South Africa in 1911, "operates a 43,000 barrel a day oil refinery in Cape Town and markets a full range of petroleum products, mostly of local manufacture, throughout the Republic." Assets at the end of 1971 totalled $103 million.[1] According to a press report, the company made pre-tax profits of R18 million ($23 million) in 1970.[2]

Chevron and Regent each own 50 percent of several concessions off-shore South Africa and Namibia (South-West Africa). They have conducted "geological and geophysical work" in each area.

Texaco Africa markets petroleum products in Angola. Since 1968, the company has been involved in both onshore and offshore oil exploration and recently in production. The Mozambique affiliate of Caltex is involved in marketing.

Relations to Government

The strategic importance of oil gives special significance to the Southern African operations of Standard California and Texaco. Oil is one of the few natural resources not yet discovered in South Africa, and the government is actively involved in the search for the "black gold." Caltex, like Mobil, has made a crucial contribution to the country's ability to function with outside oil sources. The Portuguese government is likewise eager to discover more oil reserves in Angola, where Gulf has been pumping since 1968.

According to a Texaco official:

Caltex has equity interests in two Rhodesian companies, a marketing and a refining company. Since the imposition of sanctions by the United Nations, Caltex involvement in the activities of these companies has come to an end. Rhodesia nevertheless obtains necessary petroleum products from other sources.[3]

However, a November 1967 United Nations document (No. A/6868) states that Caltex extended its storage facilities to help in the white Rhodesians' efforts to prepare for international embargoes.

Wages and Benefits

Caltex has released much less employment data than Mobil. The reply to CIC states that Caltex (South Africa) has 2,000 employees, including 700 Coloured, Asian, and Africans and 1,300 whites. No wage data was contained in the reply, but reference was made to an article in the July 1972 issue of _Fortune_, where Caltex's average black wage is said to be $139 per month; the minimum is $111, below the Poverty Datum Line.

The company states that an "increasing number" of Coloured, African, and Asian employees are moving into more skilled positions previously held by whites. These include sales representatives, truck operators, refinery operators, laboratory technicians and testers, fieldmen and gaugers, printing press operators, depot superintendents, store assistants, and clerks.[4]

The company did not provide detailed information about wages or benefits but stated that "Caltex (S.A.) has been among the leaders of local and foreign-owned companies in providing merit opportunities, pension benefits, salary and wage administration, working conditions, and safety programs." An official outlined Caltex employment policy under three points:

1. Adhere to the principles of equal opportunity and equal treatment for all racial groups and practice this principle to the best of our ability within the laws of the Republic of South Africa.
2. Pay the rate for the job irrespective of race. Hence, salary administration is based on paying the same scales of remuneration. All positions are graded by means of job evaluation procedures, and salary ranges assigned by means of periodic personal surveys.
3. Have a common pension plan to cover all employees whether skilled or unskilled, White or Non-White.[5]

Company Position on Investment in Southern Africa

CALTEX: In replying to CIC, Caltex (U.S.A.) made no statements about company policy on Southern Africa. However, the firm has expressed itself through advertisements in South African publications. For example, on October 6, 1972, the company placed a full-page ad in the _Financial Mail_ entitled "The search for South African Oil." Stating that the search is a risky venture (less than one chance in fifty of success), the ad says the risks are "well worth taking. In the interests of us all."

TEXACO made several statements in replying to CIC. The operations of Texaco in Angola have "contributed very substantially to the economic and social development of Angola and all of its people by serving industry, agriculture, and the development needs of the regions of the Territory that were once remote and inaccessible."[6]

Concerning Rhodesian sanctions:

It must be assumed that this forced withdrawal of foreign managements has worked to the detriment of the nonwhite Rhodesian population through the removal of economic opportunities. Moreover, the imposition of these sanctions during the past five years has not brought about a change in Rhodesia's racial policies.[7]

The concluding paragraphs of Texaco's letter contain some general observations about the company's approach:

> It may be of interest to you to know that Texaco operates directly or indirectly in some 135 countries and territories in the non-communist world. But the commercial presence of Texaco subsidiaries or affiliates in these politically diverse countries and territories does not necessarily indicate approval on Texaco's part of the policies of a given host government.
>
> It has always been and continues to be a strict policy of Texaco never to become involved in the politics of any country in which it operates or has an investment. It must abide by all laws and regulations of a host country.
>
> Texaco believes that a society's progress toward tolerance, human dignity, and freedom is intimately bound up with that society's economic progress. Its fundamental position on doing business in the countries and territories of Southern Africa or anywhere else is based on its conviction that Texaco's contributions to economic and social development, over the long term, will benefit all of a country's or territory's people.[8]

Company's Release of Information

Texaco, Standard Oil of California, and Caltex sent letters in response to the CIC inquiry. As evident from the text above, much information requested was not supplied by any of the firms. Texaco and Standard Oil of California gave no reply to the Diggs questionnaire.

Footnotes

1. Caltex reply to CIC; letter to Ronald L. Phillips, Research Director, CIC, from J. D. Tierney, Manager, Public Relations, Caltex Petroleum Corp., August 29, 1972.

2. Sunday Times, Johannesburg, March 14, 1971.

3. Texaco reply to CIC; letter to Ronald L. Phillips, Research Director, CIC, from Kerryn King, Senior Vice President, Texaco, Inc., September 8, 1972.

4. Caltex reply to CIC.

5. Ibid.

6. Texaco reply to CIC.

7. Ibid.

8. Ibid.

CATERPILLAR TRACTOR COMPANY
W. H. Franklin, Chairman of the Board
100 N.E. Adams Street
Peoria, Illinois 61602

Incorporated in California in 1925, Caterpillar Tractor is the nation's leading manufacturer of earth-moving and related equipment for construction (highways, airports, dams, housing), agriculture (land-clearing, harvesting), foresting, cargo handling, mining (excavation, hauling), petroleum (pipeline, oil site, and oil and gas distribution), and other industries. The company also produces diesel engines for land and marine applications. Among the largest U. S. firms and with some 65,000 employees worldwide, Caterpillar ranked 40 on the Fortune 500 list in 1971, with $2.2 billion in sales. Caterpillar also provided construction and land-clearing equipment for the war in Southeast Asia.

According to recent annual reports, equipment for the mining industry, particularly for coal, has contributed to the growth in company sales. The demand for energy sources, such as coal by utilities, both in the United States and abroad -- e.g., Japan -- constitutes an important market area for Caterpillar products. Consistent with the rapid growth in foreign business for major U. S. firms, Caterpillar is heavily dependent on foreign markets for exports and is increasing its manufacturing capability abroad as well. In 1971, the company's foreign sales accounted for nearly 49 percent of total sales. With 19 subsidiaries operating in 17 countries, including Brazil, Panama, Mexico, Canada, England, France, Belgium, South Africa, Hong Kong, Singapore, Japan, and Australia, Caterpillar also has marketing outlets in 156 countries. Over 20 percent of the company's total work force is employed abroad.

Caterpillar's multinational activity is evidenced in the variety of major projects in which its equipment is involved. Caterpillar products are used in Japan in construction of highways, railways, airports, and seaports and on industrial and residential sites through Caterpillar Mitsubishi Ltd. The company provides equipment for Southeast Asia's forest, oil, tin, copper, and nickel resources, and the company sold more than 200 machines for a new copper mine in the Solomon Islands' Bougainville copper deposit. In addition to projects in Australia, Caterpillar equipment is used for the mining of that country's rich iron ore deposits, marketed primarily in Japan. Finally, the company is extensively involved in the Brazilian Amazon River development project with jungle-clearing and road construction equipment.

It is important to note that about 75 percent of the company's outstanding common stock is held by trustees, banks, and other institutions, while 25 per- cent is held by individuals. Company directors include representatives from Mobil Oil, FMC Corporation, and the First Chicago Corporation, and company stock is listed on stock exchanges in Belgium, England, France, Scotland, Switzerland, and West Germany -- an important aspect of multinational development toward international ownership.

Sources: Annual Reports
Standard and Poor's Corporation Records, February-March, 1973

Caterpillar in Southern Africa

Caterpillar (Africa) (Pty.) Ltd. has been operating since 1962 in the Isando industrial area, approximately 10 miles east of Johannesburg. Situated in a 90,000-square-foot building, Caterpillar Africa is engaged in a small-scale parts-processing and warehousing operation. In addition, the company facilitates local procurement of replacement parts for Caterpillar equipment and provides backup service to local dealers with imported parts. About three-fourths of the subsidiary's sales are made within the Republic of South Africa,[1] largely through dealerships. Of Caterpillar's total South African sales, equipment produced in South Africa accounted for $2.4 million, while the remainder was imported. Caterpillar has $6.4 million invested in South Africa, $5.4 million through Caterpillar (Africa).[2]

Steia (Sociedade Technica de Equipamentos Industriais e Agricolas, LDA) is the Caterpillar dealer in Mozambique, which has recently sold 38 earth-moving machines to the international consortium funding the Cabora-Bassa Dam. Guaranteeing efficient service on these and potential sales, Steia has set up a branch store in Tete, a town 87 miles from the construction site.[3]

Relations to Government

Caterpillar is proud of what it terms its "product support" in the wake of its sales to the Cabora-Bassa Dam project. Having sold 38 earth-moving machines to the consortium of French, German, Italian, Portuguese, and South African companies, Steia has provided expert technical personnel to the construction site for maximum-efficiency repair service and has also directed training programs concerning the repair and operation of Caterpillar equipment. Steia supplies, in addition, a twin-engine Piper "Aztec" airplane to deliver spare parts in emergencies.

According to statistical estimates, Steia has supplied the first phase of the Cabora-Bassa project with 15 percent of its equipment (in terms of cash value).[4]

Isando-based Caterpillar (Africa) does 50 percent of its business with the South African government.[5]

Wages and Benefits

Caterpillar Tractor Company - Average Wages for 1971

Employee Category	No. Employees	Average Yearly Wage (for 1971)
White (male)	24	$7,965
White (female)	17	4,125
African (male)	51	1,670
Colored (male)	1	1,790

Note: Pay converted at the rate of 1 rand = $1.35[6]

So far as it is possible, Caterpillar seeks to avoid any racial discrimination in its employment policy, giving work to "as many Bantus as possible."[7] Operating on the principle of equal pay for equal work, Caterpillar's salaries are high for blacks, and the company claims that it is encouraging the advancement of black employees into better-salaried skilled jobs. This is possible because of special concessions made to them, allowing employment of blacks in all job classifications. The statistical breakdown above shows, however, that the ideals articulated by Caterpillar have not been realized -- skilled jobs are still controlled primarily by whites. A more detailed breakdown as of 1970 follows:

Grade	Job Category	Wages Per Month Rand	$
I	Janitor	55.03- 73.66	77.04-103.12
II	Canteen Assistant	64.34- 82.76	90.08-115.86
III	Filing Clerk II, Painter, Maintenance Helper, Stores Helper	73.66- 99.66	103.12-139.52
IV	Track Press Operator	82.76-119.38	115.86-167.13
V	Filing Clerk I, Senior Stores Helper, Truck Driver	100.96-137.79	141.34-192.91
VI	Office Clerk II (whites and non-whites)	123.00-168.00	172.20-235.20
VII	Switchboard Operator, Office Clerk II	144.00-195.00	201.60-273.00
VIII	Office Clerk, Computer Operator, Steno Secretary	168.00-288.00	235.20-403.20
IX	Order Clerk Secretary	195.00-266.00	273.00-372.40
X	Bookkeeper	228.00-310.00	319.20-434.00
XI	Assistant Buyer	226.00-362.00	316.40-506.80
	A. Stores Foreman, Programmer, Senior Bookkeeper	295.00-435.00	413.00-609.00
	B. Inventory Control, Buyer, Foreman Inspector	360.00-525.00	504.00-735.00

1 Rand = $1.40

All employees have such benefits as paid vacations, disability plan, termination pay, pension based on salary and length of service, and educational assistance plan. Raises are given every six months, and all employees are allowed to borrow company property (cars, typewriters, etc.) for personal use.

Company Position on Investment in Southern Africa

Caterpillar recognizes that its established policy of "providing equal employment opportunities without regard to race, color, creed, sex, or national origin" does not harmonize with the legal and political principles of the South African government. The fact that it remains in South Africa, however, means that the company must compromise on these long-standing policies, attempting to be a good "corporate citizen."[10]

Caterpillar speaks in its official publications of the "dilemma" that confronts it concerning its presence in South Africa but explains that careful analysis has brought it to the conclusion that its involvement in South Africa and its complicity with that nation's laws does not in fact strengthen the system of apartheid. The company insists that general industrial growth, spearheaded by corporations with progressive employment practices, will ultimately free the potential of South Africa's black labor force and bring the dissolution of apartheid:

> The processes of growth are, however, going on, and the need for more workers is increasing as a concomitant of expanding direct investments in productive industry. More than any other source, it is capital which creates jobs; and as more jobs are created they are inevitably calling for the employment of more of those available to fill them.

> The education and the skills of nonwhites are, accordingly, being upgraded, if for no other reason than to meet the needs for workers. And in the long run, it will be work as a source of income which will give the nonwhite his greatest opportunity for independence, security and dignity.

> It is, therefore, our opinion that, far from being a handicap to social-civil progress, one of the best potential avenues for accelerating the changes which we and others like us favor is job-creating investment -- from any source, local or foreign.[11]

Company's Release of Information

Caterpillar did not complete the CIC questionnaire but did send several fact sheets and position papers on the topics of both its investment in South Africa and its rationale for continuing to work within the structures of apartheid.

Caterpillar's reply to the Diggs questionnaire was categorized as nonresponsive.

Footnotes

1. Caterpillar's reply to CIC; letter and materials sent to Ronald L. Phillips, Research Director, CIC, from B. DeHaan, Public Affairs Manager, Caterpillar Tractor Company, September 5, 1972. Also from W. H. Franklin, Chairman of Board of Caterpillar, in a letter to Miss Florence Little, Treasurer, Board of Missions of the United Methodist Church, December 20, 1972.

2. Reply to CIC.

3. The Dealer (a monthly Caterpillar publication for its dealers and their employees), April, 1972, p. 4.

4. Ibid., p. 5.

5. Ian Leach and Steve Green, managing director and personnel director, Caterpillar (Africa), interviewed in Johannesburg, August 13, 1970, by Tim Smith.

6. Reply to CIC.

7. Smith interview.

8. Ibid.

9. Reply to CIC.

10. Ibid.

11. Ibid.

CHRYSLER CORPORATION
L. A. Townsend, Chairman of the Board
12000 Oakland Avenue
Highland Park, Michigan 48231
Mailing Address: P.O. Box 1919
Detroit, Michigan 48231

Chrysler Corp., formed in Delaware in 1925, is the third-largest producer of motor vehicles in the world and along with its associated companies accounted for 9.1 percent of the total world market in 1971. Chrysler ranked #7 on the Fortune 500 in 1971, with $8 billion in sales. Chrysler's automotive product line includes Plymouth, Dodge, Chrysler, Imperial, and Dodge trucks. Over half of the line (56.8 percent) is manufactured in the U.S., 9.3 percent in Canada, and 43.2 percent is manufactured or assembled in approximately 25 other countries. In 1971, the U.S. accounted for 60.4 percent of Chrysler's automotive sales, while Canada and other countries accounted for 6.2 percent and 33.4 percent respectively. Other products manufactured by the company include automotive parts and accessories, outboard motors, marine and industrial engines, and defense-space products, including tracked and wheeled vehicles, missile systems, and space boosters. Chrysler received $94.4 million in military contracts, ranking #57 in 1972. The corporation has produced combat vehicles (M-60 series tank, M-615 trucks), fire control components, projectiles, and military trucks and conducts research and development work for the government. In addition, the corporation has contracts with NASA. Defense and sales, including auto products, amounted to 1 percent of consolidated net sales for the year ending December 31, 1971, equivalent to $135 million.

Chrysler has approximately 30 wholly or partially owned subsidiaries in approximately 25 countries, which include France, Puerto Rico, Portugal, Panama, South Africa, Venezuela, Mexico, Argentina, Colombia, Kenya, the Philippines, and Australia, with net sales totaling $1.9 billion in 1971. About 43 percent of the company's total work force is employed abroad. Chrysler Canada Ltd., a wholly-owned subsidiary, is the third-largest passenger car and truck manufacturer in Canada. In the latter part of 1950, the corporation organized Chrysler International S.A., a Swiss subsidiary, and began a foreign investment program to enable it to compete in this expanding market with vehicles produced outside the U.S. and Canada. It has controlling ownership in such foreign vehicle producers as Societe des Automobiles Simca (France), with 99 percent of the shares owned by Chrysler; Rootes Motors Limited (Venezuela), with 94 percent of voting shares and 67 percent of non-voting ordinary shares owned by Chrysler; and Mitsubishi Motors Corporation (Japan), where Chrysler has a 15 percent equity.

The corporation has approximately 5,500 dealers and 129,531 employees in the U.S., of which substantially all hourly employees and 25 percent of salaried employees are included in collective bargaining units represented by unions. Chrysler manufactures a substantial share of materials and parts for its automotive line and uses more than 18,000 outside firms in the U.S. for services, materials, parts, and components.

56

Front gate of the Chrysler South African plant.

Chrysler in Southern Africa

    Chrysler South Africa (Pty.) Ltd.
    P.O. Box 411, Pretoria, South Africa

    Chrysler South Africa, established in 1958, is a wholly-owned
subsidiary of the U.S. firm. The company began production at Elsies
River, outside Cape Town, and later built a larger facility near Pretoria.
In 1972, the Elsies River plant was closed. Chrysler Park, the new
plant which opened in 1967, has an annual production output of about
24,500 vehicles.[1] The company makes a number of automobile and truck
models, as well as a range of Airtemp air-conditioning units.

    The company describes its investment as "about $45,000,000
average, variable depending on inventory levels."[2]

Relations to Government

    Chrysler Park, located on the edge of Bophuthatwana (the Tswana
reserve), is the first major automobile factory to be built outside an
urban area. It is not, however, located within one of the government's
designated "border areas," and Chrysler did not receive the tax benefits
given those companies that invest in those areas.

    Still, the move must be seen as a contribution to the government's
decentralization scheme. The large, readily available source of unskilled
labor was undoubtedly an important factor in the company's decision to
build there.

    No details are available about Chrysler's sales to the government,
although various American-made vehicles are widely used by the South African
police and army, as well as other government agencies.

Wages and Benefits

    In March 1972, the company employed 2,038 persons at Chrysler
Park--924 whites and 1,114 Coloureds and Africans. Earlier, it reported
an average annual employment of 3,700 persons. It is unclear whether
closure of the Elsies River plant resulted in higher employment figures
at Chrysler Park.

    The average African wage at Chrysler Park in 1972 was R85.50
(about $110), and the company planned a 14 percent increase during the
year. Officials emphasize that pay to black employees has risen steadily.
In 1972, the company reported that its average pay to Africans had approximately doubled since 1967.[3]

    In 1970, the government issued a proclamation which applied job
reservation specifically to the automobile industry in the area where Chrysler
is located. The determination requires the company to maintain a ratio
of 60:10:30 among African, Coloured, and white workers in the assembly
plant. It does not apply in the engine manufacturing plant. According
to Chrysler, "This determination has never been strictly applied, and
has not prevented the employment of non-whites on skilled and semi-
skilled operations."[4]

A Chrysler fact sheet outlines two ways the company is advancing the skill and responsibility levels of jobs performed by Africans and Coloureds:

> Fragmentation of Labor: Fragmenting of jobs (redefining job categories) only applies to artisan jobs. The basic method of increasing productivity of the very limited number of maintenance artisans is to provide them with unqualified helpers who work under their general direction. This technique is practiced throughout Africa, and has led to a rapid improvement of non-white skills. In effect, the artisan becomes a Supervisor/Instructor and directs the work of three or more helpers. In the absence of adequate technical training facilities, this method of advancing non-whites is practical and effective.

> Non-Whites in Supervisory Positions: During the past year, a special position called a "Team Leader" has been established in each foreman area, and non-white candidates are being trained to fill these positions. There will be approximately 112 Team Leaders when all vacancies are filled. These Team Leaders do supervisory work. As their supervisory skills improve, we foresee, in the current political climate, no difficulty in increasing the responsibility and status of these black and colored employees.[5]

Each approach is quite limited as a means of significantly changing the position of black workers. Job fragmentation, though it may improve a few skills of black employees, is essentially a means of maintaining a racially structured work force while increasing productivity. The "helpers" perform an artisan's job for a fraction of the pay, and the company's labor costs remain low despite rising wages. It also enables the company to fill vacated white positions despite a severe skilled-labor shortage without confronting the restrictions placed on skilled jobs by the government and white workers' organizations.

Team leaders perform a similar task. Their pay remains far below that of white supervisors, whose work they expedite and in some cases replace.

Company's Release of Information

The two-page fact sheet Chrysler sent CIC contained no general statement on corporate policy about South Africa. There was brief but useful data about the company's activities and labor policies, most of which is reported above. Chrysler did not reply to the Diggs questionnaire.

Footnotes

1. "Chrysler South Africa," Sunday Times Survey, Johannesburg, August 20, 1972.

2. "Facts about Chrysler South Africa," sent in reply to CIC, November 13, 1972.

3. Ibid.

4. Ibid.

5. Ibid.

FIRESTONE TIRE AND RUBBER COMPANY
Raymond C. Firestone, Chairman of the Board
1200 Firestone Parkway
Akron, Ohio 44317

Incorporated in Ohio in 1910, Firestone is a leading producer
of tires and related products for cars, trucks, aircraft, and earth-moving
equipment accounting for about 80 percent of the company's business.
Ford, General Motors, and Chrysler are major purchasers of Firestone
tires. In addition, the company produces natural and synthetic rubber
products, foam products, stainless steel and aluminum stampings, plastics,
industrial products, textiles, brake linings, chemicals, and adhesives.
The company also engages in military production, including missiles,
rubber products for aircraft and vehicles, and other equipment. With
52 subsidiaries, most of which are wholly owned, Firestone operates
plants in some 20 states, employing over 105,000 people in 1971. The
company markets products through some 60,000 dealers and 1,400 owned or
leased stores. In 1971 the company ranked #34 on the Fortune 500 list,
with $2.5 billion in sales.

Firestone views the expanding foreign market for tire products
as critical to the company's future growth. Oriented principally to
the motor vehicle industry, the company suggested in a recent annual
report that foreign growth rate per year for tire products is more than
double the U.S. rate, and the number of vehicles in foreign countries
is expected to increase by 60 percent between 1970 and 1975. With operations
in over 27 foreign countries, Firestone has carried out major expansion
plans in most overseas units, such as in Latin America (Brazil, Argentina,
and Venezuela), Canada, England, several other European nations, Africa
(Kenya, Ghana, and South Africa), and Asia (India, New Zealand, Thailand,
the Philippines, and Australia). In 1971, foreign sales accounted for
30 percent of total sales and 33 percent of total net income. Firestone
owns major rubber plantations in Liberia, Ghana, the Philippines, Brazil,
and Guatemala.

Firestone Tire and Rubber in Southern Africa

FIRESTONE SOUTH AFRICA (PTY.) LTD.
Port Elizabeth

Firestone began selling tires in South Africa in 1930 and
started manufacturing in 1936. The Port Elizabeth factory has been
expanded several times since then. In 1969, the company began construction
of a new $10-million plant at Brits, in the Transvaal. The new facility,
which supplies Johannesburg and other Transvaal areas, will help Firestone maintain its position as South Africa's leading tire and rubber
manufacturer.[1]

The company has released no figures on the size of its South
African investment, but it is probably in the $25-$30 million range.

61

Relations to Government

Firestone's Brits factory is within one of the designated "border areas." To encourage firms to locate in these areas, the government offers tax incentives and other benefits. The decentralization program is primarily an attempt to implement the government's blueprint for a racially segregated country. By locating major employers on the edge of "white" areas,blacks remain in the Bantustans while providing the labor essential to maintaining the white economy. Firestone's investment has made a significant contribution to the success of this apartheid scheme.

Wages and Benefits

No recent data is available, but in 1969 Firestone South Africa had 1,550 employees--620 whites and 930 Africans and Coloureds.[2]

A July 1972 _Fortune_ article shows Firestone's average African wage at the Brits plant as $70 per month. The minimum rate is shown at about $62. On the _Fortune_ list of 15 corporations Firestone's rates are the lowest; and they are almost equal to the average monthly wage of African industrial workers throughout South Africa.

The low wages reflect both Firestone's poor labor record and the less competitive situation in border areas. In Port Elizabeth, the company has the reputation of paying less to its black workers than other major employers. In Brits, the company has a large pool of labor to draw upon and is not forced to pay higher rates to compete for workers.

Company's Release of Information

Firestone has apparently made no policy statements about South Africa. CIC received no reply from the company. In 1969, the chairman sent a brief response to a Princeton University questionnaire, but several more recent requests for information and interviews from church organizations have met refusals or no response.

Firestone gave no reply to the Diggs questionnaire.

Footnotes

1. "The Rubber Industry," _Africa Today_, September-October, 1970; and _South African Digest_, October 24, 1969.

2. Raymond Firestone, in a letter to D. S. Bliss, Princeton University, October 2, 1969.

FORD MOTOR COMPANY
Henry Ford II, Chairman of the Board
American Road
Dearborn, Michigan 48121

While Ford Motor Company is the second-largest manufacturer of automobiles in the United States, it is the leading company in foreign sales of all U. S. auto companies and in 1971 held over 9 per cent of the auto market in the "free world." Incorporated in Delaware in 1919, Ford produces a number of different automobile models and trucks and also manufactures tractors and farm implements. Through its subsidiary Philco-Ford, the company makes household appliances, including televisions, stereos and refrigerators. Ford also is one of the nation's largest military contractors, ranking #28 in 1972, with nearly $197 billion in contracts. Primarily through Philco-Ford, the company's military products include jeeps, grenade launchers, missiles, and communication systems for the Southeast Asian war, as well as contracts for space flight and satellite-tracking station operations. Philco-Ford also constructs telecommunications installations at U. S. military bases in Belgium, Britain, Germany, Taiwan, Korea, and Okinawa. The company markets its products through about 6,900 independent dealers and both exports and assembles automobiles in foreign countries. The company ranked #3 on the Fortune 500 list in 1971, with over $16.4 billion in sales.

Because General Motors dominates the American auto market, Ford has sought to cultivate foreign markets for its business. Thus, foreign sales in 1971, not including Canada, accounted for some 25 per cent of total sales. If the Canadian market were absorbed in the company's calculations for foreign sales, the percentage would be much higher. Ford's foreign investments are currently concentrated in Canada, England, and European countries, with a smaller percentage in Latin America. In Latin America, Ford's largest operation is in Brazil and its second-largest is in Argentina. The Chilean government recently nationalized Ford assets, worth about $7 million.

The significance of foreign sales (and manufacturing) to Ford is evidenced in its recent efforts to penetrate the Asian auto market. According to the company, Asia, with over one-third of the world's population, accounts for only 2 per cent of the world's cars. In the company's 1971 Annual Report, it was reported that Henry Ford met with government and business leaders in nine Asian countries (Australia, Indonesia, Japan, Malaysia, New Zealand, the Philippines, Taiwan, Singapore, and Thailand) to discuss auto trade. Ford maintains six automotive assembly plants in the Asia-Pacific area and expects to increase that number (including a facility in Saigon) to market a low-cost multipurpose utility vehicle. Although the company has faced competition for small car imports as have other U. S. auto producers, Ford has entered into joint ventures with major Japanese auto firms, and holds minority investments in such firms.

<u>Ford in Southern Africa</u>

Ford Motor Company of South Africa (Pty.) Ltd.
P. O. Box 788, Port Elizabeth

Ford Motor Company of South Africa, a wholly-owned subsidiary of Ford
Motor Company of Canada, Ltd., was established in 1923. Ford of Canada is
81 per cent owned by Ford Motor Company of the U. S. Ford South Africa now
operates in these locations:

Location	Facility	Established
Port Elizabeth, South Africa	Administrative offices (leased)	--
Neave, South Africa	Car, van, and tractor assembly plant	1947 (replaced original plant)
Struandale, South Africa	Engine plant	1964
	Parts and service depot	1962
	Truck assembly plant (leased)	
	Car assembly plant (nearing completion but not operative until 1973)	

The company in South Africa machines and assembles engines from
locally supplied and imported components. In addition, it imports
"knock-down" kits of cars and trucks for local assembly and sale.
The South African regulations extend various incentives to companies
"manufacturing" passenger cars in South Africa. To qualify as a car
manufactured in South Africa in 1972, the car must have a local content of at least 54.5 percent.

Ford of South Africa does not extract raw materials and exports
a very limited quantity of vehicles from South Africa. For example,
252 vehicles have been exported so far this year (1972), 234 of them
to Zambia. The company sells its products to franchised dealers,
fleet operators of cars and trucks, and government agencies throughout
South Africa.[1]

Although Ford will not reveal the size of its South African investment,
the figure is probably between $80 and $100 million. Ford's share of the South
African automobile and commercial vehicle market is 15 to 20 per cent. In 1971,
the company sold over 48,000 vehicles.

<u>Relations to Government</u>

In 1965, Ford South Africa bid on a contract to supply four-wheeled-
drive vehicles to the South African government. The Canadian government decided
the items might violate the United Nations arms embargo and refused to issue an
export permit to Ford Canada. In retaliation, the South African government refused

to allow Ford to bid on contracts for the next two years. Since then, Ford has regained its position as a major government supplier and makes every effort to avoid repetition of the affair.[2]

Ford has refused to discuss the volume or type of government business it has in South Africa.

Another aspect of the company's relations with the government is the local content program. (See GM profile for details.)

Wages and Benefits

The following chart, supplied by Ford, shows the distribution by category and wages paid to the company's 3,941 employees.

Hourly Wage Structure

| Labor Grade | Per Hour | | | | Population | | |
| | Minimum | | Maximum | | White | Colored | Black |
	Rands	$	Rands	$			
1	0.40	.51	0.58	.74	0	627	165
2	0.42	.54	0.62	.79	0	777	15
3	0.44	.56	0.66	.84	0	278	100
4	0.46	.59	0.70	.90	0	432	16
5	0.50	.64	0.74	.95	1	264	5
6	0.56	.72	0.83	1.06	3	68	5
7	0.62	.79	0.88	1.13	12	95	4
8	0.69	.88	1.00	1.28	82	35	0
9	0.90	1.15	1.00	1.28	297	51	5
10	1.05	1.34	1.50	1.92	463	0	0
11	1.10	1.41	1.75	2.24	104	0	0
Apprentices (Skilled trades)					37	0	0
					999	2,627	315

1 Rand = $1.28

July, 1972

The job distribution pattern is not unusual -- blacks hold the least skilled positions. Only five of Ford's African employees are in a category in which the minimum rate is high enough to match the minimum monthly budget suggested by the South African Institute of Race Relations for Port Elizabeth (about $140 per month for an African family). Only 51 of Ford's 2,627 Colored employees fall into a category that has a minimum rate high enough to give them the recommended monthly income (about $160 per month for a Colored Port Elizabeth family).

Company Position on Investment in Southern Africa

Ford offers this explanation of its policies:

The maximum amount of pay within a labor grade is the amount set by Ford to which employees can expect to progress within that labor grade through periodic seniority and merit increases. Within labor grades with significant numbers of white and non-white employees, whites, blacks and coloreds are spread through the rate range. Within a labor trade rate range there may be, and are, some coloreds being paid more than some whites and some blacks being paid more than some coloreds and some whites due to seniority and merit increases. In fact, if one were to assume a totally static situation, viz. no promotions, no turnover and no new hires, all employees could be expected to be paid the maximum for their labor grade in two or three years' time.

It will be noted that in the higher labor grades fewer non-whites and more whites will be found. This is accounted for primarily by the fact that due to the shortage of skilled workers among non-whites, Ford employed more whites than non-whites, and the non-whites were hired primarily in the lower graded classifications. There has been a general advancement of non-whites (for example, ten years ago there were no blacks employed above grade 2) as the Job Reservation Law and union practice have been relaxed, and whites in the higher grades generally have longer service than non-whites....

However, it will be noted that there are no non-whites in labor grades 10 and 11. These grades encompass the skilled trades and are still restricted to whites by union practice and potential application of the Job Reservation Law.

According to the company, "all employees of Ford of South Africa enjoy equal opportunity to participate in the company's benefit programs."[3]

Company's Release of Information

Ford did not fill out the CIC questionnaire but instead sent a four-page letter, a wage sheet, and a copy of the industrial agreement that outlines labor policies. Most of the information requested in the questionnaire was supplied, except as noted in the text above. Almost all the data for this profile was taken from the Ford reply. The company's reply to the Diggs questionnaire was categorized as fair.

Footnotes

1. Ford's reply to CIC; letter and materials sent to Ronald L. Phillips, Research Director, CIC, from John A. Banning, Executive Director, International Governmental Affairs Staff, Ford Motor Co., October 5, 1972.

2. R. J. Scott, Managing Director of Ford South Africa, in an interview with Tim Smith, Tami Huttman, and Reed Kramer, Port Elizabeth, South Africa, July 30, 1970.

3. Ford's reply to CIC.

GENERAL ELECTRIC COMPANY
Reginald H. Jones, Chairman of the Board
570 Lexington Avenue
New York, New York 10022

General Electric Company (GE) is the largest manufacturer of electrical and electronic equipment in the United States. Incorporated in New York in 1892, GE maintains a leading position in the manufacture and sale of a wide range of products serving consumer, industrial and government markets and ranked #4 on the Fortune 500 list in 1971 with $9.4 billion in sales. Products include household electronic and electrical appliances, power-generating equipment for utilities, industries, and ships, including nuclear plants and reactors (GE and Westinghouse together hold an estimated 80 percent of the world nuclear market), and electric locomotives, among many others. GE is also one of the largest military contractors, ranking #4 in 1972, with over $12 billion in contracts. GE military products include machine guns, jet engines for fighter-bombers, radar, flight and weapons fire control systems, missiles, and other electronic components and equipment. The company has received over $8 billion in contracts since 1961.

Foreign operations are critical to GE's future growth and earnings. With over 80 manufacturing facilities in 24 countries, more than 20 percent of the company's work force is employed abroad. In 1972, the company reported foreign sales that represented 18 percent of the total and foreign net income accounting for 19 percent of the total. Reporting to stockholders in 1971, a company executive underscored the importance of foreign business for GE, noting that 60 percent of the total world market for GE-type products is outside the United States and is growing much faster than the U.S. market.

GE views its international orientation as building the "GE World System." The company has a sophisticated method of penetrating foreign markets and production processes in its line of business. For example, GE is involved in licensing agreements with many Japanese firms, providing technological know-how in the production of a wide range of electronic components, generating equipment, and military equipment. The compnay also enters into joint ventures and owns minority-stock interests in foreign firms. In Germany, for example, GE is tightly interlocked with major German electronic and power-generation (including nuclear) manufacturing companies, such as AEG Telefunken. Major foreign subsidiaries include operations in Brazil (from the early part of this century), Argentina, Mexico, Puerto Rico, Canada, several European countries, and Northern Ireland. In Asia, GE operates electronic assembly plants, mainly in Singapore, and is considering establishing plants in Indonesia.

In SAGE's plant at Benoni, black and white employees work together.
They share the work, but the white is called supervisor and paid
about five times as much as his black colleague.

General Electric in Southern Africa
_____

SOUTH AFRICAN GENERAL ELECTRIC COMPANY (PTY.) LTD.
1 Van Dyke Road/P.O. Box 5031, Benoni, South Africa

South African General Electric Company (SAGE), a wholly-owned subsidiary of the U.S. firm, began its operations in what is now called the Republic of South Africa in 1898. The subsidiary manufactures household appliances (refrigerators, freezers, washers and dryers), housewares (irons, percolators, electric kettles), industrial controls, capacitors, locomotives, and magnet wire. SAGE also markets imported items, such as lights, mobile radios, and automated drives for steel mills.[1] In September, 1972, the South African government--which belatedly decided to introduce tightly-controlled television by 1976--chose SAGE as one of the manufacturers of receiving sets. Of more than 30 applicants, only 5 were chosen, including the consortium in which SAGE is involved with AEG-Telefunken, Electra Appliances, and others.[2] In 1970, SAGE's sales volume was about $20 million per year; total investment at book value was approximately $55 million.[3]

Relations to Government
_____

GE is a major supplier of locomotives for the government-owned South African Railways (SAR) and for the Portuguese administration in Angola. According to the government-published South African Digest (June 19, 1970), SAGE has won two contracts in recent years for supplying powerful diesel locomotives to the SAR. Following the delivery of 115 locomotives for $30 million in 1970, the company was awarded a $24 million contract for another 75 machines. For the first order, the Export-Import Bank of the U.S. granted SAR a $11.7 million loan guarantee.[4] Some reports indicate that GE will build the engines for locomotives General Motors might supply SAR under a new contract.[5]

GE sold about 30 locomotives in 1967/1968 for use by two Portuguese mining companies in Angola. The Export-Import Bank gave one company a $6.8 million guarantee in 1967 and another firm a $1.1 million guarantee in 1968.[6]

SAGE has constructed 130 control relay panels costing $140,000 for the Transvaal (South Africa) terminal of the power grid for the Cabora-Bassa Dam in Mozambique.[7] The dam has been vigorously condemned by the Organization of African Unity and FRELIMO (Mozambique Liberation Front) as a scheme aimed at entrenching colonial rule, and vehement protests throughout Europe have led to the withdrawal of several European firms from participation in construction. Previously, GE had tried to sell direct current conversion equipment for the dam, but the Export-Import Bank failed to provide guarantees for the sale,[8] presumably to avoid U.S. involvement in the controversial project.

An official of the U.S. Atomic Energy Commission told the House Subcommittee on Africa last year that GE is one American firm that might compete for the contract to build South Africa's first nuclear reactor, on which construction will begin soon.[9]

Wages and Benefits

SAGE: AVERAGE MONTHLY WAGES[10]
January, 1972

Race	Category	Wages Rand	Dollars	Number of Workers	Percent of Workers
Africans	Unskilled	R55	$73	145	9.7
	Semi-skilled	R78-R123	$104-164	363	24.2
	Skilled	R160	$213	242	16.1
Coloureds				120	8.0
	Starting rate				
	male	R84	$118		
	female	R47	$63		
	Average rate	R146	$194		
Whites				630	42.0
	Unskilled	R140	$186		
	Journeymen & operators	R211	$281		
	Artisans	R302-322	$402-428		
			TOTAL	1500	100.0

SAGE belongs to the Iron, Steel, Engineering, and Metallurgical Council, the largest such statutory industrial grouping in the country. In the council and in SAGE there are a number of strong white unions. During negotiations for the current industrial agreement in 1970 (the agreement regulates almost all aspects of labor relations within the industry), employers were able to gain some relaxation in job reservation. In return, pay raises granted to union members were 3 to 4 times greater than those given Africans, who of course had no direct representation in the discussion.[11]

SAGE officials argue, without trying to justify traditional pay differentials for racial groups, that a comparison of wages must take into account differences in living costs. They say that rent paid by their African workers is less than one-tenth that paid by their white employees. And white workers pay toward their pension, death, and sick benefits, which are totally subsidized for Africans.[12]

However, these arguments do not take into account the faster increase in African living costs or the inadequacy of housing, educational, medical, and recreational facilities in the African townships. And they ignore the widening gap between pay rates for whites and blacks, which is occurring despite a rise in the skill levels of jobs performed by blacks.

GE office building in Johannesburg.

Company Position on Investment in Southern Africa

At its 1972 annual meeting, Chairman Borch explained the company's policy on South Africa. Here is the full summary which appeared in The General Electric Investor (Summer, 1972):

What position does General Electric take with regard to continuing its operations in South Africa?

Chairman Borch: We think General Electric has done a pretty good job in South Africa. A lot is yet to be done there, and we are working at it. Also, the products we export from the United States into South Africa help the Company meet its responsibilities in terms of providing jobs for minorities here in the U.S.

The Chairman also referred to previous correspondence on the subject which included the following points:

General Electric's position on South Africa is founded on the same management standards and concerns which apply in the 37 countries where we do business around the world. By turning out quality products that meet the wants of our customers, we try to provide good jobs for employees and a profit for share owners. It is our policy to try to provide equal pay for equal work and performance without regard to race, creed or color.

Achieving these goals has not been an easy task in South Africa. Intense European, Japanese and other U.S. competition for a relatively limited market has made GE's profit picture in South Africa less than satisfactory in recent years. But the Company has recognized that broad geographical representation in the marketplaces of the world is essential to GE's long-term success.

The South African affiliate has made steady progress in ensuring gains for its people in South Africa, especially its non-white employees. Continued improvements have occurred in those areas regularly used to measure progress for employees anywhere in the world: more jobs; higher minimum, average and maximum wage rates; employee benefits programs; and--perhaps most important of all-- employee training programs and the opportunity for promotion to higher-skilled jobs.

GE's South African management has been working to increase the skills of non-white employees on a continuous basis over the years. On-the-job training has been accelerated to include more employees reaching higher levels of skill. In addition, actual classroom training during working hours, at full pay, takes the worker from rudimentary training with basic tools through to an ability to read wiring diagrams and do electrical wiring and assembly work. As in the U.S., managers of the South African affiliate are developing affirmative action programs that assure continuing progress for non-white employees in South Africa.

Company's Release of Information

GE made no response to the CIC inquiry. Chairman Diggs also received no reply from the company. The above-quoted paragraph is GE's only public statement on the subject to date. However, early in 1972 the company gave full cooperation to CIC researchers who were preparing the BRIEF on GE. Both U.S. and South African personnel responded to letters that asked for corrections on data gathered during a March 1971 interview with SAGE officials at the Benoni plant. In 1973 the Board of Christian Education of the United Presbyterian Church in the U.S.A. under the Church Project on U.S. Investments in Southern Africa filed a disclosure resolution with GE; the company opposed the resolution but promised a report to shareholders.

Footnotes

1. This and much of the other data, hereafter cited as GE Data, was collected by Tami Hultman and Reed Kramer in an interview with R. E. Johnson and M. T. O'Grady, SAGE managing director and public relations officer respectively at Benoni, March 11, 1971; in a follow-up letter to Johnson on January 3, 1972; from Johnson's responses on January 17 and January 25; and from telephone conversations with A. J. Demaris at GE's New York offices.

2. Television Survey, SA Financial Gazette, October 6, 1972, p. I.

3. Figures on sales are from GE response to questionnaire from the Council on Economic Priorities (CEP), September 11, 1970; figures on investment, stated in terms of assets and turnover, are from "General Electric," Management, Johannesburg, October, 1970, p. 57. Mr. Johnson, in his letter (op. cit.) states that neither figure is completely correct.

4. Table on Eximbank exposure in Southern Africa and Portugal, Appendix 7, in Hearings before the Subcommittee on Africa of the Committee on Foreign Affairs, House of Representatives, on "U.S. Business Involvement in Southern Africa," Part I.

5. The Star, Johannesburg, January 22, 1972.

6. Table on Eximbank, op. cit.; and "Activities of Foreign Economic and Other Interests.../in/ Colonial Countries...," United Nations document A/AC.109/L.506, October 9, 1968, p. 46.

7. The Star, Johannesburg, June 27, 1970.

8. Letter from B. M. Jarrati, GE international press relations, to Janet Hooper, American Committee on Africa, June 17, 1971.

9. John J. Flaherty, General Manager of International Activities, Atomic Energy Commission, in Hearings ..., Part 2, op. cit., p. 68.

10. GE Data, op. cit.; for fuller discussion see "General Electric: Apartheid and Business in South Africa," CENTER BRIEF, Corporate Information Center, National Council of Churches, March, 1972.

11. "Main Agreement of the Iron, Steel, Engineering, and Metallurgical Industry, Republic of South Africa," Government Notice No. R 1432, Government Gazette, No. 2799, Vol. 63, September 4, 1970. More details in BRIEF on GE, op. cit., pp. 14-16.

12. GE Data, op. cit.

GENERAL MOTORS CORPORATION
Richard C. Gerstenberg, Chairman of the Board
3044 West Grand Boulevard
Detroit, Michigan 48202

Incorporated in Delaware in 1916, General Motors Corporation (GM)
has had a history of steady growth and acquisition, today holding the uncon-
tested position as the largest manufacturer of automobiles in the world.
The company controls almost 50 percent of the domestic auto market and
ranks as the largest corporation in the United States on the Fortune 500
list, with sales of $28.3 billion in 1971. A diversified, relatively
decentralized company, GM operates 118 plants in 18 states and 68 cities
throughout the United States. The company produces automobiles and trucks,
auto components (AC, Delco Electronics), household appliances (Frigidaire),
provides financial and insurance services for its products, and is involved
in other related areas of business. GM is also one of the largest military
contractors, ranking number 23 in 1972 with $255.7 million in contracts.
GM's military business has amounted to $3.3 billion since 1966, producing
such strategic weapons and components as tanks, engines and transmissions
for armored personnel carriers and howitzer artillery, missiles, the M-16
rifle, jet engines used in the Navy and Air Force's A-7 type aircraft, jungle
warfare helicopters, and the electronic surveillance E-2A aircraft. GM
employed 733,000 persons worldwide in 1971.

GM, like other U.S. auto producers, looks to the foreign market
for increased sales and earnings. According to Business Week (December 11,
1971), GM's chairman stated that the company is looking "to foreign business
as a primary source of growth and fatter profits. He notes that auto sales
abroad are expected to grow by 55 percent by 1980, compared with only 30
percent in the U.S."

Employing 180,000, or 25 percent of its total work force,
GM operates assembly plants in some 25 countries in Europe, South America,
South Africa and, most recently, Southeast Asia. Overseas operations excluding Canada brought $4.1 billion in sales, or 15 percent of total sales,
and $103 million in net earnings. Automobiles produced abroad include the
Opel (Germany), the Vauxhall and Bedford in vehicles (England), and the
Holden (Australia). GM's Brazilian, Argentinian and Mexican subsidiaries
continued to show increased sales of GM vehicles. In Brazil the U.S. accounts
for some 75 percent of foreign investment. The favorable business climate
has allowed GM to expand rapidly. In 1968, only 305 vehicles were assembled.
By 1969, the company turned out more than 25,000 vehicles and has expanded
production capability to include sheet metal, stamping, foundry, and engine
plants. The company is also planning a multimillion-dollar program in
Brazil.

While GM has felt the competition from small-car foreign imports
in the United States, the company acquired a 34.2 percent interest in Isuzu
Motors Ltd., a Japanese passenger car and truck manufacturer, and will

Segregated locker room at GM Engine Plant, Port Elizabeth.

market the Isuzu products in certain overseas markets. GM's participation in foreign firms, characteristic of U.S. corporate efforts to join with foreign "competitors," is also evidenced in its production and marketing of a vehicle for the Southeast Asian market. Like Ford, GM is looking forward to the prospect of a huge auto market in the populous Asian countries. GM opened as assembly plant in Malaysia in 1971 and acquired a 49 percent interest in a Bangkok, Thailand, distributor of GM vehicles, which will become a strategic base for production and sales in the Asia-Pacific area.

General Motors in Southern Africa

General Motors South African (Pty.) Ltd.
  P.O. Box 1137, Port Elizabeth
General Motors Acceptance Corporation
  P.O. Box 2102, Port Elizabeth

General Motors South African (GMSA) was established in 1926 and presently represents an investment of approximately $125 billion for the U.S. parent. GMSA's sales, which consisted of 2,601 vehicles in 1926, totalled 35,700 in 1971. The company offered the following description of its South African subsidiary in its "1972 Report on Progress in Areas of Public Concern," February 10, 1972.

This subsidiary has grown from a small assembly operation to a large manufacturing-assembly complex. This growth reflects the institution by the South African Government of local manufacturing content requirements for passenger cars sold in that country, as well as increased vehicle demand.

GM South African is a very large company by South African standards and represents a substantial investment in facilities. In South Africa, the subsidiary would rank 11th in terms of total assets and 41st in terms of number of employees among the top 100 public companies listed on the Johannesburg Stock Exchange.

By U.S. standards, the operation would rank about 563rd in sales in the Fortune 1000 Industrials. As part of General Motors, however, our operations in South Africa represent approximately four percent of our overseas operations and one percent of the total Corporation.

Currently, GM South African has an assembly plant and a manufacturing plant located in Port Elizabeth, approximately 750 miles south of Johannesburg, in addition to an engine manufacturing plant located at Aloes, outside of Port Elizabeth. Automotive products of GM South African include the Ranger, based on Opel design, the Opel Manta Coupe and Chevrolet Holden design passenger cars, as well as Chevrolet and Bedford commercial vehicles. Supporting the assembly of these vehicles, the subsidiary manufactures components such as engines, radiators, batteries, spark plugs, springs and many sheet metal parts.

General Motors Acceptance Corporation also conducts financing operations in South Africa through its subsidiary, GMAC South Africa (Pty.) Ltd.

Relations to Government

The South African government's local content program, referred to above, represents a major GM involvement with the regime. The program was launched in the early 1960s, following the political and financial crisis which threateened the country's stability. Its purpose was (1) to reduce the vulnerability of the economy to outside economic pressures, such as the outflow of foreign capital, (2) to reduce imports and thus improve the country's balance-of-payments position, and (3) to stimulate growth of other economic sectors. Currently, the program is in Phase III, with a projected goal of 65 percent local content by 1976.

GM has released no information about contracts with the South African government or military applications of its products. Press reports reveal that South African Railways has purchased a number of diesel locomotives from GM. Many GM vehicles are used by the South African police for general activities, including transportation of prisoners to jail. There have been reports of GM trucks being used by the South African Army.

Wages and Benefits

GMSA's wage and employment figures, as of October 1972, have been released by the U.S. parent:

EMPLOYMENT

	Hourly		Salaried	Total	
	No.	%		No.	%
White	1,072	31	1,320	2,392	50
Colored	1,839	53	14	1,853	39
African	551	16	1	552	11
Total Colored and African	2,390	69	15	2,405	50
Grand Total	3,462	100	1,335	4,797	100

Source: "General Motors and South Africa," presentation by Mr. E. M. Estes at the Council on Religion and International Affairs Seminar, October 16, 1972, Chart 7.

The high percentage of Coloured and African workers, according to GM, reflects the company's "continuing efforts, as well as the rapid and expanding industrialization in South Africa."

GM reports that GMSA appointed its first Coloured foreman on October 1, 1972: "While the number of Colored and African staff is relatively small, it is a start--and, as such, a precedent for further progress has been established."

HOURLY EMPLOYMENT BY WORK GRADE CLASSIFICATION AND RACE

| Work Grade | Total White | Colored and African | | Total |
		Colored	African	
1	-	146	196	342
2	3	233	98	331
3	2	326	110	436
4	32	486	99	585
5	5	267	24	291
6	35	107	5	112
7	50	46	4	50
8	139	173	5	178
9	268	55	10	65
10	446	-	-	-
11	92	-	-	-
Total	1,072	1,839	551	2,390

Source: Estes presentation, Chart 8

COLORED AND AFRICAN HOURLY EMPLOYMENT BY WORK GRADE CLASSIFICATION

Work Grade	October 1972	March 1971	1972 O/(U)* 1971
1	342	429	(87)
2	331	677	(346)
3	436	597	(161)
4	585	801	(216)
5	291	297	(6)
6	112	44	68
7	50	24	26
8	178	93	85
9	65	32	33
Total	2,390	2,994	(604)

*O/(U) = 1972 over or (under) 1971
Source: Estes presentation, Chart 9

As GM's charts above show, Coloured and African workers are heavily concentrated in the lowest, least-skilled categories. In defense, GM states that "many Colored and several Africans are in the upper grades...(and) GM South African is conducting extensive training programs to upgrade these race groups...."

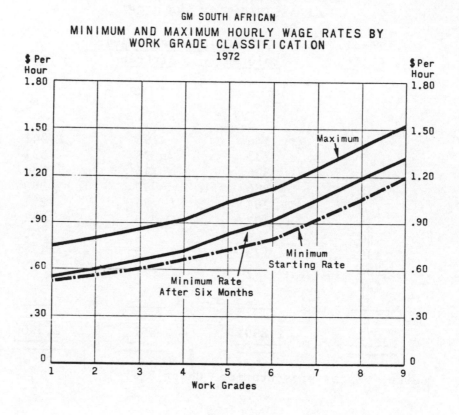

GM SOUTH AFRICAN
MINIMUM AND MAXIMUM HOURLY WAGE RATES BY
WORK GRADE CLASSIFICATION
1972

Source: Estes presentation, Chart 11

AVERAGE MALE WAGE INCREASES
GM SOUTH AFRICAN VS. OVERALL

| | 12 Months Ending | | | Memo: Mar. 1971 to |
	April 1971 %	Nov. 1971 %	April 1972 %	Oct. 1972 %
GM South African				
Colored and African	9	15	15	23
White	10	11	12	18
Overall Male Per Capita Income				
Colored, African and Asiatic	8	8	12	18
White	11	7	5	7

Source: Estes presentation, Chart 14

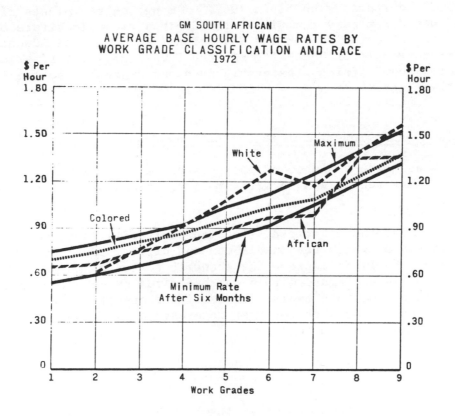

GM SOUTH AFRICAN
AVERAGE BASE HOURLY WAGE RATES BY
WORK GRADE CLASSIFICATION AND RACE
1972

Source: Estes presentation, Chart 12

The charts on the previous pages tell something about GM's new wage program. According to the company, the program has "reduced wage differential for work grades" and "increased wages to establish standardized wage structure through...narrowing the wage differential paid for a specific job (and) initiation of a standard, minimal seniority system."

Other facts, not mentioned by GM, also emerge from the charts. Over 90 percent of GMSA's African workers (categories 1-4) are paid less than the minimum effective level that the South African Institute of Race Relations has suggested for Port Elizabeth.* Based on $155 to $160 as an appropriate comparative figure for Coloureds, all of GMSA's Coloured employees in categories 1-4 and most in 5 (nearly 80 percent altogether) fall under that level.

The company has announced improvements in other areas of labor policy. Besides the black foreman already mentioned, the company appointed its first two Coloured quality control inspectors. Enrollment in various training programs has been expanded. GMSA's benefit plans are "at least equal to the average for all race groups in South Africa and, with regard to Colored and African employees, our benefits are well above those provided by most other companies in South Africa." Further, GMSA's Coloured workers are now eligible for loans to make down payments on their homes.

Another change in GMSA's policies is in the area of charitable contributions: "Reflecting a thorough examination of GM South Africa's outside educational and financial assistance programs, contributions made to Colored and African organizations this year will represent 43% of our total support, compared with 5% in 1969." Among the recipients of the new funds are Inanda Seminary for Girls, the South African Institute of Race Relations, the Association for the Educational and Cultural Advancement of the African People of South Africa, the Bureau of Adult Literacy, the United States-South African Leadership Exchange Program, and the African-American Institute.

Company Position on Investment in Southern Africa

GM has made a number of policy statements on investment in South Africa. The most recent was in October 1972, in conclusion to a report on activities:

> The South African situation admittedly involved complex issues on which reasonable men can differ. Our continuing approach is to improve the economic status of our employees and to build a climate within which desired changes can be implemented. On this basis, our continued operation in South Africa is consistent with the best interests of our stockholders and South African employees.

---

* The approximate minimum effective level is $140 per month. The computations are based on a 44-hour work week.

Although the South African economy has slowed over the past two years, indications point to an economic upturn in 1973. Similarly, the outlook for the automobile industry in South Africa is favorable. Total vehicle registrations are expected to increase to approximately 300,000 vehicles in 1973. GM South African expects to participate in this growth and to improve its overall market position. In the long-term, South Africa represents a tremendous opportunity for the automobile and commercial vehicle business.

The South African economy offers considerable opportunities for sound economic growth. The African, Colored and Asian sectors of the population should benefit as they become more closely integrated into industrial and commercial life--not only in the African homelands and border areas, but throughout the country. Employment opportunities will improve and wages and salaries will show a corresponding increase. The fact that white trade unions are allowing other race groups to occupy jobs of greater skill and importance, and the demand by the Trade Union Council of South Africa for recognition of African trade unions indicate these trends toward greater opportunities for all races.

In conclusion, General Motors believes that the steps taken during the last two years represent substantial progress in upgrading our Colored and African employees. As you have seen today, our total program for upgrading our work force is a broad one. The areas on which we can be criticized are steadily being reduced and I hope in the not too distant future you will be able to join with us in celebrating the attainment of our mutual objective-- equal opportunities in South Africa. We will continue to review all areas for further progress. General Motors will remain in South Africa and will continue to be in the forefront of progressive change.

Company's Release of Information

GM sent CIC its latest report on its South African operations, the October 16, 1972, presentation of Vice President E. M. Estes at the Council on Religion and International Affairs Seminar. Information used in this profile was taken from that address.

History of Actions Against the Company

In 1971, the Executive Council of the Episcopal Church filed a shareholder resolution with GM that would require the company to withdraw its investment from South Africa. This was the first action of this type. Management opposed the resolution, and it was defeated. However, Dr. Leon Sullivan, the first black member of GM's Board of Directors, spoke at the stockholders' meeting in strong support of the call for withdrawal. The following year, the same church filed a resolution asking the company to disclose substantial information about its South African operations. Again, management successfully opposed the move. However, in 1973, the company provided a full disclosure to its shareholders.

GOODYEAR TIRE & RUBBER COMPANY
Russell DeYoung, Chairman of the Board
1114 East Market Street
Akron, Ohio 44316

Goodyear Tire & Rubber Company, the leading tire manufacturer in the United States, was incorporated in Ohio in August, 1898. In addition to tire and related products for a variety of vehicles and aircraft, the company also makes chemicals applied to plastics, rubber processing, foam products, shoe products, film products, flooring, food-packaging materials, metals for vehicles, air conditioners, and mobile homes. The company is also a major military contractor involved in research, development, and production in such areas as missile radar, reconnaissance, guidance, electronically controlled aircraft, and laser-guided munition dispensers. In 1972, the company ranked #59 among the top 100 military contractors, with $86 million in sales. Through some 40 subsidiaries, Goodyear operates 97 manufacturing plants in 24 states and 43 in 29 foreign countries and markets products worldwide through over 165,000 dealers.

Foreign sales and investments indicate the importance of overseas operations for the company. In 1971, Goodyear's foreign sales accounted for 30 percent of the total, while income amounted to 34 percent of the total, a record high. With strong investments in Canada and European countries, such as Germany and France (in a joint venture with Michelin tires), the company is expanding its operations in the developing markets of Latin America, Africa and Asia. In Latin America, Goodyear is involved in the development plans for the Amazon basin and jungle interior. Radar developed for military uses has been applied to survey and map two million square miles of Venezuela and Brazil. The company also maintains a major tire factory and facilities for other products in Brazil, Colombia, and Mexico. In Southeast Asis, Goodyear is expanding a plant in Indonesia and has acquired a plant in Taiwan. The company also maintains plants in the Philippines and Australia. Rubber plantations owned by the company are located in the Philippines and Indonesia, as well as in Brazil and Guatemala.

Goodyear in Southern Africa

Goodyear Tyre and Rubber Company (S.A.) (Pty.) Ltd.
P. O. Box 3062, Port Elizabeth

Goodyear South Africa produces a range of products in South Africa, including car, truck, and tractor tires and tubes. In addition, it makes retread and repair materials and rubber products, such as conveyors, various hoses, and V-belts.

The subsidiary began production in 1947, although Goodyear products were sold in South Africa as early as 1913. The company also owns a 6 percent interest in a Cape Town firm, Synthetic Rubber Development Corporation.[1]

In 1972, Goodyear's South African investment totalled $15 million.[2]

Wages and Benefits

Goodyear employs about 2,300 people in South Africa. In 1970, the company's minimum wage for Africans was $.34 per hour, rising to $.56 for semi-skilled jobs. (Based on a 45-hour week, that would mean monthly rates of $61 and $101.) In 1971, Goodyear's average pay was $.63 per hour for Africans, $.84 for Coloureds, and $1.00 for whites ($113, 151, and 180 per month).[3]

These wages are lower than the minimum budget African and Coloured families need merely to maintain existence. As suggested by the South African Institute of Race Relations, minimum budgets are about $140 per month for Africans and $160 for Coloureds.

In 1969, the company reported that it offered all employees pension, hospitalization, and medical plans, paid vacations, and in-factory training.

Company Position on Investment in Southern Africa

In 1972, the American Baptist Churches filed a shareholder resolution with Goodyear requesting disclosure of certain information about its South African activities. The company opposed the move and gave this reason in its proxy statement (March 1, 1972):

It is the opinion of the Board of Directors that, based on the text of the resolution and the shareholder's statement in support of his resolution, the primary purpose of the shareholder in making his proposal is to promote social and political change in South Africa and in so doing may expose your Company to possible harassment, reprisals and adverse publicity in that country. Over the years your Company has maintained and continues to maintain business operations in many countries, and it has consistently followed a policy of being a good citizen in each country where it is doing business and observing the laws of each such country.

The successful record of your Company's subsidiary in South Africa from its establishment in 1946 demonstrates the favorable acceptance of this policy by the public in general, including our customers and employees. Your Company's continued operation in South Africa, as in any country, is largely at the discretion of that government. Consequently, in the opinion of your Board of Directors, the information required by the proposal together with the publicity to be expected as part of the shareholder's efforts to use your Company for the purpose of imposing his political and social views upon the sovereign government of a country of which he is neither a resident nor a citizen, could very well jeopardize your Company's operations in South Africa. Such activities could result in substantial losses to you as shareholders and loss of employment for our employees in South Africa.

Company's Release of Information

Goodyear did not respond to the CIC inquiry. The company's reply to the Diggs questionnaire was categorized as nonresponsive.

Footnotes

1. "The Rubber Industry," Africa Today, September-October, 1970.

2. R. E. Barnett, Goodyear Tire and Rubber Company, in a letter to E. Bulkeley Griswold, Phoenix Mutual Life Insurance Company, April 14, 1972.

3. Tim Smith, Council for Christian Social Action of the United Church of Christ, in an address at the 1972 Goodyear Annual Meeting, April 3, 1972.

GULF OIL CORPORATION
R. B. Dorsey, Chairman of the Board
Executive Offices
Gulf Building
Pittsburgh, Pennsylvania 15230

Gulf Oil Corporation[1] is one of the principal oil enterprises
in the United States. It is the fourth-largest in the world, ranking
eleventh on the Fortune 500 list in 1971, with over $5.9 billion in sales.
Incorporated in Pennsylvania in 1922, Gulf is engaged principally in the
production, transportation, refinement, and sale of crude petroleum products. In addition, the company is involved in chemical manufacturing,
coal mining, mineral exploration, nuclear fuel reprocessing, synthetic
fuel development and, most recently, a diversified activity--land development. Gulf also is a major military contractor, ranking #82 among the
1972 top 100 Department of Defense contractors.

With 57,200 employees in 1971, Gulf had over 110 principal
subsidiaries, most of which are wholly owned, and 37 affiliated companies
and owned over 13 million oil-producing acres and 219 million nonproducing
acres. In the U.S., of Gulf's eight major refineries, three--Port Arthur,
Philadelphia, and Alliance, Louisiana--produced 77 percent of the company's
average 825,000 barrels of crude oil per day.

Gulf's new subsidiary Gulf United Nuclear Electric is now the
nation's leading independent supplier of light-water reactors, with a
backlog of orders at the end of 1972 amounting to $250 million.

The Gulf Oil Real Estate Co., Gulf's newest diversification
venture, which invests in hotel, residential, industrial, and shopping
center land development schemes, plans to develop over $500 billion
worth of land in the United States alone, and will soon move into foreign
land development as well.

Gulf has foreign operations in 31 countries. Of the company's
oil-producing facilities in 16 foreign countries, 4 in Canada, Venezuela,
Kuwait, and Iran account for 70 percent of total foreign production. In
1971, 71 percent of the company's net earnings came from the Western Hemisphere and 29 percent from the Eastern. Two other important refineries
are located in the Philippines (28,200 barrels per day) and Nigeria (277,100
barrels per day). Foreign acreage is also held in Argentina and Angola,
and the company has license or agreement interests for more than 100 million
acres of Asian waters, including areas near Indonesia and Thailand.

Gulf Oil in Southern Africa

    Cabinda Gulf Oil Company
    Cabinda, Angola

Gulf Oil began exploration in 1954 in Cabinda, a small enclave
of Angola situated between the republics of the Congo (Brazzaville) and
Zaire (formerly Congo/Kinshasa). The company received its first concession

rights from the Portuguese in 1957, discovered oil in 1966, and started production in 1968. In 1971 the operation, considered by officials as "one of the major growth areas of the Corporation," achieved the production goal of 150,000 barrels per day.[2] At that rate, Cabinda Gulf's estimated reserves would last forty years. The concession is potentially the fourth-largest oil producer in Africa.[3]

Financially, Cabinda Gulf Oil is a 100-percent-owned subsidiary of the U.S. parent, but the Angolan provincial government holds 20 percent of the stock:

> This stock ownership does not involve any financial or operational participation in the company or in the concession area. It is purely a legal requirement resulting from the Portuguese Commercial Code which requires an 85 percent vote on certain matters such as consideration of farming out the concession to another oil company.... Cabinda Gulf is a Portuguese corporation as well as a U.S. corporation; therefore it is subject to the Portuguese Corporate Requirements.[4]

Under the concession agreement with the Portuguese, Gulf is also required to appoint a Portuguese citizen to be chairman of Cabinda Gulf's board of directors, to place a government-appointed director on the board, and to accept a government delegate to the company. The current board chairman is Vasco Garin, who served as Portuguese ambassador to the United Nations (1956-1963) and to the United States (1963-1971). According to a Harvard University report, "During his fifteen years in the United States Ambassador Garin was a stout defender of conservative Portuguese policies and of Portugal's role in Africa in particular."[5] The secretary-general of Cabinda Gulf is Paolo Marques, a bilingual Portuguese attorney who fought in the Portuguese army in Angola.[6]

By the end of 1970, Gulf had invested $150 million in exploration, production, and capital construction.[7] More recent expansion of various facilities and intensification of exploration activities have brought Gulf's current investment to about $200 million.

In 1972 Cabinda Gulf's production averaged about 130,000 barrels per day. Projected net income for 1972 is $30 million, considerably higher than the $5 million figure for 1971, the first year Cabinda Gulf achieved an operating profit.[8]

Relations to Government

Gulf officials argue that the company's Angolan operation is neutral in political terms. "It would be impossible to find sufficient (oil) reserves if we limited our search only to those nations with whose political philosophies we agree," says one company document.[9] Further, argues the same paper, "Invariably, because a foreign company is doing business in a developing nation, the citizens of that nation are better off than before."

In answer to critics' charges that Gulf's payments to the Angolan government help sustain Portugal's military effort, the company produced some data in its quarterly magazine, The Orange Disc (June 1972). The

CHART I

Angola: Selected Items of Government Budget Estimates as Reported by the
Gulf Oil Corporation and the Portuguese Government
(in U.S. $ million)

Budget Items	1967		1968		1969		1970		1971		Percent Change 1967-1971	
	Gulf	Official	Gulf	Official	Gulf	Official	Gulf	Official	Gulf	Official	Gulf	Official
Military	30.1	27.9	28.2	34.0	29.6	46.1	30.1	62.4	27.8	68.5	-7.6	+145.5
Education	11.0	11.0	14.3	14.3	21.1	18.8	28.9	23.2	31.6	32.0	+196.4	+190.9
Universidade de Luanda	--	1.2	--	1.8	--	3.5	--	5.2	--	8.5	--	+608.3
Servicos de Educacao	--	9.4	--	12.0	--	14.3	--	16.3	--	21.5	--	+128.7
Mocidade Portuguesa	--	0.4	--	0.5	--	1.0	--	1.7	--	2.0	--	+400.0
Health	7.0	7.4	8.2	9.2	10.3	11.5	12.7	12.6	15.1	15.4	+115.7	+108.1
Ports, Railways, other Transportation	22.5	14.3	34.5	--	44.4	31.8	48.2	--	46.5	47.8	+106.7	+234.3
Mail, Telegraph, Telephone Communications	5.9	5.0	7.9	--	9.6	5.8	10.8	--	9.1	9.0	+54.2	+80.0
Agriculture, Livestock	2.2	2.0	2.6	--	3.9	4.4	5.0	5.4	6.4	6.5	+190.9	+225.0

Sources: Gulf Oil Corporation, Fact Sheet, Cabinda Gulf Oil Company.
Portuguese Government, Budget estimates as published in official gazettes. Escudos converted into U.S. dollars
at the rate of 28 escudos per U.S. $1.00.

Note: -- indicates information not available

Compiled by: United Nations Secretariat, Department of Trusteeship and
Non-Self-Governing Territories, May 5, 1972

company claimed that "military expenses there (Angola) have been relatively stable over the past several years," while expenditures on social services have risen "commensurate with the increasing income from Gulf."

As shown in Chart I, figures published by Gulf differ from those given in the Portuguese government's official gazette. The largest discrepancy is in military expenditure. The total defense cost for Angola is now about $220 million a year, and since 1967 Angola's share of the costs have been rising--to about one-third of the total.[10] Although Gulf shows the expenditures dropping by 7.6 percent, they actually increased 145.5 percent between 1967 and 1971.

Gulf's figures on education are misleading, since one-fourth of expenditures in recent years have been for the university. According to estimates, less than 10 percent of the enrollment at the Luanda institution is black Angolans,[11] although Gulf claims that education "is available to all races equally."[12] Expenditures for the university, which increased more than six times during the five-year period, were the fastest-growing segment of the education budget. Mocidade Portuguesa, the Portuguese Youth Movement, in which there are few if any black Angolans, also received a large budget increase--400 percent, compared with 129 percent for regular educational expenditures.

Until 1968, the company's payments to the government were not very large. From 1958 through 1967 rental fees were $163,680 each year; in addition, Gulf paid $699,301 in 1966 for "concession renewal" and $34,965 in 1967 for "mining fund."[13] Between 1968 and 1971 Gulf paid the Angolan government a total of $33.2 million. Higher production and increased rates raised 1972 payments significantly, to $48.8 million. In other words, Gulf's 1972 payments were 25 percent higher than the total payments for all other years since 1958 (about $35.6 million). About 11 percent of the Angolan budget for 1972 was supplied by Gulf, whose payments are expected to rise by at least $10 million per year.[14]

A Harvard University report, which survey's Gulf's role in Angola and has a tone favorable to the company, argues that though Gulf's current level of payments is of "considerable importance" to the Portuguese, it makes little difference to the war effort:

> Since the Portuguese military effort began immediately after the uprising in 1961, it is clear that during the first eight years of struggle, until 1969, the government received revenues from Gulf that can be described as negligible at best. When more substantial revenues from the initial production and export of oil became available in 1969 ($9.4 million), 1970 ($15.7 million), and 1971 ($5.7 million), the serious military threat to Portuguese rule had long since passed and the high level of defense costs had long since been incurred.[15] (emphasis added)

In contrast, the Financial Mail, which articulates the views of South Africa's major financial interests, sees Cabinda Oil as "Angola's strength":

For Angola oil means badly needed foreign exchange,
increased government revenue, higher exports, and a more
stable balance of payments. It also means a change in the
tempo of living. Gulf's arrival in Cabinda transformed
that sleepy, tropical world's-end into a hive of activity
overnight, strained accommodation facilities and set
local construction booming.[16]

This analysis, written in 1969, before Gulf began any major payments to the
government, recognizes that the importance of Cabinda Gulf goes far beyond
a simple business transaction. In conclusion, the Financial Mail article
notes that Portugal is not the only one to benefit: "As the only country
in Southern Africa to have so far discovered oil, Angola has a special
strategic importance for South Africa."

There is no basis for the assertions that Portugal faces no
"serious military threat" in Angola or that military expenditures have
dropped--two arguments that have also been advanced by Gulf officials.
As shown in Chart II, the military budgets of Portugal and of Angola have
steadily risen. From 1965, which is before Gulf made any major payments,
through 1971, Portugal's military expenses rose 110 percent. Angola's
military budget grew by 162 percent during the same period. Since 1970,
the outlay for Angola's army has been significantly larger--an indication
of increasing, not decreasing, threats to Portuguese control by liberation
movement ground forces.

This trend is confirmed by a recent report in the French publication
Jeune Afrique (October 14, 1972). According to the article, the eastern
areas of Angola are controlled by MPLA (the Popular Movement for the
Liberation of Angola); and recently the Portuguese military staff has
grown increasingly alarmed by MPLA successes in the central region.
Noting that "the actions of MPLA are intensifying every day in the interior
of the towns," Jeune Afrique says: "It is easy to understand the anxiety
of the Portuguese, who are trying to militarize all aspects of Angolan
life in order to escape from their impasse."

Wages and Benefits

Gulf denies that "racial discrimination in employment in Angola
exists." The company's description and data on employment and benefits
are reproduced from June 1972 The Orange Disc:

Gulf's contractor employees are largely black Angolans.
(See Table of Contractor Employment.) But because of the high
level of skills required in exploration and production, the
largest percentage of Gulf's employees are still white nationals,
although this is decreasing. In the five years Cabinda Gulf
has been a direct employer of any consequence, there are now
54 Negro and 131 white nationals on the payroll. But Negro
employment increased from 18 percent of the payroll in 1970
to 29 percent this year. As a total, nationals (Negro and
white) now account for 75 percent of Gulf's total employment.

CHART II

MILITARY EXPENDITURES--PORTUGAL AND ANGOLA
(in U.S. $ million)

PORTUGAL

Year	Budget Allocations	Actual Expenditure	Percent Annual Increase in Actual Expenditure
1965	$126	$259	--
1966	143	285	10
1967	191	350	23
1968	200	382	9
1969	226	403	5
1970	227	489	21
1971	251	545	11
1972	271	--	--

ANGOLA

Year	Army	Air Force	Navy	Total	Percent Annual Change in Total
1967	$19.0	$ 6.4	$ 2.5	$27.9	--
1968	24.2	7.1	2.6	33.9	+22
1969	34.8	7.9	3.4	46.2	+36
1970	48.4	9.7	4.3	62.4	+35
1971	58.4	10.4	4.4	73.2	+17
1972	54.2	10.0	4.5	68.7	- 6

Source: United Nations Document A/8723 (Part IV) and Add. 1; and OECD Survey of Portugal, September 1972.

Note: -- indicates information not available.

And the Company has agreed that within 10 years 85 percent of all jobs and 50 percent of top management jobs will be held by Negro and white nationals. (See Tables of National Employment.)

Cabinda Gulf has Negroes earning more than whites in some salary grades, particularly in the higher Collective Bargaining Contract grades having college requirements.

To help increase further these efforts to keep raising black Angolan employment, a new training program was begun this year for unskilled and uneducated people. By March, there were seven black Angolans in this program and the plan is to hire 40 more by June. They are starting at the collective bargaining contract grade 2 which has a minimum salary of $756 a year. But Gulf is paying its trainees between $1,019 and $1,187 a year. This program is in addition to the higher level effort that sends about 10 percent of black and white national employees for training programs at Gulf's U.S., Venezuela, and Europe operations.

Equal Benefits

All Angolan Cabinda Gulf employees hold the same fringe benefits. Besides the free medicines and medical assistance by labor unions, Gulf has two doctors and two nurses to assist employees and their families. Gulf also provides limited reimbursement for medicines not provided by the unions, and pays 80 percent of doctor bills for employees and their families.

Depending upon years of service, employees get two, three, or four weeks of vacation a year. This includes a subsidy of 25 percent of the minimum salary of their grade for each week of vacation. Paid leaves of absence for three months are also provided every three to seven years of service, depending upon the salary grade. Depending upon the years of service, paid sick leave provides full pay for one to four months, 80 percent pay for the next six to twenty-four months, and 50 percent for the next six to twenty-four months.

Before Chrismas each employee receives a bonus of one month's pay, as required in the collective bargaining contract. In the case of layoffs, an employee is entitled to the Christmas Bonus, any accrued vacation pay and allowance, and a minimum of one month's pay if employed less than two years. This increases to 20 months' separation pay for 20-year employees plus two months per year for those employed longer than 20 years.

All employees are eligible for college educational assistance of up to $500 a year if the degree sought is job-related. Besides on-the-job training, all employees are taught English to help increase their learning potential in the company, and all grade 13 employees are provided six-month training programs in the U.S.

Gulf officials believe that their company directly benefits Angolans and that "real progress for Angolan people lies in more, rather than fewer jobs."[17] Gulf's impact is larger than the 185 nationals in direct employment or the 600 contract workers, according to the company's view:

Chart III

Source: The Orange Disc,
June 1972

Cabinda Gulf Oil Company—
Employment (March 1, 1972)

Expatriates	55	25%
*Nationals	185	75%
Total:	240	100%

Cabinda Gulf Oil Company—
***Nationals Employment** (December 1970 to March 1972)

Race	1970		1972	
Negro	30	18%	54	29%
White	136	82%	131	71%
Total:	166	100%	185	100%

Cabinda Gulf Oil Company—
National Employment (as of March 1, 1972)

Collective Agreement Salary Grade		Functional Job Description	Number of Employees by Race	Actual Monthly Salary Range
	2	Pipeline, Production Apprentice II (Gulf Training Grade)	7 Negro	$ 84 to $ 98
	3	Office Apprentice II, Messenger II	8 Negro	$102 to $ 158
	4	Office Apprentice I Mechanic Assistant II Office Machine Operator III	5 Negro 1 White	$151 to $ 217
	5	Typist Production Operator Helper I Radio Operator II Office Trainee Key Punch Operator Driver III	12 Negro 21 White	$191 to $ 315
	6	Laboratory Assistant Warehouseman III Production Operator Assistant Clerk III Radio Operator I Draftsman III	7 Negro 34 White	$256 to $ 354
	7	Pipeline Operator III Mechanic II Clerk II Electrician II Secretary II Nurse II	5 Negro 25 White	$315 to $ 464
	8	Clerk I Draftsman I Pipeline Operator II Electrician I Welder I Secretary I	3 Negro 13 White	$371 to $ 455
	9	Programmer II Senior Clerk	2 Negro 7 White	$434 to $ 539
	10	Senior Crane Operator Unit Head Team Head Senior Draftsman	3 Negro 12 White	$487 to $ 669
	*11-14	Foreman Assistant Supervisor Geologist Supervisor	2 Negro 18 White	$553 to $1,078

*Grades combined to protect the privacy of employees listed alone in one grade. Grade 14 is a Gulf grade, not in the Collective Agreement. All salaries are within the range listed.

**Cabinda Gulf Oil Company—
Contractors' Employment** (as of March 1, 1972)

Functional Job Description	Number of Employees by Race	Median Monthly Income
Offshore Rig, *Unskilled Labor	149 Negro	$145
Offshore Rig,. Apprentices	64 Negro 14 White	$205
Offshore Rig, Skilled Equipment Operation and Maintenance, Nurses	42 Negro 24 White	$403
Offshore Rig Service Boat Crews	56 Negro 8 White	$865
Onshore *Unskilled Labor	103 Negro 9 White	$180
Onshore Apprentices, Pipeline Workshops	49 Negro 9 White	$205
Onshore Skilled Equipment Operation and Maintenance, Nurses	26 Negro 48 White	$604
Total:	489 Negro 112 White	
	601 Total Contractor Employees	

*Lowest monthly pay for unskilled labor is $66. Due to short-term hiring needs, contractors do not operate under the Collective Agreement.

**Cabinda Gulf Oil Company—
Expatriate Employment** (as of March 1, 1972)

Functional Job Description(s)[1]	Number of Employees, Race & Nationality	Actual Monthly Salary Range[2]
Technician Supervisor Geologist I Geophysicist I Foreman	7 White, U. S.	$1,050 to $1,250
Foreman Supervisor Superintendent	17 White, U. S.	$1,113 to $1,385
Supervisor Engineer Geophysicist II Geologist II Foreman	2 White, U. K. 1 White, Canada 13 White, U. S.	$1,090 to $1,555
Supervisor Superintendent	4 White, U. S.	$1,503 to $1,754
Superintendent Supervisor	3 White, U. S. 1 White, Italy	$1,470 to $1,602
Supervisor Geophysicist IV Geologist IV Manager	6 White, U. S. 1 White, U. K.	$1,600 to $3,000
Total:	55 Expatriate Employees	

1. These jobs are above salary grades and skill requirements of collective agreement for national employees.
2. Base salary in most cases is supplemented by special allowances for extra costs of foreign service. These add about $400 to the monthly salaries listed for expatriate employees.

Economists usually figure that each production
type of job creates about eight additional jobs in the
community as the payroll cascades through the commercial
and public service channels. In a developing area such
as Cabinda, the multiplier effect is probably closer to
ten to one. Thus, the 700 jobs from Gulf operations
are creating something like 7,000 new jobs. The population
of Cabinda is only about 60,000 and the work force only
around 15,000. So it becomes apparent that Gulf gives
the local economy a tremendous boost.[18]

The isolation of Cabinda and the lack of sociological data make
it impossible to evaluate the company's wage levels or "multiplier effect"
argument. But the unreliability of other figures (as shown in the preceding section) indicates that the company's argument cannot be accepted
without further evidence. Whether the economic benefits of Cabinda Gulf
reach 185, or 700, or 7,000 people, it is doubtful that the interests
of 5,800,000 Angolans are best served by supporting the forces that deny
the entire population the rights of national independence and self-
determination.

Company Position on Investment in Southern Africa and Release of Information

In the June 1972 issue of The Orange Disc, Gulf published
detailed information on its Cabinda (Angola) operation. Management had
announced its intention to disclose the information at the 1972 annual
meeting, while also opposing a shareholder resolution requesting the
disclosure action. The resolution was filed by the Council for Christian
Social Action of the United Church of Christ. Most of the data from the
report has been included in the relevant section of this profile.

In sum, the company argues:

Withdrawal from our contract would simply leave the government with all the revenue from a well-established oil field which
the government is fully capable of operating or could contract to
another company. In either event, the Government would not be deprived of revenue. In fact, its revenue would increase substantially.... Gulf is making a special effort to hire and upgrade
black nationals, and in many other ways to make a meaningful contribution to the improved social and economic condition of the
people of Angola. Management believes that real progress for Angolans lies in more, rather than fewer skills and jobs; in more,
rather than less education; in more, rather than less medical
services. And we believe Gulf's operations are providing a major
contribution to this progress.[19]

In an official statement adopted on August 28, 1972, the Council
for Christian Social Action responded by saying:

We believe that employment practices in Angola have never been
the real issue. The major issue at stake is the charge of the Council and other church bodies that Gulf is assisting Portugal to main-

tain its colonies in Africa.... Gulf's own figures indicate that it
paid almost $18 million to the Portuguese in 1970, and sources esti-
mate that 1972 payments will top $33 million (actual Gulf figures:
$48.8 million). Such taxes are a direct subsidy to Portugal as it
fights against African movements for independence. The Council
continues to condemn such support and argues that it is a direct
investment in colonialism.... The argument used by Gulf, that if
it withdraws from Angola either some other company or the Portuguese will carry on the development of oil, does not free Gulf
from its present moral and political responsibility. Every moral
injunction in our faith urges acceptance of responsibility for our
own conduct first. U.S. companies no less than individuals operate
in the world under moral imperatives.... In general, we support
U.S. private capital development abroad where it contributes to the
overall welfare of the people and benefits the U.S. economy; but
in this case we conclude that the continued Gulf presence in Angola
prolongs the agony of a people tortured by Portuguese colonialism
whose rights to independence must not be obstructed by U.S. business or official policy.... We continue to urge Gulf to withdraw
from Angola.[20]

History of Actions Against the Company

Fall 1969--The Task Force on Southern Africa of the United
Presbyterian Church in the U.S.A., the United Church of Christ, members
of other Protestant denominations, the American Committee on Africa,
the Southern Africa Committee, and the Committeee of Returned Volunteers
organized the core of an educational campaign on the role of U.S. corporations in supporting colonial and white-majority rule in Southern
Africa and specifically on Gulf's role in Angola.

April 1970--At the Gulf annual stockholders' meeting an open
letter signed by many prominent individuals representing academic, civil
rights, church, and peace concerns was delivered from the floor. A call
was issued urging Gulf to withdraw from Angola and to discontinue its
support of Portuguese colonialism.

June 1970--The Ohio Conference of the United Church of Christ
passed a resolution opposing Gulf's support of Portuguese colonialism
and asked its members to turn in their credit cards and cease buying
Gulf products.

Fall 1970--The Council for Christian Social Action of the United
Church of Christ passed a resolution supporting the credit card turn-in
and boycott of Gulf products.

December 1971--The City Council of Dayton, Ohio, rejected a
Gulf low bid for gasoline because of the company's minority-hiring
practices and its activities in Angola.

Spring 1972--Black students at Harvard University took over the
university administration building and demanded that their university sell
its Gulf stock because of its operations in Angola.

April 1972--The Council of Christian Social Action of the United
Church of Christ presented a stockholder resolution at the annual meeting

requesting full disclosure by Gulf of its involvement in Angola. Prior
to the meeting the corporation agreed to disclose the information called
for and did so in the June 1972 issue of <u>The Orange Disc</u>.

Worldwide concern over Gulf's policies has spread: There is a
boycott group in Britain and there have been demonstrations and protests in
Scandinavia, Holland, Canada, and Nigeria.

Footnotes

1. See also "Gulf Oil--Portuguese Ally in Angola," a Center Brief published by the CIC, which contains more information on the company and particularly its Cabinda operations.

2. Christian Science Monitor, April 24, 1970; Financial Times, May 6, 1970; New York Times, January 12, 1969--all cited in "Gulf Oil in Cabinda," Africa Today, July-August 1970, p. 20.

3. Ibid., p. 20.

4. "On Doing Business in Cabinda," summary of Concession Agreement, The Orange Disc, June 1972, p. 14.

5. Stephen B. Farber (Special Assistant to the President of Harvard University), "Gulf and Angola," Harvard University Gazette, October 6, 1972, p. 6.

6. Ibid.

7. William Cox, Gulf Public Relations Officer, in a letter to Terry Ann Pristin, The Council on Economic Priorities, August 4, 1971.

8. Farber, op. cit., p. 6.

9. "On Doing Business in Cabinda--A Statement by Gulf Oil Corporation," April 1971, mimeographed.

10. Farber, op. cit., p. 6.

11. Douglas L. Wheeler and Rene Pelissier, Angola, London, Pall Mall Press, 1971, p. 237.

12. The Orange Disc, op. cit., p. 17.

13. Ibid., chart on p. 12.

14. Farber, op. cit., p. 8.

15. Ibid., p. 7.

16. "Angola-Mozambique: Power Points for Portugal," Financial Mail supplement, August 15, 1969, p. 29.

17. "Position Paper on Angola," Gulf Oil Corporation (1971).

18. The Orange Disc, op. cit., p. 17.

19. Ibid.

20. Statement of Council for Christian Social Action, United Church of Christ, August 28, 1972.

INTERNATIONAL BUSINESS MACHINES CORPORATION
Frank T. Cary, Chairman of the Board
Armonk, New York 10504

Incorporated in New York in 1911, IBM is the largest computer firm in
the world engaged in the manufacturing and marketing of information-handling
equipment and systems and related equipment services for business, science,
military, education and other areas. The company also produces textbooks and
other materials for schools and industry. In 1971, the company ranked #5 on the
Fortune 500 list, with $8.3 billion in sales. Between 1960 and 1970, IBM's
sales grew 400 percent from $1.8 billion, with an average rate of earnings of
18.8 percent annually. It is estimated that IBM controls some 70 percent of the
domestic and international computer business. Employing over 265,000 in 1971,
the company operates 17 manufacturing and 8 punch card plants, 23 research laboratories in fifteen states, and about 250 branch offices nationwide. IBM is also a
major military contractor, ranking #20 on the Department of Defense list in 1972,
with over $259 million in contracts. Since 1962, the company has ranked among the
top 34 military contractors, accumulating more than $2.5 billion in awards. Many
of IBM's products are used in the Southeast Asian war, contributing computer systems
to the "automated battlefield" and providing navigation and guidance systems for
aircraft (such as the B 52 bomber). The company also supplies data-processing and
handling systems for military communications, the Safeguard Antiballistic Missile
System (ABM), and other major weapons and support systems.

Through the company's wholly-owned subsidiary IBM World Trade Corporation
foreign business plays a crucial role in the company's earnings and future growth.
In 1971 foreign sales accounted for 41 percent of total sales and foreign net income
was 53 percent of the total. Employing some 40 percent of its total work force
abroad, IBM operates manufacturing plants in fifteen countries and sales operations
with 300 branches in 112 countries and does business in fourteen additional territories and U.S. possessions. Major foreign manufacturing plants are located in
Canada, several European countries, Japan, and Brazil. In Europe, IBM dominates
the computer business with an estimated 60 percent of the market. IBM's dominant
position in the United States and Europe has involved the company in a number of
antitrust suits filed by competing firms and efforts on the part of computer companies
in Europe to challenge the company's position. IBM is fully committed to the
developing foreign market for computers and related products. In Europe the market
is growing at a rate of 20 percent annually, while in underdeveloped areas the
market is rapidly expanding. In Brazil, for example, the use of computers doubled
between 1968 and 1970 .

IBM in Southern Africa

International Business Machines South Africa (Pty.) Limited (IBM [1]
South Africa) was established in 1951 and began marketing computers in 1960.
The company, with a reported share capital of $8.5 million, is wholly owned by
IBM World Trade Corporation. Twice in recent years, according to the Johannesburg
Rand Daily Mail, IBM World Trade has increased the capital investment in its South
African operation. The most recent addition was nearly $4 million as of January,
1971. [2]

Except for a small computer punch card plant employing six persons,
IBM South Africa is entirely a marketing operation. [3] A recent survey (1971) of
computer equipment showed that over 200 of the 530 digital units in use in the

republic were IBM models.[4] Since the list is not altogether complete, IBM's share is probably higher than 38 percent--press reports credit the company with about half of South Africa's computer sales and rentals.[5]

Almost all of IBM's data-processing is imported from Common Market countries. The bulk of this is rented or leased, not sold, to customers.[6]

In addition to computers, IBM supplies about 30 percent of South Africa's punch cards and markets and services electric typewriters and other office equipment.[7]

Although the company does not release figures on sales or revenue for any of its operations, available data suggests that IBM South Africa's annual gross income is in the $17 to $25 million range.[8] No breakdown of revenue figures is available for IBM South Africa, but four-fifths of the parent company's world-wide 1971 gross income came from selling, renting, and servicing data-processing equipment and systems. The remainder was earned by sales of other products and services, including special work for United States' space, defense, and other agencies.[9]

IBM World Trade Corporation has a sales office in Salisbury, Rhodesia. According to the company, the office formerly marketed data-processing systems, office products, and supplies but in compliance with UN sanctions all sales have ceased.

IBM Europe, a World Trade subsidiary with headquarters in Paris, has a branch office in Mozambique. There is also an office of IBM World Trade Corporation in Angola.[10]

Relations to Government

IBM South Africa depends on the South African government for about 25 percent of its business in the republic.[11] The state-controlled South African Airways uses two IBM 360/50's and a 360/30 for its $3.5 million automated ticket reservation system. An IBM advertisement describes this as "one of the biggest computer installations in Africa, a project on which an IBM specialist 'airline team' has been working for years."[12]

An IBM 360/65 is leased by the Council for Scientific and Industrial Research, the body that oversees all civilian and military research in the republic. This installation is specifically used by the National Research Inst-itute for Mathetmatical Sciences, a part of CSIR.[13]

The Department of Defence in Pretoria owns a 360/30 and two 360/40's. According to IBM officials, the machines are used for administrative purposes--payroll, inventory control, and accounting.[14]

Company officials in both South Africa and the United States have maintained that it is not IBM's policy to sell its products for military purposes in South Africa. In a letter to George Houser, of the American Committee on Africa, IBM Board Chairman T. Vincent Learson stated, "...we can frankly find no significant example whatsoever of the use of IBM hardware in South African military research."[15] When questioned about sales to the Defence Department, World Trade Vice President E.S. Groo explained that the company sees "a distinction in the use of computers between military research and operations on the one hand and administrative applic-ations such as payroll, inventory control, and accounting on the other."[16]

An IBM computer will be used in South Africa's new population registration system which will require every resident to carry a comprehensive identity document, euphemistically called a "book of life." Included in the documents will be information concerning place and date of birth, racial classification, sex, marital status, address, driver's license, firearms registration, language(s) spoken, education, and occupation. Africans' documents will contain further information, including residential district and ethnic grouping. Provision is made for future inclusion of information about each person's voting rights and dates upon which they were exercised.[17]

White South Africans have expressed some concern about the new system. One newspaper charged that it "will lay bare personal details" and "snoop on private affairs."[18] Both Parliamentary opposition parties opposed the scheme as an invasion of privacy.[19]

The Department of the Interior, which is setting up the system for whites, Asians, and Coloureds, has rented a 360/50 at the monthly rate of R31,413.38 (about $41,800).[20] African registration will be handled by the Bantu Administration and Development Department, using an International Computers, Ltd., computer.

A PARTIAL LISTING OF IBM EQUIPMENT IN USE WITH SOUTH AFRICAN GOVERNMENT AGENCIES* [21]

Agency	IBM Equipment
Departments:	
Defence	360/30; two 360/50's
Higher Education	360/50
Inland Revenue	360/40
Interior	360/40
Prisons	360/20
Social Welfare	360/40
Transport	1130
Water Affairs	1130
National Parks Board	360/25
South African Airways	360/40; two 360/50's
SA Broadcasting Corp.	360/30
SA Bureau of Standards	system 3/10
SA Railways & Harbors	360/40

*Because some government business is classified information, government use may not be completely reflected in this chart.

Wages and Benefits

IBM South Africa's two decades of involvement in the Republic of South Africa have been a time of rapid growth, as evidenced by increases in its work force:[22]

YEAR	TOTAL WORK FORCE	RACIAL COMPOSITION	
		White	African, Asian and Coloured
1952	5		
1969	750	710	40
1971	1000	938	62
1972 (January 1)	1033	953	80
1972 (April 24)	1017	933	84

Officials of IBM World Trade have described labor policy as follows: "Under company-wide personnel policies every effort is made to employ, train, and provide job security to Blacks (Africans). The company's basic premise is equal pay and benefits. In South Africa, IBM carries out these policies whenever possible."[23]

The company says it has been gradually moving Africans into positions commanding higher salaries and which were previously held by whites, Asians, or Coloureds. By March, 1972, IBM South Africa had appointed one African manager, one African supervisor, and one African personnel officer. There were no African or Coloured secretaries or computer programmers as of November, 1971, but the firm now has "limited training programs for a few Blacks (Africans) in computer operations."[24]

During 1971, nine Africans were sent to a week-long supervisory training course run by the National Development and Management Foundation, a privately operated training institute used by many South African businesses. The company intends to expand such programs during 1972. In all, approximately 10 percent of employees' time in 1970 was spent in training.[25]

Twenty percent of IBM's work force is composed of women, one of whom is an African. Thirty percent are not of South African birth, but the company has no active recruitment programs overseas.[26]

IBM expects that blacks will continue to move into more skilled work within the firm. Company officials interviewed in South Africa made clear, however, that government policy to prohibit blacks in supervisory positions over whites would place a ceiling on black aspirations.* [27]

Wage rates at IBM are primarily a matter of conjecture since, as a matter of company-wide policy, earnings are considered to be a matter between a worker and management. Theoretically, one employee never knows what another receives. Jobs are classified according to "responsibility levels" determined by management, and workers are assigned a level according to individual merit.[28] In response to questioning specifically directed toward its South African operations, however, the company has recently released some wage-related information:

Job Category		African	White
x	Number in group	7	10
	Wages per month	$213-$253	$233-$287
y	Number in group	12	3
	Wages per month	$226-$286	$266-$293

Differences among wages paid to blacks and whites can be attributed to time in the job levels and performance on the job, according to IBM.[29]

---

* Fortune magazine in a July, 1972, article pictured IBM employee Ishmael Tekane with a woman the caption called his "white secretary." The next month's issue, however, carried a letter from IBM Chairman Learson denying that Tekane has "anyone reporting to him directly."

The company has further revealed that the average wage of its African employees is $247 per month. The figure is for skilled and semi-skilled work, as all unskilled labor, such as cleaning, is done by contract. Thus, maintenance workers[30] are employees of companies that contract with IBM for the job and not of IBM itself. IBM also cites a study conducted by "an independent South African group" showing that out of 110 companies surveyed, IBM blacks are paid 35.5 percent above the average.[31] In a letter to Fortune magazine in August, 1972, IBM Chairman T. Vincent Learson stated that IBM is "still paying a few blacks--less than half a dozen--a monthly salary of between $170 and $180."

There are no unions at IBM South Africa or in any other IBM subsidiaries. The company prefers what it calls "the man/manager approach" to employee relations and prides itself as being open to hear the grievances of any employee at any time. There is, therefore, no "works committee"--form of African employee organization recognized under South African law.

In the area of employee benefits, IBM would appear to be an undisputed leader. Benefits offered to all workers, regardless of race or sex, include holidays and vacation, retirement, sickness and accident, disability, life insurance, medical checkup, travel accident insurance, stock purchase option, tuition refund, suggestion and awards program. In addition, IBM provides four further benefits to Africans: (1) free medical aid, (2) free transportation to work, (3) home improvement loans, and (4) company assistance to guarantee high school places for employees' children (long waiting lists for available places frequently make enrollment difficult or impossible for black children). A one-year no-interest loan is offered to meet costs of school fees.[32]

Company Position on Investment in Southern Africa

IBM's "Response to Stockholder's Question on Operations in the Republic of South Africa," reported in IBM, Annual Meeting, April 24, 1972:

> In view of the racial discrimination that is a stated policy of the Republic of South Africa, how can IBM justify continued business operation there?

The management of IBM is against any practice that discriminates against people based on their race or color. There has been growing concern about South Africa and its treatment of the huge non-white population living within its borders. Some stockholders have questioned whether IBM should continue to conduct its business in South Africa. We have shared this concern, closely monitored the activities of IBM there, and wish to report these facts:

Although IBM South Africa provides less than one-half of one percent of our world-wide revenue, it is a fast-growing, profitable subsidiary. We are proud of the sales and service organization we have there.

IBM South Africa today employs 1,017 people -933 white, 84 black, Asian, or colored. Though these numbers reflect the impact of custom and law, we believe they are too low. Accordingly, we have determined to increase them. While a slight decline in total employment is planned for 1972, we expect to end the year with 14 additional black employees. In 1973, while increasing total employment somewhat, we intend to increase our black headcount by 20. These are our minimum goals, and we will achieve these increases. However, we shall be vigilant for additional ways in which we can increase our black employment, continuing the effort beyond 1973.

As in all countries where we operate, we give all our employees--white, black, colored, Asian--equal pay for equal work.

For example, in one job level, where we have 7 blacks and 10 whites in comparable jobs, the blacks earn from $213 to $253 per month, the whites earn $233 to $287 per month. In another job level, where we have 12 blacks and 3 whites in comparable jobs, the blacks earn from $226 to $286 per month, the whites earn from $266 to $293 per month. The differences reflect time in the job levels and performance on the job.

We give all employees equal access to the Company's retirement, vacation, training, voluntary education, stock purchase, and SPEAK UP! and Open Door programs--the last two programs giving any employee access to any level of management, either anonymously or in person. In addition, because of their special needs, we give black IBMers free medical aid, schooling assistance for dependents, assistance in traveling to and from work, and home improvement loans.

Blacks are increasingly receiving more responsible jobs in IBM South Africa. We have two black managers managing blacks and a black personnel officer. We have a black telephone operator, our first black female employee. We have blacks working on our Data Center computers. A programmer is now in training.

In order to understand the situation in South Africa, T.J. Watson,Jr., Chairman of the Executive Committee of IBM; Gilbert Jones, Chairman of the IBM World Trade Corporation; and several members of the management team visited South Africa recently. A strong majority of the leaders the group talked to--both black and white, government and non-government--urged IBM to continue in South Africa. Some students we talked to, both white and non-white, would prefer all foreign investment to leave. To us, withdrawal would most certainly hurt the blacks and our 1000 IBMers the most. It would help no one except our competitors.

IBM has always taken the position that a corporation must leave the practice of international politics and diplomacy to the official representatives of the United States Government. We believe that if the law of the United States does not prohibit trade with another country, a corporation, by doing business there, is properly serving its stockholders and its country.

To try to apply economic sanctions to a particular country in the absence of a clear national policy to do so appears to us to be dangerous and indefensible corporate political action. We believe that corporations should be politically neutral, and we intend to continue this policy.

Wherever IBM does business we want to be profitable and we want to offer our employees equal pay for performance, better futures, and respect and dignity as individuals. In that way, we believe our stockholders are best served.

Company's Release of Information

IBM officials cooperated fully with CIC in preparation of an earlier report on the company's South African operations. (See IBM in South Africa, CIC,

September, 1972.) The company's reply to the Diggs questionnaire was categorized as "non-responsive."

In 1972 and again in 1973, IBM was one of the companies chosen by the Church Project on Investments in Southern Africa in its efforts to learn more about the activities of U. S. corporations in Southern Africa. In 1972, as a member of the project, the Executive Council of the Domestic and Foreign Missionary Society of the Protestant Episcopal Church in the United States of America notified IBM of its intention to file a shareholder resolution. Because company officials agreed to disclose information voluntarily about its South African operations, the resolution was not offered for formal action by shareholders. However, IBM failed to respond to questions posed in the resolution, offering instead the minimal data contained in the report to shareholders of the 1972 annual meeting. As a result the resolution was filed again in 1973.

Footnotes

1. This and much of the information in this paper was obtained from interviews with IBM officials. On March 4, 1971, T. Hultman and R. Kramer met with Morris Cowley, managing director of IBM South Africa, and four other officials in Johannesburg. In an effort to obtain accurate data, they have corresponded with, and on two occasions met with, E. S. Groo, vice-president of IBM World Trade. Information received in this manner will be cited as IBM Data. Where information comes specifically from one of the interviews or a particular letter, it is cited.

2. Roy Levine, "More money pumped into IBM," Rand Daily Mail, January 30, 1971. In this case, South African Rands were converted to U. S. dollars at a rate of R1 = $1.40, since this would more accurately reflect the value invested.

3. IBM Data.

4. Management, Johannesburg, February, 1972, p. 44.

5. Sunday Times, Johannesburg, January 25, 1970, and August 23, 1970.

6. Interview with Morris Cowley, managing director, and other IBM South Africa officials, Johannesburg, March 4, 1971.

7. Financial Mail, Johannesburg, December 3, 1971.

8. Management (Johannesburg, November, 1971, p. 37) estimates that computer sales in South Africa total R35 to R50 million annually. Thirty-eight percent of the lower figure and 50 percent of the higher produce the approximate range given in the text. According to IBM personnel, the company's South African operations account for less than .5 percent of IBM's gross revenue. Since .5 percent of the 1971 gross income is about $40 million, the range may be a little low.

9. IBM Annual Report, 1971, p. 21.

10. From IBM's response to questionnaire from Council on Economic Priorities, attached to letter from R. J. Currie, August 18, 1970.

11. IBM Data.

12. _Sunday Times_, Johannesburg, October 31, 1971.

13. _Management_, Johannesburg, February, 1972, p. 44; and _South African Digest_, July 5, 1968.

14. _Management_, Johannesburg, February, 1972; and IBM Data.

15. Letter to George Houser, American Committee on Africa, from Vincent Learson, September 30, 1971.

16. Letter from E. S. Groo, Vice President of IBM World Trade, to Tami Hultman and Reed Kramer, August 11, 1972.

17. _Hansard_, South African Parliament record, Reply of the Minister of Interior, March 2, 1971, p. 346; and "Population Registration Amendment Act 1970," _Republic of South Africa Government Gazette_, Vol. 62, No. 2779, August 21, 1970.

18. _Sunday Times_, Johannesburg, November 11, 1971.

19. Muriel Horrell, compiler, _A Survey of Race Relations in South Africa_, January, 1971, p. 27.

20. _Hansard_, _op. cit._

21. _Management_, Johannesburg, February, 1972.

22. IBM Data and _Sunday Times_, Johannesburg, December 5, 1971.

23. IBM Data.

24. _Ibid._, and meeting between Cowley and members of Ecumenical Church Delegation (U.S.), Johannesburg, November 13, 1971.

25. IBM Data.

26. _Ibid._

27. Cowley interview.

28. _Ibid._

29. IBM "Report on 1972 Annual Shareholders Meeting," p. 17.

30. IBM Data.

31. Letter to Mr. David Bliss, Princeton University, from Mr. T. J. Watson, Chairman of the Board of IBM, September 4, 1969.

32. IBM Data.

INTERNATIONAL TELEPHONE AND TELEGRAPH CORPORATION
Harold S. Geneen, Chairman of the Board
320 Park Avenue
New York, New York 10022

International Telephone and Telegraph Corporation[1] (ITT) is one
of the nation's largest conglomerate companies, ranking #9 on the Fortune
500 list in 1971, with sales of $7.3 billion. A longtime leader in the foreign
communications industry, with the manufacture, sale, leasing, and servicing
of electronic and telecommunications equipment and systems, ITT initiated
a program of diversified expansion in 1960 into areas unrelated to communications. From 1960 to 1970 sales increased over 700 percent, while net income
increased over 1,000 percent. The company holds a 50 percent or more
interest in over 300 subsidiaries, with over half located in Europe, over
100 in the United States and Canada, and others located in Latin America,
Africa, and Asia. Consumer-oriented businesses have involved the company
in the manufacturing and marketing of equipment for the automotive, construction, and process industries, paper pulp, lumber and wood-derived
chemicals, and foods (Wonder breads, Hostess cakes, Morton frozen foods,
and Genuine Smithfield hams), and in housing construction, book publishing,
tourism (Sheraton hotels), car rentals (Avis), insurance, among other areas.
Antitrust settlements challenging ITT's acquisitions have resulted in
an agreement that ITT will divest, over a period of time, several major
acquisitions, including Avis, Levitt (housing), and some insurance company
interests. ITT is also a major military contractor, ranking consistently
among the top 31 companies over the last several years. In 1972, the company
ranked #21, with $257 million in contracts. ITT has been a longtime contractor
for such operations as the early-warning radar systems, missile testing,
and services provided the Vandenburg Air Force base and Houston and
Kennedy space center. In addition, ITT supplies strategic weapons systems and components and services for the "automated battlefield" in
Southeast Asia, with the potential application of this form of electronic warfare to other parts of the world. ITT produces such military
systems and components as aircraft navigation and fire control systems,
electronic countermeasures, ground surveillance, and communications and
image-intensifier equipment and is involved in major military communications
systems.

Diversification over the last decade has diminished ITT's heavy
reliance on foreign business for sales and income. The company's foreign
business began in the 1920's as a result of acquiring assets that American
Telephone and Telegraph was compelled in antitrust proceedings to divest
in Europe and the Caribbean. With assets in Germany, Belgium, and England,
ITT quickly expanded holdings in other European nations, as well as in
Latin America, Africa, the Middle East, and Asia. Nationalization of
manufacturing and utility operations have characterized much of the company's history (China, Cuba, Czechoslovakia, Hungary, Poland, and Rumania),
some without compensation. The company's foreign political involvements
have been dramatized in its efforts to prevent Chile's President Salvadore
Allende from carrying out his elected position and has encouraged the U.S.
Senate Foreign Relations Committee to conduct a full-scale investigation.

In 1960, foreign business accounted for about 80 percent of revenues, whereas in 1971 the figure dropped to about 44 percent of sales. Employing 398,000 worldwide in 1971, roughly half ITT's work force is abroad. Nevertheless, with the application of antitrust rulings on ITT's domestic expansion, the company is rapidly expanding its foreign holdings. Reflecting such a direction is the company's plan to increase tourist facilities through its Sheraton holding, which already owns or operates hotels in the Caribbean and several Latin American nations, including Brazil, Peru, and Argentina. Expansion plans are set for Norway, Germany, India, and Singapore. In addition, the company is buying the SWF Group of German auto-part makers, and has also acquired the Frankfurt-based firm Alfred Teves, which handles 51 percent of the European disc brake market.

ITT is heavily invested in by banks and other institutional investors. In 1970, the 30 largest banks in the nation held some 33 percent of total stock and together with other fiduciaries more than 45 percent of the common stock.

International Telephone and Telegraph in Southern Africa

South Africa:
Standard Telephone and Cables (South Africa) Ltd.
   (owned by ITT's British subsidiary, STC)
African Telephone and Cables (Pty.) Ltd. (wholly owned by STC/SA)
Miller's Electrical Line (Pty.) Ltd. (wholly owned by STC/SA)
Speedwriting and Houghton Commercial College
   (owned by U.S. ITT subsidiary Speedwriting, Inc.)
Avis Rent-a-Car (40 percent owned by the U.S. Avis Corporation)
Maister Directories (Pty.) Ltd.
ITT Supersonic Africa (Pty.) Ltd.
South Atlantic Cable Company

Zimbabwe:
Supersonic Radio Manufacturing Company

Portugal (Angola and Mozambique):
Standard Electrica SARL Portugal
   (owned by ITT subsidiary International Standard Electric Corp.)

Standard Telephone and Cables (STC), ITT's major Southern African investment, is one of South Africa's largest electrical manufacturing concerns. During 1970, STC is said to have increased its assets from $16 million to $23 million. At the end of 1970, the company announced plans to spend $4 million to build an additional 30,000 square feet of factory space. Between 1966 and 1971, STC's sales trebled and annual turnover reached $42 million. Profits in 1970 totalled $1.225 million, and, based on the average annual growth rate of 12 percent, should reach about $1.5 million in 1972.[2]

African Telephone and Cables, an STC subsidiary, manufactures electric wire and telephone cable. Another subsidiary, Miller's Electrical Line, is a wholesale distributor of industrial and general electrical installation material, cables, switchgear, motors, domestic appliances and hardware, and switchboards.

Speedwriting and Houghton Commercial College are Johannesburg secretarial schools, open only to white students. Avis, which uses the familiar "We try harder/we're no. 2" advertisements although it is the leader in South Africa, has eleven offices, including one in Windhoek, Namibia.[3] Maister Directories prepares the "Yellow Pages" for the telephone books.

ITT Supersonic Africa, initially the marketing agent for Supersonic Radio Manufacturing Company of Rhodesia, is now manufacturing radio equipment. Construction began in 1971 on a $650,000 factory in Pietersburg, 200 miles north of Johannesburg. By 1975, the factory will be able to supply all of South Africa's requirements for Supersonic radios. No more equipment or components will have to be imported, since the radios will have 100 percent local content (the transistors will come from STC's Boksburg factory).[4]

South Atlantic Cable Company played a major role in construction of the Cape Town to Luanda cable link.

Supersonic Radio Manufacturing Company makes portable and automobile radios, portable and console radio/record players, stereo players and amplifiers, and television sets at its Bulawayo factory. Its products are exported for sale in South Africa and Namibia, although this will cease when Supersonic's South African factory reaches full production (see above).[5]

The giant ITT subsidiary International Standard Electric Corporation (ISEC) is "a holding company which controls overseas manufacturing and service companies that, together, constitute one of the largest producers and suppliers of electronic and tele-communications equipment outside the U.S." and is primarily engaged in selling communications systems to governmental agencies.[6] In 1970, ISEC paid about $15 million for Grupo Oliva, a Portuguese-registered firm, which operated four metallurgical and metal mechanical companies in Mozambique.[7] ISEC-owned Standard Electrica SARL Portugal opened a new semiconductor plant in its industrial complex near Lisbon.[8] According to press reports, ITT had invested more than $6 million in the complex, including the new facility, and planned to spend another $36 million in Portugal and the African colonies during the Third Development Plan (1968-1973).[9] Sheraton, an ITT subsidiary, is constructing a hotel in Luanda, the Angolan capital.

Relations to Government

ITT's relationship with the South African government has a lengthy, cordial history. According to the Financial Mail (September 27, 1968), the vital importance of the electronics industry, particularly as "a key to an up-to-date defense force," was only realized by the South African government about 1955 "because of anti-South African activities abroad." To boost the industry, the Post Office signed ten-year "telecommunications agreements" with STC and two other firms, all of whom were then suppliers of imported equipment.

In return for guaranteed minimum purchases of R30 million ($42 million) to be divided on a roughly equal basis, they were asked to launch crash local manufacturing programmes, each getting the right to supply its own 'speciality lines.' The companies had to establish factories and increase local content yearly....

Recently all the companies have branched into manufacture of electronic components...and, of course, some make equipment for the SA Defense Force--about which little is known and less can be said.

Of this process, STC's then-managing director (present chairman), Louis Wilder, is quoted, in the same article, as saying:

Most important of all we're completely self-sufficient as far as trained personnel and know-how are concerned. For example, there's no local demand yet for the latest, most sophisticated electronic components like the minute integrated circuits used in computers. But we have the facilities and designers to make them or any other equipment required.

ITT's affiliates have contracts with a number of governmental agencies, which account for a large portion of the company's Southern African business.* Some of the major departments with which it has contracts are:

South African Police and Military: Because of STC's role in supplying communications equipment for the police, many employees must have security clearances for their jobs.[11] No figures are available on the volume of business involvement.

At the Simonstown Naval Base, STC provides telecommunications equipment. The company also recruits and employs engineers and maintenance supervisory personnel to operate the equipment.[12] Evidently, neither ITT nor the U.S. government regards this work as a violation of the official arms embargo against South Africa.

South Africa recently announced plans to build the French "Mirage" jet in the country, and since ITT's subsidiary in France makes flight simulators for that (and other) aircraft,[13] this may mean more business for ITT.

South African Post Office Department and Television: The Post Office Department, which operates the telephone system as well as delivering the mail, may be ITT's best customer in the country. According to ITT official Peter Loveday, "Approximately half of our business (STC) is with the Post Office for the purpose of supplying telecommunications equipment." STC constructed postal automation machinery, which when fully installed is expected to reduce the staff required for sorting mail to 12 percent of the former total.[14] Most of the department's microwave telephone equipment is provided by STC, which also makes various other telephone-related materials on Post Office contracts.[15]

---

* A 1970 STC symposium on conductors was attended by representatives of the government of the Defense Force (includes Army, Navy, Air Force).[10]

African Telephone and Cables manufactures a large portion of the department's cable requirements. Maister Directories is on contract from the Post Office to produce the "Yellow Pages."[16]

Angola and Mozambique: Standard Electrica is a major supplier of telephones, telephone exchanges, cable, and other equipment in Angola and Mozambique.[17]

Rhodesian Regime: Supersonic Radio Company has continued operations since the regime's illegal Unilateral Declaration of Independence and the imposition of international sanctions by the United Nations. Under Emergency Power Regulations, the white government appointed Supersonic's managing director as its "agent" and ordered him to maintain production.[18] In 1969, the company advertised a long list of products for sale (see description above). STC officials in South Africa told interviewers that sanctions had disrupted coordinated ITT operations in Southern Africa but indicated that there are exchanges between the STC Boksburg plant and Supersonic's Bulawayo facility.[19]

Cape Town to Lisbon Undersea Cable: The link, inappropriately labeled "The Cable of Good Hope" by South African Prime Minister Vorster, was designed and constructed by STC (Britain) with much assistance from its South African affiliate.[20]

Wages and Benefits [21]

Statistics are available for STC operations only. Mr. Peter Loveday, managing director of STC, in his address to the United Presbyterian Church and the National Council of Churches in New York on January 18, 1973, stated, "Our policy has always been one of developing people to be productive and committed members of our company. The underlying theme is the full recognition of the dignity of the individual. Our policy encompasses equal pay for equal work." However, due to the laws of the country and the strong labor unions from which blacks are excluded, Africans cannot be employed in any of the top four wage categories (A, AA, B, C). Africans could be employed in Grade D jobs beginning only in December 1972. The legal minimum monthly wage for Grade D jobs is $267, while the minimum for the next grade, DD, is $191. However, the average pay for Africans in Grade DD paid by STC is $282, or 47.6 percent above the legal minimum.

Average Monthly Wages Paid by STC Compared to Legal Minimum
January 1973

Job Grade	A	AA	B	C	D	DD	DDD	E	F	G	H
Legal Minimum Wage	$368	$314	$284	$276	$267	$191	$142	$126	$93	$76	$68
STC Wages:											
Whites	535	510	362	342	312	257	195				
Asians		330		278	271	221	169	148	133		
Coloureds		330	284	306	287	220	168	148	134	132	
Africans						282	170	171	171	120	116

Straight average monthly pay in 1973 for all salaried employees is
$640.75; for all hourly employees it is $239.97. The monthly average for all
whites is $546.66 and for all blacks, $172.54. The average monthly straight
pay for Africans only as of June 1972 was $125, which is only $27 above the
"official" Poverty Datum Line (PDL) of 1972 and only $10 above the PDL of
$115 in 1973. However, in 1973 STC for the first time has no black employees
earning wages below the PDL, while in 1965 20 percent of its black employees
were below this level.

Employee fringe benefits are available for all employees regardless
of race without any distinction, according to Mr. Loveday. These include a
retirement pension fund, medical services, holiday and vacation bonus plans,
legal assistance, canteen service, educational assistance, some transportation
aid, housing aid for everyone except Africans, a subsidized children's Christmas party, sports and social club, and subsidized vacations for a portion of
the black employees.

While STC pursues a policy of advancement on merit alone, this policy
is limited severely by legal restrictions and prevailing white racial attitudes.
First and second line supervision, up to foreman, is now about 40 percent black
supervision of black employees, an increase of 13 percent since 1970. No whites
are supervised by black employees.

"For a number of years, ITT has been doing business in accordance with
U.S. policy set by the State Department, and operating under the laws of the
host country as is our practice in some 90 nations. ITT believes its economic
presence in South Africa is our greatest contribution to continued progress in
that country."

Standard Telephone and Cables

STC employed a total of 1,800 persons in mid-1971.[22] Of the 1,400
employed at the Boksburg plant, there were 800 Coloureds (primarily women)
and 100 Africans. Wages were R 0.40 ($0.56) per hour for Coloureds and
slightly lower for Africans.[23] Based on a forty-five-hour week, Coloured
wages were R 72 ($101) per month. As of December 31, 1972, Mr. Loveday stated
that there were 1,960 STC employees in South Africa; 24.4 percent (478) were
immigrants, 33.3 percent (653) were South African whites, 22.7 percent (445)
were Coloured, 10.1 percent (197) were Asians, and 9.5 percent (187) were
Africans.

The average pay for black workers in mid-1972 was $135 per month.
Peter Loveday, STC managing director, told Fortune that he raised black salaries by 10 percent in the preceding year and is working toward "wage parity,"
for sound business reasons. "Breaching the color bar" is the title Fortune
(July 1972) gave to a picture showing Asian women bonding transistor elements
under a microscope at the STC plant. This and all areas of the factory are
rigidly segregated. A primary reason for the segregation, according to an
STC official, is the company's desire not to alienate a major customer--the
South African government.[24]

South Africa's labor shortage creates problems for STC. White workers
have a high turnover rate, so the company seeks to give as many jobs as possible
to Coloured and Asian workers. STC imports skilled technicians (whites only)
both by assigning them from other STC plants and by recruitment in Europe.[25]

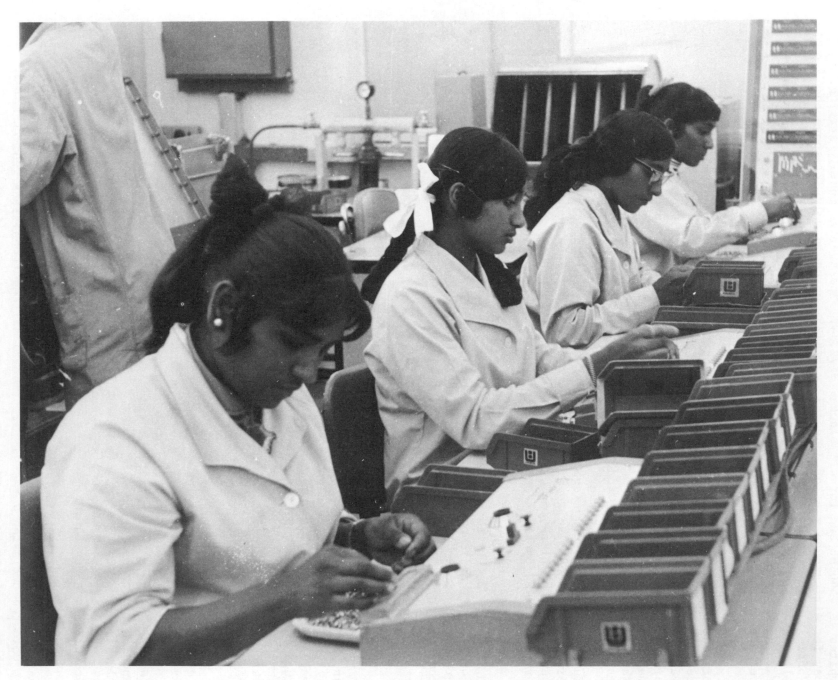

STC Plant at Boksburg. Employees are divided racially in the
plant. These Indian women are assembling intricate circuits.

According to *Fortune* reporter John Blashill, managing director
Loveday vehemently condemns the practice of paying low wages to black
employees. "In practically every situation where you've got whites and
nonwhites doing the same job, you're dealing with the cream of the
coloreds and blacks (Africans), and the dregs of the whites," he is
quoted as saying. Yet, blacks receive lower wages because powerful white
trade unions protect the interests of their members. Asians and Coloureds
who belong to the few multiracial, but white-dominated, unions benefit
not nearly so much as white members of the same organization. Africans,
with no bargaining power, remain far below in wages and benefits. At
STC, white unions have imposed a closed shop rule (which allows only
union members to perform jobs above a certain skill level) and prohibit
their members from training blacks.[26]

ITT Supersonic

ITT Supersonic will rely heavily on African labor, since it is
located in a "border area." Pietersburg, where the company has just built
a new factory to replace its old, rented facility, has been called one of
the "true border areas in the wider terms of government ideology"[27] (apartheid),
in contrast to the "border areas" near major cities. Those near cities
contribute little to the government's plan for removing all Africans to distant "homelands," but economically they have been more successful. From
1960, when first declared a "border area," until 1969, Pietersburg grew
very slowly. Faster growth since then is at least partially attributable
to Supersonic's investment.[28]

The company's black workers are drawn from the township of Seshego,
seven miles outside Pietersburg, on the edge of the areas comprising the
"homeland" for northern Sotho-speaking Africans. Victims of the government's
efforts to draw a "neater" racial map, the township's residents were recently
displaced from their homes in Pietersburg's municipal location and a nearby
area where Africans had land-owning rights, which are not available to
Seshego's dwellers.[29] Residents now have the benefit of a school that
trains health instructors and one that gives technical instruction, but it
is reported that those who receive training in trades such as welding cannot
use their skill in Pietersburg factories but only within the "homeland,"
where there are almost no industries.[30]

Standard Electric SARL Portugal

1,000 employees (1968).

Company Position on Investment in Southern Africa

ITT's attitude toward South Africa has been expressed in various
ways within the country. Through full-page advertisements in a business
magazine, the company stressed its important role in strengthening the
country. "STC manufactures in Boksburg for export to the African Continent
and the rest of the Southern Hemisphere--Good for South Africa," reads
one ad of 1968 (Financial Mail, September 20, 1968). Another gives
a longer list of STC achievements:

> Standard Telephone and Cables (SA) (Pty.) Ltd. is an
> associate of an exciting world-wide organization--International
> Telephone and Telegraph Corporation--which has been responsible

for many of the world's important communications projects....
      This partnership is important to South Africa, because
it enables us to share in the tremendous progress being
made in world-wide telecommunications and electronics.
It enables STC (SA) to make a significant contribution
to South Africa's economy by...
      Contributing substantially to our telecommunications
        and electronics industry
      Exporting
      Employing 1500 people
      Saving foreign exchange[31]

      In early 1970, STC announced its intention to apply for a listing
on the Johannesburg Stock Exchange, enabling it to sell a portion of its
stock to the South African public.[32] One year later, a press report said
that STC expected to sell 30 percent of its equity by the end of 1971--
either on the Johannesburg Stock Exchange or through financial institutions.[33]
Making the 1970 announcement, the then-managing director, L. Wildman,
said the move was an indication of ITT's close identification with the
country. There has been no report on sale of any STC stock.

Footnotes

1. See also"ITT - Apartheid and Business in Southern Africa," Center
Brief, Corporate Information Center, National Council of Churches, March 1972.

2. Sunday Times, Johannesburg, December 6, 1970, and May 16, 1971.

3. "Only Number 1," Management, April 1972, p. 49.

4. South African Financial Gazette, April 23, 1971.

5. The Classified South African Business Telephone Directory, 1969,
Johannesburg, p. 35 (Rhodesian section); and advertisement preceding Rhodesia
section.

6. Moody's Industrials 1971, p. 2781.

7. United Nations document A/8398/Add. 1, December 6, 1971, p. 96.

8. ITT Annual Report, 1968, p. 15.

9. Primeiro de Janeiro, June 27, 1968; and Diario de Lisboa, June 26,
1968, both cited in "Allies in Empire--the U.S. and Portugal in Africa,"
Africa Today, July-August, 1970, p. 12.

10. Star, Johannesburg, airmail weekly edition, March 7, 1970.

11. D. Roodendaal, public relations official of STC, interviewed during
plant tour by Tami Hultman and Reed Kramer, March 11, 1971.

12. Ibid.

13. ITT Annual Report, 1968, p. 25.

14. *Financial Mail*, October 30, 1970.

15. *DailyNews*, Durban, February 24, 1971.

16. "The Post Office," Business Times Special Survey, *Sunday Times*, Johannesburg, July 23, 1972, p. 2; and "Yellow Pages" from various South African telephone directories.

17. "The Mozambique Market," British National Export Countil (BNEC), December 1970, p. 32; "Report of the BNEC Mission to Angola, January 15-February 1, 1969," p. 42; and *Star*, January 29, 1972.

18. *Foreign Economic Interests and Decolonization*, a United Nations Report, New York, 1969, p. 16.

19. Roodendaal interview, *op*. *cit*.; and interview with L. T. Wildman, STC chairman and former managing director, Johannesburg, March 4, 1971.

20. *STC Quarterly Review*, Standard Telephones and Cables, Ltd., London, Spring 1969.

21. Peter Loveday, Managing Director, STC (SA) Ltd., "ITT and South Africa," New York, January 18, 1973, p. 39.

22. *Sunday Times*, May 16, 1971, and Wildman interview, *op*. *cit*.

23. Wildman interview, *op*. *cit*.

24. Roodendaal interview, *op*. *cit*.

25. *Ibid*.

26. *Fortune*, July 1972, p. 53.

27. *Property Mail*, supplement to *Financial Mail*, January 15, 1971.

28. *Ibid*.

29. *Survey of Race Relations in South Africa*, South African Institute of Race Relations, various annual issues between 1960 and 1970; and M. Horrell, *African Reserves in South Africa*, SAIRR, 1969.

30. *Sunday Times*, September 27, 1970, cited in *Survey of Race Relations*, 1970, p. 107.

31. *Financial Mail*, October 17, 1969.

32. *Star*, March 7, 1970.

33. *Sunday Times*, May 16, 1971.

MINNESOTA MINING & MANUFACTURING COMPANY
Harry Heltzer, Chairman of the Board
3M Center
St. Paul, Minnesota 55101

Minnesota Mining and Manufacturing Company (3M), first incorporated in Minnesota in 1902 and then in Delaware in 1929, is a leading manufacturer of a diversified line of consumer and industrial products. The company manufactures and markets such items as abrasives, adhesives, chemicals, traffic control signs, surfacing for tennis courts, recording and video tapes, medical and surgical equipment, copiers, films and printing devices, and related products. Brand names include Auto-Pak and Sand-Pak abrasives, Scotch tapes and recording tapes, Scotch-Brite scouring pads, 3M Brand copiers, and Wollensak tape recorders. With plants in 25 states (principally Minnesota) and over 180 sales offices nationwide, 3M has grown over the last 20 years through a process of acquisition, making the company currently #57 on the Fortune 500 list in 1971, with sales of $1.8 billion. Employing 71,000 people worldwide in 1972, sales for that year increased to $2.1 billion, with a net income of $244 million.

International operations are important to the company's continuing growth. In 1972, international sales doubled from the preceding five years, and overseas markets made 1972 one of the company's most profitable years. In 1972, overseas sales accounted for 38 percent of total sales. With some 30,398 employees, or 43 percent of the work force, located abroad, 3M also reported that one out of every eight domestic jobs is a result of overseas activity. 3M operates over 77 manufacturing plants in 37 countries, including Canada, England, France, Germany, South Africa, Brazil, Argentina, Australia, Mexico, Colombia, Japan, Italy, Venezuela, and New Zealand. Foreign facilities produce most of the products assembled in the United States, and the products are marketed through sales offices in 256 cities outside the United States. In 1971, about half the total capital expenditures figure of $127.5 million for new plant construction and expansion was overseas, in such countries as Belgium, Italy, France, Spain, Mexico, and Australia. About 85 percent of the company's foreign market is accounted for in Europe, Canada, and Australia. 3M, defining itself as a multinational corporation since 1950, when it first established manufacturing facilities abroad, views the multinationalism in its 1971 Annual Report as potentially "the strongest bond between nations that man has ever known."

Minnesota Mining and Manufacturing in Southern Africa

Minnesota Mining and Manufacturing Co. (South Africa) Pty. Ltd.
P.O. Box 10465
Johannesburg

Minnesota Mining and Manufacturing (South Africa) (3M (SA)) is a wholly-owned sales and manufacturing subsidiary of the U.S. firm. No investment figures have been released by the company, but press reports estimate that 3M's Elandsfontein plant cost about $8 million.[1] 3M's South African operations began in 1958; its factory was constructed about ten years later.

Many 3M products are manufactured in South Africa, and most others are sold there. 3M (SA) also develops new lines to meet special needs in South Africa:

A leading South African fertiliser company was planning to pack fertilisers in heat sealed plastic bags. But this presented a problem because the fertilisers gave off gases which burst the bags. 3M developed a machine which applied tape to two parts of the bag, thereby allowing the gases to escape harmlessly.[2]

In early 1970, 3M bought the Capetown photographic firm Africolor Holdings, which had a sales volume estimated at more than $3 million. About a year later, 3M purchased Screenprint, a Durban firm that had handled lettering for 3M's Scotchlite road sign business.[3] With the acquisition of Riker Laboratories of California in 1970, 3M took over Riker Laboratories Africa (Pty.) Ltd. Riker's Capetown operation markets muscle relaxants, pain relievers, and a line of drugs for bronchial asthma.[4] 3M has no mining interests in South Africa, according to E. C. Woods, the managing director of 3M(SA).[5]

Relations to Government

No information is available on what the volume of 3M(SA)'s sales is to various government agencies and departments. The company's huge product range includes a number of items that require an advanced level of technological development that would not be available to South Africa without 3M's presence there.

3M has obtained several government exemptions under the Physical Planning Act allowing it to increase the number of African workers.[6]

Wages and Benefits

3M employs almost 1,000 persons in South Africa, of whom about 60 percent are African. There are a small number of Asian and Coloured employees. Its work force has grown steadily in recent years, from 750 in early 1970 and 890 in mid-1971.[7]

The company has released almost no data about its wages in South Africa. In a March 1971 interview, Managing Director Woods gave a rough estimate of some pay levels:

ESTIMATED MONTHLY AFRICAN WAGES AT 3M--1971

	Rand	U.S. Dollars
unskilled	66	92.40
semi-skilled	87	121.80
skilled and foremen	129	180.60

A 3M official in St. Paul said that the head office kept no wage data on the South African operations and therefore could not validate or update the figures.[8]

A Wall Street Journal article (December 11, 1969) noted that 3M, whose white employees are not unionized, can more easily advance black workers to more skilled positions:

American companies with their training programs often operate against the upper limits of job reservations, though non-union companies (in South Africa) like Chrysler and 3M are better placed to use black labor effectively than those firms who have to deal with white unions.

The company states its labor policies in South Africa in these terms:

The subsidiary's employment practice is to treat all employees in as non-discriminatory a manner as possible. 3M South Africa is precluded from having non-white employees in most skilled and supervisory positions; nevertheless, the subsidiary takes an aggressive approach toward the placing of nonwhite employees in such positions and negotiates with the appropriate authorities to do this on a case-by-case basis. 3M South Africa has nonwhites both as foremen and skilled production workers. Nonwhites share equally in the subsidiary's pension benefits program.[9]

Company position on Investment in Southern Africa

As to apartheid itself, this company believes that those who urge a pullout of U.S. firms from South Africa would, if successful, actually be reinforcing the institution, because the result would be the unemployment of presently employed nonwhites and their forced transfer from the cities to the rural Bantustans and so-called special areas.

In addition, because of the acute shortage of skilled workers and supervisory talent in the expanding South African economy, 3M has noted a tendency on the part of the authorities toward an informal relaxation of the rules as regards industrial employment of nonwhites, although to our knowledge, no clear statement of policy on this point has been issued by the government there to date.

On balance, we feel that 3M's presence in South Africa is to the advantage of all 3M employees there, since the South African operation provides opportunities for all groups, including nonwhites.[10]

Company's Release of Information

3M responded to CIC's request by saying: "Much of the information requested in the questionnaire is far more detailed than we publicly disclose, for purely private reasons relating to business competition." Instead of returning the questionnaire, a 3M official sent a copy of the company's response to the AF-LOG (Africa Catalogue) and copies of two letters written to individuals on the subject of South Africa. The AF-LOG write-up contains only minimal information, essentially a one-sentence description of the South African subsidiary and partial figures on employees and percentage of sales.

The letters, written in 1970 and 1971, argue the beneficial aspects of 3M's presence in South Africa as quoted above. Thus, almost none of the information requested by CIC was supplied by 3M.

The staff of the House Subcommittee on Africa has described 3M's reply to Chairman Diggs' inquiry as "non-responsive to questionnaire." In 1973 the National Council of Churches in the U.S.A. under the Church Project on U.S. Investments in Southern Africa filed a disclosure resolution with the company. 3M subsequently issued an extensive report to its shareholders.

Footnotes

1. _Financial Mail_, special survey, "The Fabulous Years," July 14, 1967, p. 103.

2. Cliff Feltham, "Ready to do business anywhere, any time--that's 3M," _Sunday Times_, Johannesburg, May 3, 1970.

3. _Rand Daily Mail_, Johannesburg, February 20, 1970; _Sunday Times_, March 7, 1971; and Feltham, _op. cit._.

4. Feltham, _op. cit._.

5. E. C. Woods, interviewed in Johannesburg by Tami Hultman and Reed Kramer, March 12, 1971; see also Feltham, _op. cit._.

6. Woods interview, _op. cit._.

7. Figures for 1970 from Feltham, _op. cit._; for 1971 from letter to Richard L. Ramey, Assistant to Senator Birch Bayh, from L.N. Sarbach, International Public Relations official of 3M, August 12, 1971, enclosed with 3M response to CIC; for 1972, from 3M response to AF-LOG, _op. cit._.

8. L. N. Sarbach, in telephone conversation with CIC, November 27, 1972.

9. L. N. Sarbach, in a letter to R. L. Ramey, _op. cit._.

10. _Ibid_.

MOBIL OIL CORPORATION
Rawleigh Warner, Jr., Chairman of the Board
150 East 42nd Street
New York, New York 10017

Mobil Oil Corporation was incorporated in New York in 1882 as
Standard Oil of New York and through various mergers was known as Socony-
Vacuum and Socony-Mobil. Originally owned by Standard Oil of New Jersey,
the stock was distributed to shareholders as a result of an anti-trust
dissolution decree in 1911. The company's present name was adopted in 1966.

Ranking #6 on the Fortune 500 list, Mobil's sales totaled more than
$8.2 billion in 1971. The company's diversified product line consists of over
5,000 petroleum and chemical products, including plastics, for transporation
industries (auto, truck, bus, aviation and aerospace, marine, and railroads),
agribusiness, household furnishings, and industrial equipment. Among the
chemical products are interior and exterior paints, Hefty plastic bags, herbicides, and other crop chemicals. Mobil is also a major military contractor,
ranking #51 among the top 100 in 1972, with over $110 million in contract
awards. The company employed 75,300 persons worldwide in 1971.

The company owns over 20 refineries and has an interest in 20 more,
over half of which are overseas, in such places as Singapore, Venezuela,
Australia, and Indonesia. The petroleum is transported through 38,587 miles
of pipelines, with 8,457 miles wholly owned in the U.S. Mobil also produces
crude oil in 15 countries, refines crude in 22 countries, and markets petroleum
products in over 100. The company has an interest in 71 gas-processing plants
and markets through nearly 48,000 gasoline retail outlets, with slightly more
than half in 40 states and the remainder abroad. There are domestic reserves
in 21 oil-producing states and Mobil's refineries in the U.S. have a daily
crude capacity of 797,400 barrels per day. Mobil's major chemical facility
is at Beaumont, Texas, although it now has 36 domestic and 16 foreign chemical-
producing plants, including 2 in Canada, 2 in the Far East, 3 in Latin America,
and 7 in Western Europe.

More than 56 percent of Mobil's net income of $541 million in 1971
came from outside the United States. Mobil owns 50 percent of the Near East
Development Corp., which holds 23.7 percent of Iraq Petroleum Co. and associated
companies and has a joint venture with four Japanese oil companies for exploration in Iran through the National Iranian Oil Company. In 1948 it acquired
10 percent of the Arabian-American Oil Company and the Trans-Arabian Pipeline
Co. The remaining interests in these companies are Exxon, Standard Oil of
California, and Texaco, with 30 percent each. Mobil also owns an 8.68 percent
interest in the proposed 800-mile Trans-Alaska Pipeline. The company wholly
owns 33 ocean-going tankers (6 registered in the U.S., 27 in foreign countries),
charters 96, and has 15 under construction.

<u>Mobil Oil in Southern Africa</u>

> Mobil Oil Southern Africa (Pty.) Ltd.
> Hans Strijdom Avenue, Cape Town
>
> Mobil Refining Company Southern Africa (Pty.) Ltd.
> 465 Tara Road, Wentworth, Durban
>
> Mobil Oil Company
> Lourenco Marques, Mozambique
>
> Mobil Oil Company
> Luanda, Angola

In South Africa, where Mobil has been operating since 1897, the company's business is conducted through two subsidiaries. Mobil Refining Company operates a refinery in Durban. Marketing is handled by Mobil Oil Southern Africa. Mobil also holds 25 percent interest in a petroleum prospecting license for certain offshore areas. Its partners are Compagnie Francaise des Petroles, British Petroleum, and Shell. The company's most recent South African venture is a 32.9 percent interest in South African Oil Refinery (Pty.) Ltd., which will operate a lubricating-oil refinery in Durban.

In Angola and Mozambique, Mobil markets its products and owns an oil terminal in Luanda.

In 1969, Mobil reported that its Southern African investments were valued at $87,500,000;[1] the company has issued no new figures.

<u>Relations to Government</u>

The contribution of Mobil and other oil firms to the economy of the republic is widely recognized in South Africa. The <u>Financial Mail</u>, a major business weekly in South Africa, made the observation in a recent oil supplement that "without the massive resources of the big international oil companies, applied through their South African subsidiaries, the oil industry in the republic would not have built into a R700 ($900 million) business."[2]

Oil is one of South Africa's most important resources for its future yet is a resource for which that nation is 100-percent dependent on outside sources. "Oil is too significant to be left to oilmen"[3] is the way one government minister has put it. Feeling vulnerable to outside pressure as long as such an important industrial requirement is not produced locally, the government is engaged in a massive search for exploitable reserves, a search aided by Mobil and other international petroleum companies. In a 1971 special issue of the <u>Financial Mail</u>, Mobil ran a back-cover color advertisement called "The Power Seekers," saying, "Everyone is conscious of South Africa's need for its own supply of crude oil--and Mobil is doing something about it."[4]

In a partnership with Royal Dutch Shell, British Petroleum, and Total, Mobil has an agreement with quasi-governmental agencies for offshore exploration. The company also is the leading supplier of fuels and lubricants to the oil rigs and drilling ships. In one 1969 contract alone, Mobil agreed to supply the drillers with 100,000 gallons of diesel oil every month.[5]

Equally important is Mobil's expertise transferred to South Africa for oil exploration technology. In 1971 a commentator explained, "Five years ago SOEKER (the government-established exploration corporation) had practically no personnel trained in these very specialized technical and technological fields and was largely dependent upon imported skill and experience. Today the corporation, almost completely independent of overseas consultants, maintains a high standard of work."[6]

Mobil has not been shy about its contribution to the security of Southern Africa's white governments. "Nas Horas Boas E Nas Mas"("In the Good Hours and in the Bad") reads a 1964 advertisement in the Portuguese military journal Jornal do Exercito. The company pledges that it "could not be absent" from the sacrifices imposed in quelling "the wave of terrorism which treacherously attacked the North of Angola."[7] In the 1970's, Mobil is still proud to help. "From Cape Agulhas to the Mozambique Channel, wherever offshore drilling is taking place, Mobil is there."[8]

Wages and Benefits

In July 1972, Mobil published a four-page report on its South African activities, concentrating heavily on labor practices. (For more details about the background see History of Actions Against the Company below.) The following chart, compiled from Mobil's data, shows the changes in Mobil's work force from 1962 to 1972.

CHART I							
MOBIL'S WORK FORCE **NUMBER AND PERCENT OF WORKERS IN EACH EMPLOYMENT CATEGORY**							
Salary Group/Type Position*	Number of Africans, Asians, Coloureds			White 1972	1972 Total** All Employees	1972 Percent (%) Total Africans, Asians, Coloureds	Whites
	1962	1968	1972				
1 Unskilled laborers	687	387	365	NONE	365	100%	– %
1A	342	267	271	NONE	271	100	–
2	157	145	143	NONE	143	100	–
2A	78	142	82	15	97	84.5	15.5
3 Semi-skilled	NONE	22	37	41	78	47.4	52.6
3A	NONE	12	36	110	146	24.7	75.3
4	NONE	NONE	42	114	156	26.9	73.1
5	NONE	6	48	301	349	13.8	86.2
6 Skilled	NONE	6	16	279	295	5.4	94.6
7 Supervisory & Skilled	NONE	NONE	NONE	219	219	–	100
8 Supervisory & Artisan	NONE	1	5	132	137	3.6	96.4
9-12 Supervisory & Skilled	NONE	NONE	1	409	410	0.2[1]	99.8
13 and above Managerial	NONE	NONE	NONE	186	186	–	100
TOTAL EMPLOYEES	1,264	989	1,046	1,806	2,852	36.7	63.3

* Details of what the position entails is reported by Mobil but generalized here.

** Computed by adding number of white workers to number of African, Asian and Coloured workers when necessary.

[1] Mobil reports 1.2 percent.

Mobil's employment record between the years 1962 and 1972 indicates improvement in promoting and providing greater benefits for African, Asian, and Coloured workers. Yet recognition of this "improvement" cannot be interpreted to mean that Mobil is seriously dealing with the apartheid system. The issue is not the "material well-being" of the African, Asian, and Coloured people in South Africa but rather the right ot these people to determine their own lives and share fully in the fruits of their own economic development. Examination of Mobil's employment record reveals more the tragic condition of apartheid than a sign of substantial change.

Mobil reported that in 1972 it had a total work force of 2,852. Of this number, 1,046--or about 37 percent--were "non-white." The low percentage of African, Asian, and Coloured indicates that Mobil depends increasingly on skilled workers and machines for its operations.[9] The Durban refinery utilizes expensive machinery,[10] and in Capetown, headquarters for Mobil's marketing operations, the company recently installed an IBM 360/30 computer to perform a variety of tasks.[11]

The highly-mechanized nature of Mobil's operations denies the company's contention that increased investment means more jobs for African, Asian, and Coloured people. In fact, according to Mobil figures represented in Chart I, employment among African, Asian, and Coloured workers decreased 18 percent over the last decade. The report does not indicate, however, if white employment increased over this same period.

Table A of the Mobil report displays information on African, Asian, and Coloured employment in over 13 job categories for the years 1962, 1968, and 1972, with statistics for the number of whites and percent of "non-whites" in each job category for 1972. Charts I and II in this profile are based on information provided in Table A of the Mobil report. It is immediately apparent from these charts that 100 percent of the jobs available in the lowest three job classifications are occupied by Africans, Asians, and Coloureds. These classifications represent nearly 75 percent of Mobil's 1,046 African, Asian, and Coloured work force. The fourth lowest and still unskilled category (2A) shows a small percentage of whites (0.8 percent of a 1,806 white work force) but increases the total African, Asian, and Coloured workers in the bottom four classifications to 83 percent of Mobil's work force.

Although it can be said that since 1962 some African, Asian, and Coloured workers have minimally advanced, the percentages of their occupancy in job categories from the semiskilled (3), especially skilled (6), and supervisory (7-12) positions fall rapidly. There are no African, Asian, or Coloured workers in managerial positions (13 and above), and only six are employed in supervisory positions. It should be noted that Africans make up less than 1 percent of the 5 supervisory and skilled groups (6-12) (see Chart II).

Mobil has no trade unions in any of its South Africa operations. For Africans, there is a consultative committee at the refinery, where less than 25 percent of the African, Asian, and Coloured work force is employed. In 1970, Mobil officials told interviewers that there were no committees at any other Mobil installations, and the recent report gives no indication that this situation has changed.

125

CHART II

MOBIL'S WORK FORCE 1972
SKILL DISTRIBUTION BY RACIAL CATEGORIES

Salary Title	Salary Classification	Percent African	Percent Asian	Percent Coloured	Percent of Total A,A,C	Percent White
Unskilled	1, 1A	69	--	41	61	--
	2, 2A	24	--	17	22	0.8
Semi-skilled	3, 3A	5	5	14	7	8
	4, 5	1	86	22	9	23
Supervisory and skilled	6-12	0.9	9	5	2	58
Managerial	13-15	--	--	--	--	10

Note: Totals may not equal 100 percent because of rounding.

The committee "communicates to management issues relating to working conditions that it considers deserve management's attention." It has no bargaining power. All strikes by Africans are illegal.

However, Mobil's policy in this area not only does not violate South Africa's very restrictive labor legislation, it does not even come to the edge of what is permissible under the apartheid system. Although African unions are not recognized in South African law, they are not forbidden. Mobil could allow establishment of an African union among its employees. Short of that, the company could make sure that all its employees have access to the consultative apparatus in operation at the refinery. One U.S.-controlled corporation, a Namibian mining firm, recently pledged not to prosecute African workers for breach of contract, including strikes. Mobil's report contains no indication whether it would respect the "right" of Africans, Asians, and Coloureds to strike or bargain collectively.

Mobil states that its policy is "equal pay for equal work," although this may be somewhat affected by "local customs and practices." The report also claims that "in South Africa the company pays salaries well above the minimum required by law" and that "Mobil's salary structure puts it among the leaders in industry in that country."

However, the apparently progressive "equal pay for equal work" slogan has been used as a method of preserving white privilege in South Africa. White workers demand it to ensure that employers do not hire blacks at lower pay when there are whites available to fill a job.

Mobil's reference to "the legal minimum" is misleading because South Africa has no national minimum wage. The only restrictions on Mobil are those for the liquid fuel and oil trade by a government body called the Wage Board. Africans are not allowed to attend meetings of the board but are represented by a government-appointed white official. (According to law, the appointee must be white.)

CHART III[12]

AVERAGE SALARIES IN 1972 (in U.S. Dollars)

Group	Monthly Salary Averages*			
	African	Asiatic	Colored	White
1	123	--	127	--
1A	139	--	140	--
2	158	--	164	--
2A	190	--	190	210
3	214	--	217	219
3A	251	250	257	251
4	277	288	304	285
5	317	320	324	333
6	362	--	380	386
7	--	--	--	471
8	429	452	450	489
12	--	656	--	721

*Salaries reflect an extra month's pay given to all employees each year as a Christmas bonus.

CHART IV[13]

AVERAGE MONTHLY WAGES AT MOBIL IN 1972

	13-month	Without Christmas Bonus
Africans	$148	$137
Asians	312	287
Coloureds	212	195
Whites	388	358
Average African, Asian, Coloured	167	154

A useful criterion for judging wages is the Effective Minimum Level (E.M.L.), determined by the Institute of Race Relations in South Africa as the least income required by an African family to maintain life. For Durban and Capetown, where the bulk of Mobil's employees live, the E.M.L. is about $146 to $150 per month. Average salaries in Categories 1 and 1A, in which about 69 percent of the Mobil African workers are positioned, are $123 and $139 respectively, well below the $146 figure. The average salary for Africans in the next category (2), in which another 15 percent of the total African work force is employed, is $158, only slightly higher than the E.M.L. Thus, about 84 percent of Mobil's African work force is below or at parity with an income determination reflecting what is necessary only to maintain life.

The E.M.L. for Coloureds in Capetown is $170 per month. Again, at Mobil half of the Coloured employees (those in 1, 1A, and 2) are in groupings in which the average wage is below $170.

The report also points to the difference between the rate of increase of minimum pay and the Consumer Price Index (C.P.I.). However, there is no mention of the fact that the C.P.I. is based on a white family. There is no official index of African cost-of-living increases, but available information suggests that the cost of living is rising much faster for Africans than for whites. For example, three times during the past six years the Johannesburg Non-European Affairs Department has prepared a minimum budget for a Soweto family based on samplings of costs. Between June 1967 and June 1969, while the C.P.I. rose 4.3 percent, the department increased its budget estimates by 12 percent. From June 1969 to July 1971, the department again raised its figure 17 percent, although the C.P.I. went up by only 12.9 percent. Between the years 1967 and 1971, living costs increased about 31 percent for Africans, while the C.P.I. rose 17.7 percent.

The Mobil report shows that all benefit plans, including those formerly open only to whites, are now available to all employees. These include: pension plan, ill-health retirement, recognition of long service, vacation leave, sick leave, medical aid plan, medical policy, aviation travel accident insurance plan, home ownership plan, suggestion plan, transfer expense and transfer reimbursement policies, and educational assistance for employees and children. However, only selective information about these plans is presented in the report. Mobil includes a long list of what it offers to workers but does not show how many employees are enrolled in various programs.

For example, there is no data on the number of African, Asian, and Coloured employees interested who are able to afford the contributory pension plan. Nor is there information about the number of workers' children assisted by the educational loan program or the number of persons who are able to take advantage of subsidized education for employees.

With regard to medical care, Mobil states, "Many non-whites elect not to participate in this plan because of the excellant (sic) state health service available to them." Yet no matter how good the facilities are (and most African doctors feel they are inferior), access to them is very limited. While there is a doctor for every 455 white South Africans, the ratio for Africans is one doctor for every 100,000.[14]

Nor does Mobil explain the operation of its "home ownership plan." In no urban area or African area anywhere near Capetown or Johannesburg are Africans allowed to own their own homes. Umlazi, about 25 miles from Mobil's Durban refinery, is considered a part of the Zulu homeland, and there home ownership is available to a small number. However, few, if any, Mobil employees live in that township.[15]

Mobil's commitment to the advancement of African, Asian, and Coloured employees could logically be expected to be reflected in its training programs. However, from 1962 through 1970 the company trained only 4 Africans and 22 Asians and Coloureds, compared with 992 whites. Presently, since the programs are open only to employees in group 3A and above, only 14 percent of African, Asian, or Coloured employees are eligible even for training.

The 15 Africans enrolled in training during 1971 and 1972 were all learning heavy-vehicle driving. Coloured trainees were also concentrated in that category, as were whites. Opportunities to advance to other skilled or supervisory jobs are therefore very limited.

Company Position on Investment in South Africa

Mobil policy toward South Africa, as stated in the July 1972 report, is as follows:

> There are differing views among Americans with respect to whether, or how, U.S. corporations should invest and do business in South Africa. As individual Americans, various of us may disapprove of laws or customs of other countries--just as many of us disapprove of many U.S. laws and customs. Wherever a Mobil affiliate operates, however, it must comply with the laws of the host country--just as U.S. affiliates of foreign corporations must comply with applicable U.S. laws.
> Some Americans urge that U.S. corporations with interests in South Africa should "disinvest"--that is, simply pull out and leave the country. Mobil's position is that pulling out of South Africa would not be in the best interests of non-whites there nor in the interest of our shareholders.
> What is most needed for the continued improvement of the material well-being of non-whites in South Africa is not disinvestment but greater investment. Over the long term, only economic growth can create additional jobs, more job mobility, and greater opportunities for human advancement. And capital investment is the catalyst of economic growth. With further economic growth, more

and better jobs will become available for non-whites.

We believe Mobil's record in providing wages and benefits to non-whites in South Africa is good; that it has improved appreciably in recent years; and that it will continue to improve. In short, we are convinced that our presence in South Africa is clearly beneficial to the non-white as well as the white population of that country and to our shareholders.

Company's Release of Information/History of Actions Against the Company

In 1972, the United Church Board for World Ministries of the United Church of Christ filed a shareholder resolution with Mobil requesting disclosure of certain information about the company's South African activities. In response, the company agreed to provide the information to its shareholders, and the resolution was withdrawn. The resulting report, "Mobil in South Africa," has been the source for much of the information used in this profile.

The company's reply to the Diggs questionnaire was categorized as "non-responsive." In 1973 agencies of the United Church of Christ filed a resolution with Mobil requesting the company to adopt worldwide "principles of fair employment." The resolution was opposed by the company.

Footnotes

1. Most of the information comes from "Mobil in South Africa." The investment figure was supplied by Mobil in its response to a Princeton University Questionnaire, 1969.

2. "Oil: The Great Gamble," Financial Mail special survey, March 5, 1971, p. 24.

3. Cape Times, August 1, 1970.

4. Advertisement in Financial Mail, survey, back cover.

5. Sunday Times, July 12, 1970.

6. "What About South Africa," Auge of Mexico, April 1971, p. 302.

7. Africa Today, July-August 1970, inside back cover, from Jornal do Exercito, December 1964.

8. Advertisement in Financial Mail, survey, back cover.

9. W. F. de la H. Beck and William Greenwood, managing director and personnel relations manager of Mobil Oil Southern Africa (Pty.), Ltd., interviewed in Capetown, August 4, 1970, by Tami Hultman, Reed Kramer, and Tim Smith.

10. Mobil response to questionnaire from the Council on Economic Priorities, late 1971.

11. <u>Management</u>, Johannesburg, February 1972, p. 6.

12. Chart III is reprinted from the Mobil report.

13. Chart IV is compiled from Charts I and III.

14. "Are Things Getting Better in South Africa?" by Don Morton, Ecumenical Commission on Southern Africa, 475 Riverside Drive, New York, N.Y. 10027, p. 5.

15. Based on conversations with several Mobil employees during late 1970 and early 1971 in Durban.

UNION CARBIDE CORPORATION
F. Perry Wilson, Chairman of the Board
Union Carbide Building
270 Park Avenue
New York, New York 10017

Union Carbide Corporation is the second-largest chemical company in
the United States. Incorporated in New York in 1917, the company is
primarily involved in the mining and refining of metals and the manufacturing of petrochemicals, plastics, carbons, gases and related products,
as well as in the production of electronic components and consumer products
(such as Eveready batteries, 6-12 insect repellent, Glad Bags, Preston
anti-freeze, and other products).[1] The company operates 250 plants in the
United States and another 175 in foreign countries. Ranking #25 in 1971 on
the Fortune 500 list, with over $3 billion in sales, Union Carbide is also
a major contractor with the Atomic Energy Commission. The company operates
the Oak Ridge nuclear energy facilities in Tennessee and Kentucky, which
involves work on uranium production and research for the military. The company
employed over 99,000 persons worldwide in 1971, excluding several thousand more
connected with the Oak Ridge facilities and employment in minority-owned firms.

Union Carbide's international business is continually expanding and constitutes an important sector in the company's future growth and earnings, with
over 60 international subsidiaries and affiliates in 40 nations. Of the $729
million in total construction expenditures for 1970-71, some 25 percent was
invested in foreign facilities. In 1971, foreign business accounted for over
$906 million, or 30 percent of total sales, and over $44 million, or 28 percent
of total net income. The company employed some 43 percent of its total work
force abroad in 1971. Union Carbide maintains facilities in Canada, 9 European
countries, 12 countries in the Far East (including Thailand, Malaysia, Indonesia,
Singapore, the Philippines, and Japan), 7 Latin American nations, and 7 in Africa
and the Middle East.

One of the company's largest petrochemical complexes is located in Brazil
and another in Puerto Rico, a highly industrialized haven for U. S. oil and
petrochemical refining companies. Union Carbide also operates several mines
in foreign countries extracting such strategic metals as manganese and tungsten
(in Brazil) and chromium in South Africa and Rhodesia. The U. S. is virtually
100 percent dependent on foreign sources for these metals and is over 50 percent
dependent on many others. While the company had imported most of its chromium
from South Africa and the Soviet Union, the U. S. decision to relax enforcement
of UN sanctions on imports from Rhodesia has provided a cheaper source for the
metal.

In its 1971 Annual Report, a company executive described the company's
"internationalization" to stockholders in terms of the future of Carbide-type
products. Birny Mason referred to the "great, worldwide middle class: an
immense cosmopolitan group that will demand new and better products."

Union Carbide in Southern Africa

South Africa:

    Chrome Corporation (South Africa) (Pty.) Ltd.
        P. O. Box 8194, Johannesburg
    Ruighoek Chrome Mines (Pty.) Ltd.
    Ucar Chrome Company (South Africa) (Pty.) Ltd.
        (formerly Jagdlust Chrome Co.)
    Ucar Minerals Corporation
    Union Carbide South Africa (Pty.) Ltd.
        P. O. Box 8194, Johannesburg
    Elektrode Maatskappy Van Suid Africa (Eiendoms) Beperk
        (translation: Electrode Company of South Africa (Pty.) Ltd.)

Rhodesia:

    African Chrome Mines Ltd.
    Rhodesian Chrome Mines Ltd.
    Union Carbide Rhomet (Private) Ltd.
    Mitimba Estates

Chrome Corporation (South Africa), Ruighoek Chrome Mines, and Ucar Chrome Company operate several chrome mines in the Transvaal region of South Africa. Their combined output, which was increased by about 50 percent following imposition of sanctions against Rhodesia, reportedly accounts for one-fifth of the country's chrome production.[2] Only the USSR produces more chrome than South Africa -- whose output accounts for about 31 percent of world production and whose reserves, though not of high quality, make up about 74 percent of total estimated world reserves.[3]

Union Carbide's major South African subsidiary is Ucar Minerals Corporation, which operates a vanadium mine and processing plant near Pretoria. In 1970, Ucar launched a $3.5 million expansion program to convert its plant from production of vanadium pentoxide to vanadium carbide, which Union Carbide calls "carvan." Carvan is simpler and cheaper for production of ferro-vanadium, a steel alloy, and was only produced within the United States before Ucar started making it. According to South African press reports, carvan offers a "big boost" to the country's mineral exports and "should earn considerable foreign exchange."[4]

Union Carbide South Africa (Pty.) Ltd. markets the company's products in South Africa. These include plastic raw materials, industrial and agricultural chemicals, silicones, coating and adhesive resins, graphite electrodes, special alloys, industrial gases, and pharmaceuticals.[5] Elektrode Maatskappy makes carbon products.[6]

Union Carbide began operating in Zimbabwe (Rhodesia) in 1923, only seven years after the company was incorporated in New York. In 1969, the president of the Mining and Metals Division told a House Subcommittee, "We first went to Rhodesia because it was, and still is, the source of the finest metallurgical chrome ore that has ever been found."[7]

133

The company places its gross investment there at $17 million, although from other sources it would appear to have an actual value of $40 to $45 million.[8]

Rhodesian Chrome Mines and its wholly-owned subsidiary African Chrome Mines produce most of Rhodesia's chrome ore. Their combined total output in 1965 (the last year for published figures) was 490,000 tons -- 78 percent of the total for that year.[9] During 1967, production was cut back at the African Chrome Mines, northwest of Salisbury, and it was placed on a "care and maintenance basis."[10] Rhodesian Chrome was awarded several prospecting concessions in 1968, not only for chrome but also for nickel, platinoids, and copper. In 1971, the company was reportedly prospecting in the Gwelo region for chromium and nickel.[11] Current chrome production probably remains at about the same level as it was when sanctions were enacted.[12]

Union Carbide Rhomet operates a ferroalloy plant near Que Que. The facility's two electric furnaces have a production capacity of at least 40,000 tons of ferrochrome, an iron alloy including 60 to 75 percent chromium and up to 10 percent carbon, used to make stainless and specialty steel as well as other alloys.[13] The ferrochrome industries of Rhodesia and South Africa have grown rapidly in the last year, and ferrochrome has been the major import affected by the U. S. relaxation of sanctions.

Mitimba Forests grows trees and supplies timber for mine supports.

Relations to Government

United Nations sanctions, and particularly their enforcement by the United States government, have changed Union Carbide's relationship with its Rhodesian subsidiaries. J. Clayton Stephenson, president of the Mining and Metals Division, told a House subcommittee how his company has operated:

> On February 8, 1966, the de facto Rhodesian government directed our local management, pursuant to the Emergency Power Regulations, to continue to produce, sell, and export chrome and appointed the individual then serving as Managing Director of both (Union Carbide subsidiary) companies its agent to effect this purpose. As a result, the local management of our Rhodesian affiliates continued to operate the mines and ship ore to ports in Mozambique.[14]

Later, according to Mr. Stephenson, at the request of the State Department, which the company had kept "fully informed," the Mozambique shipments were stopped. Subsequently, the Rhodesian government directed the company to sell all its produced chrome to a state-controlled trading corporation.

Union Carbide has employed several methods to lessen the detrimental effects that sanctions have produced for the company. A special committee of the United Nations General Assembly noted that several foreign companies sought to maneuver around sanctions by moving large supplies of minerals to Mozambican ports just before the boycott became officially in force:

In this connection special mention must be made of the
Union Carbide Company of the U. S., which was reported
to have imported significant amounts of chrome from its
stockpile of an estimated 140,000 tons in Mozambique.[15]

The company took other precautions in 1966, besides stockpiling in
Mozambique, in case the threatened embargo was initiated. In November,
the U. S. parent transferred $2 million to a South African subsidiary,
Ruighoek Chrome Mines. On December 16, the day the United Nations adopted
mandatory sanctions, Union Carbide sent another $1 million to Ruighoek;
and five days later Ruighoek forwarded $2,680,000 to Rhodesian Chrome Mines
as advance payment for chrome ore. Later, the company applied to the U. S.
government for permission to import 150,000 long tons on the premise that
it was purchased before the U. S. enacted sanctions.[16]

The request was denied by Johnson administration officials but in
September, 1970, the Treasury Department announced that under "hardship
provisions" of the law, companies would be allowed to import any chrome ore
that was purchased before President Johnson signed the executive order im-
plementing sanctions on January 5, 1967. The department issued a license to
Union Carbide for the importation of 150,000 tons.[17] (In 1973, during con-
firmation hearings, several Senators suggested that there might have been a
connection between the decision reversal and Kenneth Rush, newly-appointed
Deputy Secretary of State. Before President Nixon appointed his former law
professor as ambassador to West Germany in 1969, Rush had been president of
Union Carbide. Rush denied any role in the decision to allow his former
employer to import chrome and pledged nonparticipation in Southern African
questions in his new post.)

Union Carbide has also supported legislative efforts to abolish or relax
U. S. enforcement of sanctions. Two other organizations active in this campaign were Foote Mineral Company, whose Rhodesian subsidiary is the other
major chrome producer in the territory, and the Rhodesian Information Service,
the illegal regime's mouthpiece in the U. S. The Rhodesian Information Service
has reportedly spent over $9 million since 1967 in an effort to weaken U. S.
support for international sanctions.[18]

In 1971, these efforts bore fruit when Congress passed Section 503 of
the Military Procurement Bill. The measure, sponsored by Representative James
Collins and Senator Harry Byrd, had failed to pass either the House Foreign
Affairs Committee or the Senate Foreign Relations Committee but was added as a
rider to the Military Bill. It prohibited the President from banning importation of a "strategic" material from a "free world" country as long as it was
being imported from a "Communist" country. Its effect was to allow entry of
14 different minerals produced in Zimbabwe -- all on the list of 72 strategic
items.

Passage of the measure could hardly have been better timed for the illegal
Ian Smith regime, which at that time was negotiating for an agreement with the
British government. As a reporter for London's Sunday Times observed, "coming
as it did just four days before (Foreign Minister) Sir Alex Douglas-Home left

to negotiate with Ian Smith, (the Congressional action) was <u>the death knell of Britain's non-violent</u> 'solution' of the Rhodesian problem" (emphasis added).[19]

Union Carbide officials and Congressional supporters of the Byrd amendment concentrated their arguments on the strategic importance of chrome ore. In testimony before the House subcommittee on Africa (June 22, 1971), Fred Kroft, Jr., president of Union Carbide's Ferroalloys Division, outlined the reasons his company supported the Byrd amendment. He stressed the dangers of U. S. reliance on the USSR "for more than 50 percent of its supplies of a critical and strategic material"; and he predicted that continued enforcement of sanctions might result in "employee layoffs in the ferroalloys and steel industries."

However, the importation of Soviet chrome has continued at the same level since the Byrd amendment was passed, and many ferrochrome workers have lost their jobs as a result of the inflow of cheaply-mined and processed Rhodesian materials. U. S. government figures for the first eleven months of 1972 show that 58 percent of metallurgical grade chromium imported came from the USSR -- the same amount as in 1968, 1969, 1970, and 1971.[20]

"In short, chrome ore was never the real object of passing the Byrd Amendment," notes Edgar Lockwood, director of the Washington Office on Africa. "Ferrochrome was more important but it was in fact never mentioned."[21] Since the United States lifted sanctions, there have been only four shipment of chrome ore received in the country, compared with twenty shipments of some form of ferrochrome. Imports of ferrochrome during the first eleven months of 1972 were 70 percent higher than for all of 1971 and twice as much as the annual average for 1966-71 (while sanctions were in force).[22]

As mentioned above, Union Carbide Rhomet produces ferrochrome in its Rhodesian plant. Also, much Zimbabwean chrome is being used in South Africa's ferrochrome industry. Ferrochrome imported from Rhodesia and South Africa is cheaper than domestically produced ferrochrome, despite the much greater shipping costs. As a result, ferrochrome plants in Steubenville, Ohio (Foote Mineral), Brilliant, Ohio (Ohio Ferro-Alloy Corp.), and Charleston, South Carolina, are closing down, affecting the jobs of about 1,000 workers.[23]

The actual result of Union Carbide's policies, including support for ending sanctions, is to allow the company to obtain Southern African ferrochrome at the cheapest prices, regardless of the consequences for American and African workers.

Wages and Benefits

Union Carbide refused to provide any wage data to the CIC; but in a 1970 interview, the head of the company's Southern African operations gave these figures:[24]

Rhodesia	South Africa

Rhodesia

Whites: $122.50 monthly minimum
$750.00 monthly for management

Africans: $47 for unskilled monthly
$50 -- approximate average
$130 -- craftsman rate
(same for whites)

South Africa

Whites: $140 monthly minimum

Africans: $48 -- unskilled
$55 -- average
$160 -- skilled

Average wages for men were 25 percent higher than those for women.

A company fact sheet states that "over the past three years, alone, wages of our black employees in the mines (in South Africa) have increased more than 50 percent."[25]

In 1970, the average annual earning for full-time workers in the U. S. mining industry was $9,262.[26] In South Africa, the average for all workers involved in mining was $852.[27] Based on the figures above, Union Carbide's African workers in South Africa (who make up over 90 percent of the work force) made an average annual wage of $660. Thus, it is easy to understand how Union Carbide profits by shifting production of ferrochrome and other materials from the United States to Rhodesia and South Africa, where the minority regimes keep wages low by political repression, population control, and the denial of basic trade union rights.

Company Position on Investment in Southern Africa

In replying to the CIC, Union Carbide provided the following statement regarding Southern Africa:

Union Carbide's Position

Union Carbide is a commercial, not a political entity. As such, its presence in, or business involvement with, a foreign country should in no way reflect an endorsement of that country's government, governmental policies, laws and/or customs. Union Carbide currently has production facilities in some 30 foreign countries and sales operations in more than 100. A significant number of these countries have political systems, policies, laws and/or customs which many Americans may find morally unacceptable. For that matter, many Americans today are in moral conflict with some of the laws, policies, and practices of our own country.

Union Carbide recognizes its obligation to conduct its business affairs in a morally-responsible manner as its past record, particularly regarding its operations in Southern Africa, will bear out. It also recognizes that if it is to survive as a commercial entity -- if it is to continue to provide for the economic well-being and security of its nearly 100,000 employees worldwide, remain a vital force in our nation's economy and continue to support social progress both at home and in the countries in which it operates -- it must fulfill its basic obligation to its shareholders to conduct its business in a sound and profitable manner.

If it is to continue to grow and prosper in today's highly competitive business world, a corporation can ill-afford to sit in moral judgment of the countries of the world or to attempt to interfere in the political affairs of the countries in which it operates. If compatibility with the moral, political, and social beliefs and values of the American people were to be the sole criterion, some case probably could be made against U. S. corporations investing in or doing business with any foreign country.

Basic to any consideration of the "morality" of U. S. corporations doing business in the white minority-run countries of Southern Africa is the inescapable fact that, through their presence in these countries, U. S. corporations are ministering to the basic needs -- shelter, clothing, medical care, and education -- of hundreds of thousands of Southern African blacks.

From the very beginning of its involvement in Southern Africa, Union Carbide has worked tirelessly to improve the quality of life for its black employees there. For example, it brought medical attention to literally thousands of black Rhodesians -- many for the first time. Thanks to Union Carbide's medical care efforts in the largest community in which it operates, infant mortality has been reduced from 50 per cent to less than 1 per cent, life expectancy has increased dramatically, and diseases which historically have been epidemic for the black population have been brought under control.

Union Carbide built a hospital -- the first, and still the only one in the area -- and staffed it with two full-time physicians who not only minister to the medical needs of our employees, but to those of many non-employees in the surrounding trust area, as well.

It built and maintains day care centers for preschool children, one of the best school systems in the entire country, a fine trade school where black Rhodesians are acquiring necessary skills for further advancement. It even established an adult educational program covering such subjects as reading, writing, arithmetic, nutrition, and hygiene.

It provided its black employees and their families with permanent, multi-room housing with running water, and electricity. And it replaced the nutritionally poor, high starch diet common to black Africans with a nutritionally balanced diet which includes milk, fresh vegetables and meat.

Union Carbide did all this and more not because it was required to, certainly, and not because of public pressure since these programs were established before the present public outcry made it fashionable and politic to do so. It did this because it recognized its responsibility to improve the quality of life in the communities in which it operates.

138

In South Africa our task has been made considerably more difficult by the nature and location of our principal operation there. Mining is an extremely labor-intensive industry. Our chrome deposits, however, are located in remote, sparsely-populated regions of South Africa. This factor, coupled with the critical shortage of skilled manpower throughout South Africa, has forced us to rely heavily on unskilled workers recruited from economically-depressed areas of South Africa and neighboring countries. The raw and transitory nature of this kind of work force poses special problems with regard to wage levels, benefits, advancement opportunities, educational and training programs, and the like.

Nonetheless, considerable progress is being made in each of these areas. For example, over the past 3 years, alone, wages of our black employees in the mines have increased more than 50 percent. Fringe and other employee benefits also have been improved significantly. In addition, Union Carbide is currently considering moves which could lead to the development of a more stable mining work force, hence, more and better job opportunities for its black employees.

Union Carbide does not attempt to interfere in the political affairs of any foreign country in which it operates and doubts that any sovereign nation would long tolerate such outside interference. However, consistent with sound business practices and South Africa law, it will continue to work to improve job opportunities, wages, benefits, and educational opportunities for its black employees.

In sum, then, Union Carbide is convinced that, through its presence in Southern Africa, it is helping to improve the quality of life for tens of thousands of Southern African blacks and that its withdrawal from Southern Africa would serve neither the cause of humanity nor the interests of the black people of Southern Africa.

Company's Release of Information

Union Carbide's reply to the CIC was a three-page paper, "Union Carbide in Southern Africa." The document contained one-half page of "background," giving a brief sketch of the company's Southern African involvement, and one-half page outlining the "issue" of U. S. corporate activity in the area. The rest was the company's position, which is quoted in the preceding section.

History of Actions Against the Company

Union Carbide has been critized for support given the minority regimes through its investments and through its lobbying activities. The company's 1972 shareholders meeting was picketed by a group of demonstrators protesting Union Carbide's role in breaking UN sanctions. Inside the meeting, representatives of several religious organizations condemned the company's Southern African involvements. Lyle Tatum, from the American Friends Service Committee, told the officers and shareholders, "Today we have a strange reversal of roles. Demonstrators for law and order, led by a judge, are protesting in the streets outside while the international law breakers meet here."

Representative Charles Diggs (D. Mich.), chairman of the House Subcommittee on African Affairs, though not a stock owner, attended the meeting "to express the outrage of the Congressional Black Caucus and indeed of a growing number of black Americans all over this country that Union Carbide should be an accomplice in breaking international sanctions against Rhodesia."

Management responded with the same argument as above: Union Carbide's presence is bringing benefits to all segments of the population. But African leaders do not agree. During a visit to New York early in 1972, Bishop Abel Muzorewa, of Zimbabwe, told American church leaders about his people's feelings on the matter:

> My people are dismayed that the U. S. has _failed_ them through its decision to relax sanctions and allow the importation of chrome ore from Rhodesia . . . . Sanctions must remain. Sanctions are the only weapon we have.[28]

Muzorewa is the bishop of the United Methodist Church in Zimbabwe and president of the African National Council, an organization formed to present the views of Africans and work for peaceful change to majority rule. Following visits to the U. S. A. and Great Britain, Bishop Muzorewa had his passport revoked by the Rhodesia regime.

Footnotes

1. _Discovery_, Union Carbide, (no date).

2. _Tempo_, South African Foundation, No. 75, December 1969/January 1970.

3. _Minerals Yearbook_ 1970, U. S. Department of Interior.

4. _Sunday Times_, Johannesburg, March 1, 1970; and _South African Financial Gazette_, June 11, 1971.

5. "South Africa," _Trade List_, U. S. Department of Commerce, August, 1971, P. 34.

6. Union Carbide's reply to CIC; letter and position paper sent to Ronald L. Phillips, Research Director, CIC, from R. S. Prochnik, Director of Public Relations, Union Carbide Corp., September 29, 1972.

7. J. Clayton Stephenson, President of the Mining and Metals Division of Union Carbide, in a statement to the House Subcommittee on African Affairs, October 31, 1969 (photocopy).

8. The United States government places the total value of U. S. investment in Zimbabwe at $57 million and the value of the chrome ore assets at $50 million. --David Newson, _United States Foreign Policy for the 1970's_: Hearings Before the Africa Subcommittee of the House Foreign Affairs Committee, p. 176 (Africa section). The two companies with the chrome assets, Union Carbide and Foote Mineral, state the book value of their Rhodesian holdings as $17 million for Union Carbide (Stephenson, _op. cit._) and about $2 million for Foote Mineral (Foote

Annual Report, 1971, p. 10). Using these figures to determine each company's share of the more useful $57 million figure, the value of Union Carbide's holdings is $40-$45 million.

9. Stephenson, op. cit.

10. Minerals Yearbook 1967, U. S. Department of Interior, Vol. IV.

11. Minerals Yearbook 1967, Vol. IV.

12. Financial Mail, October 18, 1968; and "Rhodesia Supplement," Financial Mail, April 30, 1971.

13. Financial Mail, March 17, 1972.

14. Stephenson, op. cit.

15. Foreign Economic Interests and De-colonization, United Nations, 1969.

16. Stephenson, op. cit.

17. United Nations General Assembly Document A/8398/Add.1, December 6, 1971, p. 145.

18. Tony Geraghty, "U. S. Churches Helped Rhodesia Break Embargo," Boston Sunday Globe, December 12, 1971, p. 1.

19. Tony Geraghty, "Why the U. S. Gave Smith a Chromium Polish," London Sunday Times, January 30, 1972.

20. Edgar Lockwood, Director of the Washington Office on Africa, in a statement submitted to the House Subcommittee on African Affairs and the Subcommittee on International Organizations and Movements, February 22, 1973, p. 2.

21. Ibid., p. 4.

22. Ibid., p. 5.

23. Information collected by the Washington Office on Africa.

24. Logan Emlet, interviewed by Tim Smith, Tami Hultman, and Reed Kramer, Johannesburg, July 17, 1970.

25. Union Carbide's reply to CIC, op. cit.

26. Minerals Yearbook 1970, U. S. Department of Interior, Vol. I, Table 27, p. 40.

27. Bulletin of Statistics, quarter ended June 1972, Pretoria, South Africa.

28. Quoted in "Sanctions and Rhodesian Chrome," Ecumenical Commission on Southern Africa (no date).

ADDRESSOGRAPH-MULTIGRAPH CORP.
Tower East
Shaker Heights, Ohio 44120
216 731-8000
Chairman: Frank H. Woods

Fortune 500 #274	agencies with investments: 2
foreign 30.7% of total sales	response to CIC: none

Addressograph-Multigraph (Pty.) Ltd.

$ invested: not known   employees: not known

Addressograph-Multigraph markets a wide range of products in South Africa, including the Total Copy Systems, typesetting equipment and Datek tape preparation equipment.

AMERICAN METAL CLIMAX, INC.
1270 Avenue of the Americas
New York, N.Y. 10020
212 757-9700
Chairman: Ian MacGregor

Fortune 500 #162	agencies with investments: 5
foreign 14.2% of sales	response to CIC: good
52.7% of earnings	

Tsumeb Corp. (Namibia)
O'okiep Copper Co. (South Africa)

$ invested: not known   employees: not known

See profile.

ARMCO STEEL CORP.
703 Curtis Street
Middletown, Ohio 45042
513 425-6541
Chairman: C. William Verity, Jr.

Fortune 500 #66	agencies with investments: 7
foreign 13.6% of total sales	response to CIC: none

ARMCO (Pty.) Ltd.

$ invested: not known   employees: not known

ARMCO manufactures and markets steel products at its Isando factory, opened in 1961. It is the country's only producer of galvanized corrugated steel piping. Ten to fifteen percent of its products are exported. In 1971, the company announced a $3-$4 million expansion of its Isando plant, as well as new involvements in mining ventures, purchasing agreements, and partnerships.

142

BETHLEHEM STEEL CORP.
701 East Third Street
Bethlehem, Pennsylvania 18016
215 694-2424
Chairman: Steward S. Cort

Fortune 500 #29   agencies with investments: 7
                                     response to CIC: none

Prospecting office in Namibia
Reported active in prospecting in Namibia
Received a mining concession in Mozambique

$ invested: not known   employees: not known

BRISTOL-MYERS CO.
345 Park Avenue
New York, New York 10022
212 644-2100
Chairman: Gavin K. MacBain

Fortune 500 #118   agencies with investments: 7
foreign 24.7% of total sales   response to CIC: good

Bristol-Myers Group (Pty.) Ltd.

$5-$10 million invested   employees: 185 white
                                              150 African and Coloured

Company offices are located in Johannesburg and plants are in
Germiston and Wadeville. Bristol-Myers has only small operations and no
assets in Rhodesia. Company officials state that all company employment and
benefit policies apply worldwide. However, while espousing an equal opportunity
employment policy, they grant employees "benefits which are appropriate
to the country in which they work."

BURLINGTON INDUSTRIES, INC.
301 North Eugene Street
Greensboro, North Carolina 27401
919 379-2000
Chairman: Charles F. Myers, Jr.

Fortune 500 #65   agencies with investments: 9
foreign 10.3 % of total sales response to CIC: none

<u>Burlington Hosiery Mills (S.A.) Ltd.</u>

$ invested: not known   employees: not known

      Burlington is a minority shareholder in the Cape firm, a producer of women's hosiery.

BURROUGHS CORP.
Burroughs Place
Detroit, Michigan 48232
313 972-7000
President: Ray W. Macdonald

      Fortune 500 #136   agencies with investments: 9
      foreign 41% of total sales   response to CIC: none

<u>Burroughs Machines</u>
P.O. Box 3996, Johannesburg

$ invested: not known   employees: 530 total
                                             40-50 blacks
                                           480-490 whites

      This subsidiary is managed through Burroughs of Great Britain and accounts for 8-9 percent of the computers installed in the country. Burroughs' major customers include DeBeers (mining), Ford, Redbank, and Union Steel. Burroughs has donated equipment and money to white universities but none to African, Coloured, or Indian colleges. In a March 1971 interview, officials stated that most black employees perform menial tasks and are making only very slow progress toward skilled positions. Wages for black workers are considerably below wages for whites, and although women are paid equally for equal work, they are largely relegated to clerical positions. Burroughs recruits white skilled labor from Britain and has training programs that involve only a few blacks. Burroughs is strongly opposed to withdrawal and is proud of its contribution of technical expertise to the development of the country. The company disclosed some information on its operations in 1973 in response to a request from the Commission on Ecumenical Mission and Relations of the United Presbyterian Church in the U.S.A. as part of the Church Project on U.S. Investments in Southern Africa.

CATERPILLAR TRACTOR CO.
100 N.E. Adams Street
Peoria, Illinois 61602
309 675-1000
Chairman: William Blackie

      Fortune 500 #40   agencies with investments: 12
      foreign 49% of total sales   response to CIC: fair

<u>Caterpillar (Africa) (Pty.) Ltd.</u>

$6.4 million invested   employees: 93

      See profile.

CHASE MANHATTAN BANK
1 Chase Manhattan Plaza
New York, New York 10015
212 552-2222
Chairman: David Rockefeller

      Fortune #3 of 50 largest banks   agencies with investments: 13
      foreign 34.3% of earnings   response to CIC: good

<u>Standard Bank of South Africa Ltd.</u>
<u>Banco Standard Totta de Mozambique S.A.R.L.</u>
<u>Banco Totta-Standard de Angola S.A.R.L.</u>

    $ invested: not known   employees: not known

      Chase has a 13.77 percent interest in the London-based Standard and Chartered Banking Group, which controls Standard Bank of South Africa and has a minority interest in the Angolan and Mozambiquan banks.

CHRYSLER CORP.
341 Massachusetts Avenue
Detroit, Michigan 48231
313 956-5252
Chairman: Lynn Townsend

      Fortune 500 #7   agencies with investments: 4
      DOD #57   response to CIC: fair
      foreign 23.8% of total sales

<u>Chrysler South Africa (Pty.) Ltd.</u>

    $45 million invested   employees: 2,038

    See profile.

COLGATE-PALMOLIVE CO.
300 Park Avenue
New York, New York 10022
212 751-1200
Chairman: George Lesch

      Fortune 500 #93   agencies with investments: 1
      foreign 58% of total sales   response to CIC: none

<u>Colgate-Palmolive Ltd.</u>
<u>Lakeside Laboratories (S.A.)(Pty.) Ltd.</u>

      Colgate-Palmolive began sales to South Africa in 1929. The East London factory was built in 1937, the Boksburg plant in 1957. The company produces a range of toiletries, soaps, and detergents and household cleaners. Lakeside Labs produces pharmaceuticals.
      $ invested: not known   employees: about 850

CONTROL DATA CORP.
8100 34th Avenue South
Minneapolis, Minnesota 55440
612 888-5555
Chairman: William Norris

Fortune 500 #215   agencies with investments: 5
DOD #73   response to CIC: good
foreign 41% of total sales

                        Control Data (Pty.) Ltd.
                          P.O. Box 185, Randburg

$5 million invested   employees: 100 (over 90% white)

This wholly-owned subsidiary markets the company's line of computer
systems, products, and services and provides customer support with a variety
of services. All products sold in South Africa are imported; none are manufactured or assembled there. Its contracts with government-related agencies
include: Iron and Steel Corp., Electricity Supply Comm.,South African Airways,
and Council for Scientific and Industrial Research (the National Institute
for Defense Research being one of the fields in which CSIR coordinates
study). Control Data operates no training programs in South Africa and has
not made charitable grants to organizations. Company policy at present does not
address the social problems of South Africa but is directed toward building
resources that may provide an opportunity to confront social problems at
a later date.

DEERE AND CO.
John Deere Road
Moline, Illinois 61265
309 792-8000
Chairman: William Hewitt

Fortune 500 #108   agencies with investments: 8
foreign 18.8% of total sales   response to CIC: none

                        John Deere (Pty.)Ltd.

$14 million invested   employees: 360 total
                                                 130 African
                                                  30 Coloured
                                                 100 white

Deere manufactures and assembles tractors and tractor parts,
chisel ploughs, subsoilers, and other farm and industrial equipment. About
10 percent of its products are locally manufactured. The company has
achieved a substantial increase in exports to neighboring African countries,
Britain, and the United States. In 1970, exports were about $2 million; return
on investment was about 17 percent. Minimum pay was $0.27 per hour.

DOW CHEMICAL CO.
Midland, Michigan 48640
517 636-1000
Chairman: C.B Branch

Fortune 500 # 46   agencies with investments: 7
foreign 41.8% of total sales   response to CIC: good

Dow Chemical Africa(Pty.) Ltd.

$22,000 invested   employees: 38
(in office furniture)

The company was set up in 1959 to sell agricultural, mining and general industrial chemicals and plastic raw materials. Products are sold in South Africa, Mozambique, Angola , as well as in Zambia, Malawi, Kenya, Uganda and Tanzania.

MONTHLY WAGES ($)

	1962		1968		1972	
	No.	Average Wage	No.	Average Wage	No.	Average Wage
Africans:						
non-skilled	0	-	5	$78	4	$222
semi-skilled	1	$ 78	2	$107	2	$289
Coloured/Asian:						
semi-skilled	0	-	0	-	2	$303
White:						
semi-skilled	1	$106	1	$167	0	-
skilled	7	$232	25	$416	21	$594
supervisor	3	$508	3	$647	6	$852
manager	2	$762	2	$860	3	$1,314

ENGELHARD MINERALS
& CHEMICALS
299 Park Avenue
New York, New York 10017
212 752-4000
Chairman: Alfred G. Blake

foreign 44.8 % of total sales   agencies with investments: 1
                                    response to CIC: none

Engelhard Industries International Ltd.

$ invested: not known   employees: not known

The late Charles Engelhard was an important financial supporter of South Africa, both through Engelhard Minerals and Chemicals Corp. and through the family-controlled Engelhard Hanovia. His intervention during the financial crisis of 1961 was particularly important to South Africa. Now,

the giant South African mining house Anglo American holds 30% of Engelhard
Minerals and Chemicals' stock. In mid 1972 the company contracted with
Ford to supply South African platinum for pollution devices.

EXXON CORP.
30 Rockefeller Plaza
New York, New York 10020
212 974-3000
Chairman: J.K. Jamieson

Fortune 500 #2   agencies with investments: 20
DOD #25   response to CIC: good
foreign 39% of total sales

Esso Standard South Africa (Pty.) Ltd.
Esso Chemical(Pty.)Ltd.

$16 million invested   employees: 224 total
                                                  148 White
                                                   67 African
                                                    5 Coloured
                                                    4 Asian

        Predecessor companies of Esso have been in South Africa since
1907. Since 1962, when a joint-interest company with which the company was
associated was dissolved, Esso has maintained only a small marketing operation
in South Africa. Terminals are located in Johannesburg, Durban, and Capetown.
There are about 50 service stations and rural supply points. "Because of regulations and skill levels, at the present time there are no non-whites employed
in the same positions as whites." The company says it "is working to upgrade
the skills of all employees and seeking government approval for employment of
non-whites in higher job classifications." Exxon has a permit to explore offshore Angola.

FIRESTONE TIRE AND RUBBER CO.
1200 Firestone Pkwy.
Akron, Ohio 44317
216 379-7000
Chairman: Raymond Firestone

Fortune 500 #34   agencies with investments: 5
foreign 30% of total sales   response to CIC: none

Firestone South Africa (Pty.)Ltd.

$25-$30 million invested   employees: 1,550
   (estimate)

        See profile.

FIRST NATIONAL CITY BANK
399 Park Avenue
New York, New York 10022
212 559-1000
Chairman: Walter B. Wriston

Fortune 500 #2 (50 banks)   agencies with investments: 14
foreign 54% of total sales   response to CIC: fair
    (1970)

First National City Bank (South Africa) Ltd.

                                   employees: 230 (12 % "non-white")

        Citibank's South African subsidiary was established in 1958.
It now has eight branches in Cape Town, Johannesburg, Durban, Pretoria, Isando
and Port Elizabeth. Citibank states that in South Africa it "has always given
equal pay for equal work without regard to race." Most non-whites are initially
employed in non clerical jobs. Non-whites account for 6% of Citibank's clerical
staff. Between 1960 and 1971 the average starting salary for non-white employees
more than tripled, rising from R35($49) to R110($154) per month.

FORD MOTOR CO.
The American Road
Dearborn, Michigan 48121
313 322-3000
Chairman: Henry Ford II

        Fortune 500 #3   agencies with investments: 9
        DOD #28   response to CIC: good
        foreign 25% of total sales

            ### Ford Motor Company of South Africa (Pty.) Ltd.

$80-$100 million invested   employees: 4,000
    (estimate)

        See profile.

GENERAL ELECTRIC CO.
570 Lexington Avenue
New York, New York 10022
212 750-2000
Chairman: F.J. Borch

        Fortune 500 #4   agencies with investments: 19
        DOD #4   response to CIC: good
        foreign 16.8% of total sales

        ### South African General Electric Company (Pty.) Ltd.

$55 million invested   employees: 1,500
    (estimate)

        See profile.

GENERAL FOODS CORP.
250 North Street
White Plains, New York 10625
914 694-2500
Chairman: C.W. Cook

Fortune 500 #38   agencies with investments: 5
foreign 13.4% of total sales   response to CIC: fair

General Foods (Proprietary) Ltd.
c/o Food Corporation (Proprietary) Ltd.

$3 million in sales   employees: none

General Foods Ltd. has had contracts since 1948 with Food Corporation Ltd., a subsidiary of South African Breweries, to operate certain pieces of manufacturing equipment in the production of certain General Foods products. General Foods pays a fee for this operation of equipment to Food Corporation. The company claims no employees in South Africa. General Foods also uses varying amounts of green coffee beans grown in Angola.

GENERAL MOTORS CORP.
General Motors Building
Detroit, Michigan 48202
313 556-5151
Chairman: Richard Gerstenberg

Fortune 500 #1   agencies with investments: 25
DOD # 23   response to CIC: good
foreign 14.5% of total sales

General Motors South African (Pty.) Ltd.

$125 million invested   employees: 4,800

See profile.

THE GILLETTE CO.
Prudential Tower Building
Boston, Massachusetts 02199
617 261-8500
Chairman: Vincent Ziegler

Fortune 500 #171   agencies with investments: 3
foreign 45.2% of total sales   response to CIC: none

Gillette South Africa (Pty.) Ltd.

$ invested: not known   employees: not known

Gillette South Africa was set up in 1931 and began manufacturing in 1953. The company's Springs plant produces toiletries and cosmetics.

Imported razor blades are packed there for sale in the country.

GOODYEAR TIRE AND RUBBER CO.
1144 East Market Street
Akron, Ohio 44316
216 794-2121
Chairman: Russell De Young

Fortune 500 # 19   agencies with investments: 4
DOD #59   response to CIC: none
foreign 30% of total sales

Goodyear Tyre and Rubber Co. (South Africa) (Pty.) Ltd.

$15 million invested   employees: 2,300

See profile.

GULF OIL CORP.
Gulf Building
Pittsburgh, Pennsylvania 15219
412 391-2400
President: B.R. Dorsey

Fortune 500 # 11   agencies with investments: 5
DOD #82   response to CIC: good
foreign 29.1% of total net
         earnings

Cabinda Gulf Oil Co., Angola

$200 million invested   employees: 240 total
                                             55 white expatriates
                                            131 white nationals
                                             54 "Negro"

See profile.

HOLIDAY INNS OF AMERICA, INC.
3742 Lamar Avenue
Memphis, Tennessee 38118
901 362-4001
Chairman: Kemmons Wilson

                                    agencies with investments: 2
                                    response to CIC: none

franchise to Amalgamated Hotels
(associated with Wits Industrials)

$ invested: not known   employees: not known

Six Holiday Inns are currently in operation, with more in the
process of being planned or built. By the end of the program there are intended to be 3,000 rooms available throughout Southern Africa. Domestic
service and hotel work employees are unorganized for trade union purposes,
but no reliable information on wage scales is currently available. A new
Holiday Inn at Jan Smuts Airport, Johannesburg, has certain interracial facilities, but mixed racial groups using facilities must not move outside of the
hotel. None of the other hotels allow non-white guests, and visitors to the
Holiday Inn in Swaziland have reported witnessing the use of African women
as prostitutes for white guests. Tourism is South Africa's third-biggest
foreign exchange earner, following gold and wool.

HONEYWELL, INC.
2701 49th Avenue South
Minneapolis, Minnesota 55408
612 332-5200
Chairman: James H. Binger

Fortune 500 #53   agencies with investments: 7
DOD #18   response to CIC: good
foreign 37.6% of total sales

<u>Honeywell Automation (Pty.) Ltd.</u>
Port Road, Robertsham, Johannesburg
<u>Honeywell Computers South Africa Ltd.</u> and
<u>Honeywell Information Systems South Africa Ltd.</u>
14 New South Street, Johannesburg

employees: 144 white
            25 black
            (1972)

Honeywell Automation, established in 1969, is wholly-owned by
Honeywell U.S.A. and imports automatic controls for industrial processes.
Formerly, for forty years Honeywell products had been sold by local agents.
Honeywell Computers was launched in 1970 with National Funds Investment Ltd.,
which supplied about 56 percent of the original $1.15 million outlay. In
August, 1970, Honeywell purchased the N.F.I. share to take full control.
Total Honeywell sales in South Africa during 1971 were $3,438,000 and the
company paid $69,000 in taxes to the South African government. Blacks are
employed only in non- or semi-skilled positions, but whites and blacks in semi-
skilled positions have the same average monthly earnings ($216). Honeywell
stated to CIC that it has no plans to invest in any other Southern African
countries because of small markets and because of the undesirable political
and economic climate. Honeywell's position concerning investment in Southern
Africa is to keep "lines of communication open and trying to understand the
reasons for opposing points of view." Consequently, it feels it will accomp-
lish more for South African blacks by remaining in the country and expanding
operations there. The company further states, "We believe that South African
trade per se should not be a factor in measuring American corporate responsibility."

INGERSOLL - RAND CO.
11 Broadway
New York, New York 10004
212 797-2700
Chairman: W.L. Wearly

Fortune 500 # 156   agencies with investments: 2
                                     response to CIC: poor

Ingersoll-Rand Co., South Africa (Pty.) Ltd.
P.O. Box 3720, Alberton
Ingersoll-Rand LDA
Portugal

Ingersoll-Rand has had operations in South Africa since the 1880's
and in Portugal since 1926. In South Africa, operations center around marketing
a wide range of industrial equipment, and one of their tunnel machines is
currently involved in the Orange-Fish River irrigation project. In Portugal
Ingersoll- Rand has sales and service operations and a production center for the
Torrington sewing machine needle, which is exported worldwide. In reply to
C.I.C., W.A. Mackie, executive vice-president, wrote that he could not complete
the questionnaire because "Our company in South Africa is an autonomous operation
and we do not have at our disposal the very detailed type of information you
require."

INTERNATIONAL BUSINESS MACHINES CORP.
Old Orchard Road
Armonk, New York 10504
914 765-1900
Chairman: T. Vincent Learson
Chairman Executive Committee: T. J. Watson, Jr.

Fortune 500 # 5   agencies with investments: 27
DOD # 20   response to CIC: good
foreign 41.2% of total sales

International Business Machines South Africa (Pty.) Ltd.

$8.5 million invested   employees: 1,020
       (estimated)

See profile.

INTERNATIONAL HARVESTER CO.
401 North Michigan Avenue
Chicago, Illinois 60611
312 527 0200
President: Brooks McCormick

Fortune 500 # 26   agencies with investments: 11
DOD #97   response to CIC: poor
foreign 24.1% of total sales

153

International Harvester (South Africa) (Pty.)Ltd.

employees: 1,000 (approximately)

International Harvester assembles some trucks but is primarily involved in marketing imported products. International Harvester also owns 51 percent in a farm-implement manufacturing firm. In 1971, International Harvester began constructing a new $2.8 million factory in Pietermaritzburg, a designated border area.

INTERNATIONAL TELEPHONE AND TELEGRAPH CORP.
320 Park Avenue
New York, New York 10022
212 752-6000
Chairman: H.S. Geneen

Fortune 500 #9	Agencies with investments: 12
DOD #21	response to CIC: good
foreign 38.1% of sales	

See profile list of subsidiaries.

$50-$70 million (estimate)   employees: 2,000 for all subsidiaries
(estimate)

See profile.

JOHNSON AND JOHNSON
501 George Street
New Brunswick, New Jersey 08903
201 524-0400
Chairman: P. B. Hofmann

Fortune 500 #113	agencies with investments: 6
foreign 31.1% of sales	response to CIC: none

Johnson and Johnson (Pty.) Ltd.
Ethnor Laboratories (Pty.) Ltd.

$ investment: not known   employees: not known

Johnson and Johnson makes a full line of baby products, surgical dressings, and hospital products in South Africa, exporting the same also to Rhodesia. Ethnor Labs manufactures the complete line of pharmaceutical products, veterinary products and surgical sutures for the medical profession in South Africa and also Rhodesia.

EASTMAN KODAK CO.
343 State Street
Rochester, New York 14650
716 325-2000
Chairman: Gerald B. Zornow

Fortune 500 #28   agencies with investments: 20
DOD#62   response to CIC: none
foreign   32.6% of total sales

Kodak (South Africa) (Pty.) Ltd.

$6.5 million invested   employees: 500 (about 300 blacks)
        (approximately)

Kodak, which began operating in South Africa in 1913, has film -
processing laboratories and distribution units in South Africa, Rhodesia,
Zambia, and Kenya. From South Africa, the company exports about $150,000
worth of merchandise to Angola, Mozambique, and Malawi.   Kodak has no manufacturing operations in South Africa but built a new $1.4 million headquarters in
Cape Town in 1970.   The photographic business in South Africa is dominated by
Kodak. The company disclosed details of its operations in 1973 in response to a
request from the World Division, Board of Global Ministries of the United Methodist Church as part of the Church Project on U.S. Investments in Southern Africa.

ELI LILLY AND CO.
307 East McCarty Street
Indianapolis, Indiana 46206
317 636-2211
Chairman: Eugene N. Beesley

Fortune 500 #172   agencies with investments: 3
foreign   31.1% of total sales   response to CIC :   good

Lilly Laboratories (South Africa) (Pty.)Ltd.

$2 million invested   employees: 103 total
                                                    79 whites
                                                    24 blacks

Lilly started exporting to South Africa in 1924, set up its subsidiary in 1957, and began manufacturing in 1964. At the 38,000 square-
foot Isando factory, the firm produces pharmaceutical, agricultural, and
cosmetic products.

The company provided the following information on wages:

Our South African affiliate recently participated in a nationwide
survey on salaries and benefits received by Bantu workers in all
industries. The survey, which was conducted by the Productivity
and Wage Association, involved 1,086 completed questionnaires
covering 188,233 Bantu employees. The following table compares
average Lilly monthly salaries with those in the East Rand area
where we are involved.

Job Category	*Average Monthly Salary 1971-1972		Average % Increase Over 1970 -1971	
	Lilly	**East Rand	Lilly	East Rand
Janitor, Gardener	R90,00	R49,96	16%	4.59%
Stores Packer, Maintenance, Packer	R111,00	R61,44	16	6.17
Capsule Operator, etc.	R145,00	R66,34	11	6.59
Driver, Chef etc.	R123,00	R92,73	7	6.95
Laboratory Asst.	R195,00	R100,87	6	6.36
Clerk	R160,00	R117,82	8	6.92

*Exact conversion of rand to U.S. dollars cannot be given for this time period because of fluctuating exchange rates. Until December, 1971, R1 was approximately equivalent to $1.40. From December, 1971, to June, 1972, R1 was approximately $1.33.
**East Rand is the immediate community in which Lilly operates.

<u>Elizabeth Arden</u> (recently acquired by Lilly)
$ invested: not known   employees: 100

MINNESOTA MINING AND MANUFACTURING CO.
3M Center
St. Paul, Minnesota 55101
612 733-1110
Chairman: Harry Heltzer

Fortune 500 # 57   agencies with investments: 9
foreign   38% of total sales   response to CIC: fair

<u>Minnesota Mining and Manufacturing Co. (South Africa) (Pty.) Ltd.</u>

$12 million invested   employees: 1,000
     (estimate)
   See profile.

MOBIL OIL CORP.
150 East 42nd Street
New York, New York 10017
212 883-4242
Chairman: Rawleigh Varner, Jr.

Fortune 500 # 6   agencies with investments: 21
DOD#51   response to CIC: good
foreign   61.5% of total sales

Mobil Oil Southern Africa (Pty.) Ltd.
Mobil Refining Southern Africa (Pty.) Ltd.
Mobil Oil Company (Angola &Mozambique)

$87.5 million invested   employees: 2,852

See profile.

MONSANTO CO.
800 North Lindbergh Boulevard
St. Louis, Missouri 63166
314 694-1000
Chairman: Charles H. Sommer

Fortune 500 #42   agencies with investments: 5
foreign 17.8% of total sales   response to CIC: poor

Monsanto South Africa (Pty.)Ltd.

$ invested: not known   employees: 16 (2 blacks)

Monsanto South Africa imports and markets a range of products, primarily plastic fibers and agricultural chemicals. It neither owns nor operates manufacturing facilities in the country.

MOTOROLA, INC.
9401 West Grand Avenue
Franklin Park,Illinois 60131
312 451-1000
Chairman: Robert Galvin

Fortune 500 # 137   agencies with investments: 1
DOD   #74   response to CIC: none

Motorola South Africa (Pty.) Ltd.

$invested: not known   employees: not known.

Motorola South Africa was formed in 1965 to manufacture the company's products. The U.S. firm owns 40 percent; the rest of the shares are held by a Johannesburg firm, T.P.H. Engineering. The South African Police is the major customer for the company's mobile two-way radio sets. Motorola is also the major producer of alternators for cars. In 1971, it launched a $1.3 million expansion program. Other products include a range of electronic, measuring, recording, and control instruments.

NATIONAL CASH REGISTER CO.
Main and K Streets
Dayton, Ohio 45409
513 449-2000
Chairman: Robert Oelman

Fortune 500 #79   agencies with investments: 3
foreign 45% of total sales   response to CIC: none
        (1970)

National Cash Register South Africa (Pty.)Ltd. (NCR/SA)
P.O. Box 3591, Johannesburg

employees: 1,300 (approximately)

National Cash Register in South Africa began operations in 1892 and
has continually expanded. From 1968 to 1970 sales doubled and National Cash
Register /South Africa became the sixth-largest National Cash Register
subsidiary among 120 throughout the world. National Cash Register/South Africa
has reported an annual sales volume of $14 million on cash registers and
adding machines; annual computer revenue is probably about $3 to $4 million
(low estimate), and it has supplied about 14 percent of the computers in the
country. National Cash Register/South Africa is building a $15 million
complex between Johannesburg and Pretoria, which will contain executive
offices, a computer center, and a computer training center. National Cash
Register has released almost no employee information or labor policy data but
has sent a number of employees (probably all white) overseas for highly
specialized training. Since National Cash Register issues no statements on its
involvements in South Africa, none of its positions are known.

NEWMONT MINING CORP.
300 Park Avenue
New York, New York 10022
212 PL 3-4800
Chairman: Plato Malozemoff

See AMAX-Newmont profile on Tsumeb.

OWENS-ILLINOIS, INC.
P.O. Box 1035
Toledo, Ohio 43601
419 242-6543
Chairman: Raymon H. Mulfod

Fortune 500 #77   agencies with investments: 8
foreign 16.9% of total sales   response to CIC: good

Consolidated Glass Works Ltd.(16% interest)

Owens Illinois acquired the 16 percent interest in Consolidated Glass Works "as a collateral part of the negotiations leading to a technical assistance agreement." The U.S. firm provides the assistance by training Consolidated personnel who are sent here from the South African company. Consolidated,which has a Rhodesian subsidiary, makes glass containers, table-ware, and plastics. Consolidated's 1971 Annual Report states that Owens-Illinois helped the South African firm obtain two unsecured loans in Euro-Dollars from Barclay's Bank and Owens-Illinois Overseas Capital Corporation.

PFIZER AND CO., INC.
235 East 42nd Street
New York, New York 10017
212 573-2323
Chairman: John J. Powers, Jr.

Fortune 500 #133   agencies with investments: 8
foreign 48.6% of total sales   response to CIC: none

Pfizer (Pty.)Ltd.
P.O. Box 7324, Johannesburg
Pfizer (Pty.) Ltd.
P.O. Box 1600,Johannesburg
Rhodesia: Central African Pfizer (Pty.)Ltd.
Box 3295, Salisbury
Portugal: Laboratorios Pfizer, S.A.R.L.
Coina, Seixal

$6 million in 1970 in   employees: 400 persons in South
South Africa only   Africa in early 1971

A major factor in the company's South Africa performance is the Coty cosmetic division. Sales increases from 1968 to 1971 led Pfizer to plan construction of manufacturing facilities valued at over $5million. In 1967,Pfizer built a $3.5 million factory in Pietermaritzburg. No infor-mation is available about Central African Pfizer or Laboratorios Pfizer or about Pfizer's employment policies in Southern Africa. Pfizer has actively participated in the South African government's decentralization efforts and has made no policy statements about Southern Africa.

PHELPS DODGE CORP.
300 Park Avenue
New York, New York 10022
212 751-3200
President: George Munroe

Fortune 500 #177   agencies with investments: 2
                                response to CIC: poor

Black Mountain Mineral Development

This subsidiary owns several land options in the northern Cape area of South Africa, where large copper deposits are thought to exist. In August, 1972, Phelps Dodge announced discovery of a copper body in the area, purchased land, and will open a mine. In 1973 the company announced it would withdraw from prospecting in Namibia because of the legal complications concerning the territory.

PHILLIPS PETROLEUM CO.
Phillips Building
Bartlesville, Oklahoma 74003
918 336-6600
Chairman: W.W. Keeler

      Fortune 500 # 37   agencies with investments: 10
      foreign 17.4% of total sales   response to CIC: poor

Phillips Carbon Black Company (Pty.)Ltd.(50%)
Phillips Petroleum

Phillips owns 50 percent of Phillips Carbon Black, South Africa's only producer of the commodity, which is used as a binder for rubber. Carbon black, essential for automobile production, is being exported to Angola, Mozambique , and Zimbabwe. Phillips is also part of a consortium involved in oil exploration offshore of Namibia. A disclosure resolution filed with the company in 1973 by the Protestant Episcopal Church as part of the Church Project on U.S. Investments in Southern Africa received more than 4 percent of the shareholder vote.

POLAROID CORP.
549 Technology Square
Cambridge, Massachusetts 02139
617 864-6000
Chairman: Edwin Land

      Fortune 500 #229   Agencies with investments: 7
                                  response to CIC: fair

Frank and Hirsch (Pty.)Ltd.(distributor,no ownership)

In January 1971, as a result of demands by Polaroid workers in the U.S. that the company withdraw from South Africa, it launched a one-year experiment involving wage increases and contributions to black eduction. Declaring the experiment at least a partial success, the company announced continuation of its South Africa program at the end of 1971. Polaroid's actions have been seen by many as a public relations stunt with little real impact. Wages remain lower than those of some other U.S. firms.

SINGER CO.
30 Rockefeller Plaza
New York, New York 10020
212 581-4800
Chairman: Donald Kircher

       Fortune 500 #41   agencies with investments: 7
       DOD #35   response to CIC: poor
       foreign   38.5% of total sales

                    Singer South Africa (Pty.) Ltd.
                    Friden (South Africa)(Pty.)Ltd.

                              employees: 850

       Singer produces sewing machines, parts, knitting machines, radios
and high fidelity equipment. Friden markets office and data-processing equipment.

SPERRY RAND CORP.
1290 Avenue of the Americas
New York, New York 10019
212 956-2121

       Fortune 500 #63   agencies with investments: 5
       DOD#15   response to CIC: poor
       foreign   30.6% of total sales

              Sperry Rand South Africa (Pty.)Ltd.
                40 DeBeer Street, Johannesburg

$5.8 million invested

       Sperry Rand's direct involvement in South Africa began in 1955 and
in 1969 its Vickers division began manufacturing in the country. In mid-1970
a Univac division was established with the goal of capturing 20 percent of
the South Africa computer market. There are now four Sperry Rand divisions in
South Africa: Vickers(industrial equipment); Remington Rand(business machines);
Remington shavers(shavers and household utensils); and Univac (computers),
which by the end of 1971 had sold or leased over $15 million worth of equipment.
Sales for the year ending March, 1972, totaled over $7 million, and over the next
five years the company plans to expand greatly by reinvesting earnings and
adding as much as $20 million in outside funds. No data is available on
Sperry Rand's employment practices in South Africa. J.H. Garwood, vice president of the U.S. parent, summarized Sperry Rand policy in a letter ,stating
that it intended to continue and expand operations as a good member of the
community and increase training programs,"thus providing opportunity to lead
to a better environment."

STANDARD OIL CO. OF CALIFORNIA
225 Bush Street
San Francisco, California 94104
415 894-7700
Chairman: Otto Miller

    Fortune 500 #12   agencies with investments: 8
    DOD#39   response to CIC: poor
    foreign 24% of total sales

                Caltex Oil (South Africa) and others

        See Caltex profile.

TEXACO INC.
135 East 42nd Street
New York,   York 10017
212 953-6000
Chairman: Maurice Granville

    Fortune 500 #8   agencies with investments: 7
    DOD#48   response to CIC: poor
    foreign 40% of total sales
                    (1970)
                Caltex and others

        See Caltex profile.

TENNECO, INC.
P.O. Box 1687
Wilmington, Delaware 19899
302 655-6231
Chairman: N.W. Freeman

    Fortune 500 #32   agencies with investments: 9
    DOD #13   response to CIC: none

            South African Paper Chemicals (Pty.) Ltd.
                        J.I. Case

    $invested: not known   employees: not known

        J.I. Case makes tractor, agricultural implements, and construction
equipment. South Africa

UNION CARBIDE CORP.
270 Park Ave.
New York, New York 10017
212 551-2345
Chairman: F. Perry Wilson

Fortune 500 #25   agencies with investments: 7
foreign 22.4% of total sales   response to CIC: poor

See profile list of 10 subsidiaries (South Africa-6, Rhodesia-4).

U.S. STEEL CORP.
71 Broadway
New York, New York 10006
212 558- 4444
Chairman: Edwin Gott

Fortune 500 #13   agencies with investments: 11
                                         response to CIC: poor

Ferroalloys Ltd. (31%)
Zeerust Chrome Mines (30%)
Prospecting and Development Co. (Pty.)Ltd.
African Triangle Mining (30%)

U.S. Steel has numerous and increasing investments in South
African mining, primarily through companies associated with Anglo-Transvaal
Consolidated Investment Company, a major South African mining group. U.S.
Steel is involved in developing South Africa's ferro-chrome industry through
Ferroalloys, which has recently constructed a new plant in the eastern Trans-
vaal. The Prieska mine, developed by African Triangle, has a large copper
deposit. Africa Triangle also owns concessions in Namibia.

WEYERHAEUSER CO.
2525 South 336th Street
Federal Way, Washington 98002
206 383-3361
Chairman: Norton Clapp

Fortune 500 #97   agencies with investments: 9
                                         response to CIC: good

Barlow Weyerhaeuser Packaging Investments(Pty.) Ltd.

$1.8 million (Weyerhaeuser   employees: 800, 2/3 black, 1/4 white
   investment in Barlow   remainder "coloured" or
   Weyerhaeuser)   Asian.

Weyerhaeuser initially invested in Barlow Weyerhaeuser Packaging
Investments in 1964. Investment involves the manufacture and sale of corrugated shipping containers within South Africa. The company owns four plants,
one of which is located in a border area. This company notes that " we are
operating under a 1965 Board of Directors policy that all investments shall
be reviewed to determine that they do not serve to strengthen apartheid."

Average individual wage is slightly in excess of $200 per month; basic unskilled wage is $100 per month, plus $25 in benefits. There is no race-based wage differential as such. However, the "no differential" policy does not really guarantee equal pay for equal work, or equal opportunity.

XEROX CORP.
Stamford, Connecticut 06904
203 329-8711
Chairman: C. Peter McColough

Fortune 500 #52   agencies with investments: 18
DOD #92   response to CIC: poor
foreign 33.8% of total sales

Rank Xerox (Pty.) Ltd.

Xerox owns about 75 percent of the shares in Rank Xerox and controls 51 percent of the voting power. Rank Xerox controls 35 percent of South Africa's copying industry and has assets of about $14 million. Its earnings have grown rapidly in recent years.

The company disclosed information to shareholders on its operations in 1973 in response to a request from the American Baptist Home Mission Societies as part of the Church Project on U.S. Investments in Southern Africa.

Complete List of All Corporations with Southern African Operations

A. AMERICAN FIRMS OPERATING IN
THE REPUBLIC OF SOUTH AFRICA AND NAMIBIA

Abbott Laboratories
Abelman Agencies Ltd.
Addressograph-Multigraph Corp.
AFAMAL-Quadrant (The Interpublic
  Group of Companies, Inc.)
AFIA (American Foreign Insurance
  Association, Aetna)
Alcan Aluminum
Allied Chemical Corp.
Allis Chalmers
Amalgamated Packaging Industries,
  Ltd. (National Amalgamated
  Packaging, Ltd.)
American Abrasives, Inc.
American Bank Note
American Bureau of Shipping
American Celanese Co.
American Chicle
American Cyanamid Co.
American Express Co.
American Home Products
American Insurance Co.
American International Under-
  writers
American Metal Climax Inc. (AMAX)
American Motors Corp.
American Pacific
American South Africa Investment
American Steel Foundries
Ampex Corp.
Amrho International
Amrho International Underwriters
Arthur Andersen and Co.
Anderson, Clayton and Co.
Anikem (Nalco Chemical Co.)
Applied Power Industries
ARCO (Atlantic Richfield Co.)
Argus Africa Ltd.
Argus Oil
Armco Steel Corp.
Armour-Africa, Ltd. (International
  Packers, Ltd.)
Armstrong Cork Co.
Artnell International (Artnell
  Exploration Co. & Mono
  Containers)
Ashland Oil and Refining Co.
  (Valvoline Oil Co., Ltd.)

Audco Rockwell (Rockwell Mfg. Co.)
Ault and Wiborg (Inmont Corp.)
Automated Building Components
Avco
Avis-Rent-A-Car
Ayerst Laboratories (American
  Ethicals, Ltd.)
Azolplate Corp.
Badger Co., Inc.
Balkind Agencies, Ltd.
Bankers Trust Co.
Barlow Oshkosh (Oshkosh Motor Truck Co.)
Baxter Laboratories
Bechtel Corp.
Beckman Instruments, Inc.
Bedaux, Charles and Associates
Beech-Nut Life Savers, Inc.
Bellows, W. S. Construction Co.
Berkshire International Corp. (Berkshire
  Knitting Mills)
Bethlehem Steel
Bethlehem Steel Export Corp.
Big Dutchman, Inc. (United States
  Industries)
Black Clawson Co.
Black and Decker Manufacturing Co.
Boeing Corp.
Borden Inc.
Borg-Warner Corp.
Born Africa (Born Engineering)
Boyles Drilling Co.
Braun Transworld Co. (C. F. Braun
  and Co.)
Bristol-Myers Co.
Buckner Industries, Inc.
Bucyrus-Erie
Budd
Bundy
Burlington Industries
Burroughs Machines Ltd. (Burroughs
  Corp.)
Butterick Publishing Co., Ltd.
  (Butterick Co., Inc.)
Calabrian Co., Inc. of New York
California Packing Corp.
Caltex (Standard Oil of California
  & Texaco, Inc.)
Canada Dry International Inc.

Carbone Corp.
Carborundum Co.
Carlane Corp.
Carnation Co.
Carrier Corp. (Airco Engineering
   Ltd.)
Carrier International
Carter Products Division
J. I. Case Co.
Caterpillar Tractor Co.
Celanese Corp. (Buffalo Paints
   Ltd.)
Champion Spark Plug Co.
Charter Consolidated
Chase Manhattan Bank
Chemical Bank New York Trust Co.
Chemical Construction Corp.
Chesebrough-Pond's Inc.
Chicago Bridge & Iron Co.
Chicago Pneumatic Tool Co.
Christrani & Nielsen Corp.
Chrysler Corp.
Cities Service
Clark Equipment
Coca-Cola Export Corp.
Colgate-Palmolive International, Inc.
P. F. Collier Inc.
Collier-Macmillan, Ltd. (The
   Macmillan Co.)
Collins Radio Co.
Colloids, Inc.
Columbia Broadcasting System
Columbus McKinnon Corp.
   (McKinnon Chain, Ltd.)
Combustion Engineering
Computer Science (Computer Services
   Corp.)
Connell Bros. Co. Ltd.
Consolidated Equipment & Mfg. Co.
   (Clipper Mfg. Co.)
Consultant Systemation
Continental Grain Co.
Continental Illinois National
   Bank and Trust
Continental Insurance Co.
Control Data Corp.
Corn Products Co. (Robertsons Ltd.)
Crane-Glenfield, Ltd. (Crane Co.)
Crown Cork & Seal Co., Inc.
Cutler Hammer International
Cyanamid International
Dana
Dean Export International Ltd.

Deere & Co. (John Deere & Co.)
De Leuw, Cather & Co. International
   Investments
Del Monte Corp. (South Africa
   Preserving Co. Ltd.)
Denver Equipment Co. (Joy Mfg. Co. Inc.)
Derby & Co. Ltd. (Engelhard Minerals
   & Chemical Corp.)
Diamond H. Switches Ltd. (Oak Electro-
   netics Corp.)
Diner's Club International, Ltd.
Dodge & Seymour Ltd.
Dolein Corp.
Donaldson Co., Inc.
Doughboy Industries, Inc.
Dow Chemical Co.
DuBois-Dearborn-Vestol Chemical Co.
Dunn & Bradstreet Co.
Dunlop
Du Pont Chemical Co.
Duroplastic Penta Industries (Engelhard
   Hanovia Inc.)
E. C. DeWitt & Co.
East Newark Industrial Center
Eastern Stainless Steel Corp.
Eastman Kodak Co.
Eimco Corp.
Electric Storage Battery
Electro-Nite Co.
Eltra Co.
Emery Air Freight Corp.
Encyclopedia Brittanica Inc.
Engelhard Hanovia
Engelhard Minerals and Chemicals
   Corp.
Endo Drug Corp.
Ernst & Ernst (Whitney, Ernst &
   Ernst)
ESB Incorporated
Essex Corp. of America
ESSO Standard Ltd. (Standard Oil
   of New Jersey)
Eutectic Welding Alloys Corp.
Ewing, McDonald & Co.
Max Factor & Co.
Fairbanks, Morse & Co.
Farrell Lines Inc.
Ferro Enamels Ltd.
Fiberglass, Ltd. (Owens Corning
   Fiberglass Corp.)
Firder Inc.
Firestone Tire & Rubber Co.
First Consolidated Leasing Corp. Ltd.
   (First National City Overseas
   Investment Corp.)

First National Bank of Boston
First National Bank of Chicago
Flintkole Co.
Fluor Co.
FMC Corp.
FNCB Services Corp. (First National
  City Bank of New York)
Ford Motor Co.
Fordom Factoring Ltd. (Walter
  E. Heller International Corp.)
Forsyth Udwin Ltd.
Fram Filters Corp.
Fruehauf
George A. Fuller Co.
Gabriel International Inc. Ltd.
Galion
Gamlen Ltd. (Sybron Corp.)
Gardner-Denver Co.
Gates Rubber Co.
General Electric Co.
General Foods Corp.
General Motors Corp.
General Signal Corp.
General Tire & Rubber Co.
George Angus Co.
J. Gerber & Co., Inc.
A. J. Gerrard & Co.
Getty Oil Co.
Gilbarco Ltd. (Gilbert & Barker
  Mfg. Co.)
Gillette Co.
Gillsevey Co.
Glair and Kestler Co.
Glidden-Durkee
Goodyear Tire and Rubber Co.
W. R. Grace & Co.
Grant Advertising Inc.
Graver Tank & Mfg. Co.
Grolier Inc.
Gulf Oil Corp.
Harnischfeger International Corp.
Harsco
Haskins & Sells
Heinemann Electric Co.
Helena Rubinstein Inc.
Walter E. Heller International
  Corp.
Hertz Rent-A-Car Co.
Hewitt-Robins Inc. (Litton Indus-
  tries)
Hewlett Packard Ltd.
Hochmetals Ltd. (South American
  Minerals & Merchandise Corp.)
Holiday Inns of America
Home Products International, Ltd.
Honeywell Inc.

Hoover Co.
Howe Richardson Scale Co.
Hyster Co.
IBM World Trade Corp.
Industrial Chemical Products (Amchem
  Products, Inc.)
Infilco Division of Fuller Co.
Ingersoll-Rand Co.
Insurance Co. of North America
Interchemical Corp.
International Banking Corp.
International Bank of Reconstruction &
  Development (World Bank)
International Flavors and Fragrances Inc.
International Group of Companies
International Harvester Co.
International Latex Corp.
International Nickel
International Packers, Ltd.
International Staple & Machine Co.
International Telephone & Telegraph Corp.
Irving Chute Co., Inc.
Jeffrey-Galion Mfg. Co. (The Jeffrey Co.)
Johns-Manville International Corp.
Johnson and Johnson
S. C. Johnson & Son Inc.
Kellogg Co.
Kelly-Springfield Tire Co.
Kendall Co.
Kennedy Van Saun Mfg. & Engineering
  Corp.
Kewanee Overseas Oil Corp. (Etosha
  Petroleum Co.)
Keystone Asbestos Corp.
Kidder, Peabody & Co., Inc.
Kimberley-Clark Corp.
Koret of California
K. R. C. Resources (King Resources)
Lakeside Laboratories Inc.
E. J. Lavino & Co. (International
  Minerals & Chemical Corp.)
Lease Plan International Corp.
Leo Burnett Co.
A. R. Lilly & Son
Eli Lilly International Corp.
Link-Belt Co.
Litton Industries
Litwin Corp.
Loftus Engineering Co. (Western
  Gear Corp.)
Lovable Co.
Lubrizol Corp.
Lykes Brothers Steamship Co., Inc.
  (Lykes Lines Agency, Inc.)
Mack Trucks Worldwide

Mahon International Inc.
Manhattan Shirt Co.
Manufacturers Hanover Trust
Maremount Corp.
Masonite Corp.
Master Mechanics Co.
McGraw-Hill Inc.
Mechanite Metal Corp.
Merck, Sharp & Dohme International
Merkan Enterprises
Merrell National Laboratories
Metro-Goldwyn-Mayer
    International Inc.
Meyer Mfg. Co. (George J.
    Meyer Co.)
Midlands Oil
Millburg Industrial Painters
Mine Safety Appliances Co.
Minerals & Chemicals Phillipp
    Corp.
Minnesota Mining & Mfg. Co.
Mobil Oil Corp. (Socony, Ltd.)
Monarch Cinnabar
Mono Containers (J. C. Allen)
Monsanto Co.
Moore-McCormack Lines, Inc.
Morgan Guarantee & Trust
Morrison-Knudson
Motorola Inc.
MSD (Merck & Co., Inc.)
Muller & Phipps International
    Corp.
National Cash Register Co.
National Standard Co.
National Trust & Savings
    Association
Navarro Exploration Co.
Newmont Mining Corp. (O'Okiep
    Copper Co. Ltd.)
New Wellington
A. C. Nielsen Co.
Nordberg Mfg. Co.
North American Rockwell
Norton Co.
Nuclear Corp. of America
Ocean Science & Engineering Inc.
Olin Mathieson Chemical Corp.
Otis Elevator Co.
Owens Corning
Owens-Illinois
P. E. Consulting Group (Kurt
    Salmon Assoc. Inc.)
Robert Page & Assoc.

Palabora Mining Co. Ltd. (Newmont
    Mining Corp.)
J. J. Palmer & Co.
Pan American World Airways Inc.
Paragon Keylite Chemicals (Keylite
    Chemicals)
Parke, Davis & Co.
Parker Pen Co.
Pegasus International Corp.
Pepsi Cola International
Permatex Co. Inc.
Perth Products
Charles Pfizer & Co. Inc.
Phillips Petroleum Co.
Pillsbury Co.
Pipe Line Technologists Inc.
Placid Oil
Playtex Corp.
Plough Inc.
P. M. Products
Polaroid Corp.
Potter & Moore (DeWitt Drug & Beauty
    Products, Inc.)
Precision Spring
Preload International Corp.
Premix Asphalt Co.
Prentice-Hall Publishers Inc.
Prestolite International
Proctor & Gamble Co.
Publicker International Inc.
Radio Corp. of America (R.C.A.)(owns
    Hertz)
Ramsey Engineering Co.
Reader's Digest
Reichhold Chemicals, Inc.
Reliance-Toledo
Remington Rand
Revlon, Inc.
Rexall Drug & Chemical Co.
Rheem International Co.
Rheem Mfg.
Richelieu Corp. Inc.
Riker Laboratories
Ritepoint Corp.
Ritter Pfandler Corp.
River Brand Rice Mills Inc.
R. M. B. Alloys
H. H. Robertson Co.
Rockwell International
Rockwell Standard
Rohm & Haas Co.
Royal Baking Powder Ltd. (International
    Standard Brands)

Royal Crown Cola Co.
A. S. Ruffel Ltd. (Smith,
   Kline & French Laboratories)
Schering Corp. (Scherag Ltd.)
Schlesinger Organization
Scholl Mfg. Co.
W. F.Schrafft & Sons
Scripto, Inc.
G. D. Searle & Co.
Seaway Associates Inc.
Security Resources
Servac Laboratories (Miles
   Laboratories Inc.)
Sheffield Corp.
Shell Oil Co.
Simplicity Pattern Co., Inc.
Singer Sewing Machine Co.
Skil Corp.
A. O. Smith Corp.
Southwire Co. of Georgia
   (Phalaborwa Mining & Union
   Steel Corp.)
Sperry-Rand Corp. (Vickers-West &
   DuToit Ltd.)
Squibb Beechnut Corp.
Standard Oil Co. of California
   (Caltex)
Standard Oil Co. of New Jersey
   (Exxon)
Standard Pressed Steel Co. (Gordon
   Webster & Co.)
C. V. Starr & Co.
States Marine Lines
Stauffer Chemical Co.
Stein, Hall & Co. Inc.
Steiner Co.
Sterling Drug Inc. (Sterling
   Products & Winthrop Labs)
St. Regis Paper Co. (National
   Packaging Co., Ltd.)
D. A. Stuart Oil Co.
Symington Wayne Corp. (Vitreous
   Enamelling Corp.)
Systematics Services Pty.
Tampax, Inc.
Tedd-Hill Products
Tedd McKune Investments
Tenneco Chemicals Inc.
   (Superior Oil)
Thermo-Electric Co. Inc.
Thompson Remco (TRW Inc.)
J. Walter Thompson Co.
Thor Power Tool Co.
3M Corp.

Tidewater Oil Co.
Time International
Timken Roller Bearing Co.
Titan Industrial Corp. (Pantheon
   Industries, Inc.)
Tokheim Corp.
Toledo Scale Corp. of Ohio
Touche, Ross, Bailey & Smart -
   International
Transalloys Ltd. (Air Reduction Co.
   Inc.)
Trans World Airlines, Inc.
Triton Chemicals Ltd. (Rohm & Haas
   Co.)
Tuco Ltd. (The Upjohn Co.)
Tupperware Home Parties
Twentieth Century Fox Films Corp.
Underwood (Olivetti-Underwood)
Unimark International
Union Carbide Corp. (Chrome Corp., Ltd.)
Uniroyal Inc.
United Artists Corp.
United Cargo Corp.
United Shoe Machinery Corp.
United States Steel Corp.
Universal Mineral Discoveries
Valenite-Modco Ltd. (The Valeron Corp.)
Valvoline Oil
Van Dusen Aircraft Supplies Ltd.
The Vendo Co.
Vick Chemical, Inc.
Vick International (Richardson-
   Merrill Inc.)
Wallace International (Sam P. Wallace
   Co.Inc.)
Warner Bros.-Seven Arts Corp.
Warner-Lambert Pharmaceutical Co.
J. R. Watkins Products Inc.
Wayne Pump Co. (Symington Wayne Corp.)
Western International Hotels
Western Knapp Engineering Co. (McKee
   of Panama)
Westinghouse Air Brake Co.
Westinghouse Electric International
   Corp.
Weyerhaeuser Co.
Whitney Co.
Wilbur-Ellis Co.
H. B. Wilson Co.
Worldtronic Inc.
Worthington Air Conditioning Co.
Xerox Corp.
X-Ray International Ltd.
Arthur Young & Co.
ZOE

B. AMERICAN FIRMS OPERATING IN ZIMBABWE (RHODESIA)

Affiliated Exporters, Inc.
American Foreign Insurance
  Association (AFIA)
American Metal Climax, Inc.
Arbor Acres Farms, Inc.
Bardahl Mfg. Corp.
Burroughs Corp.
California Texas Oil Corp.
Canada Dry International Inc.
Carbourundum Co.
Celanese Corporation
Chesebrough-Pond's Inc.
Chicago Pneumatic Tool Co.
China American Tobacco Co.
Christian Science Publishing
  Society
Chrysler Corp.
Coca-Cola Bottling Co. of
  N.Y., Inc.
Continental Ore Corp.
Dibrell Bros. Inc.
Dillon Read & Co.
Eastman Kodak Co.
Eimco Corp., Division of
  Enviro Tech Corp.
Electric Storage Battery Co.
  of America(ESB)
Falls City Tobacco Co. Inc.
Foote Mineral Company
Fort Dodge Laboratories
Gardner-Denver Co.
Goodyear Tire & Rubber Co.
Grant Advertising Intl.,Inc.
Haskins & Sells
Hoover Company
IBM World Trade Corp.
Ingersoll-RAND Co.
Insurance Company of North America
International Basic Economy Corp.
International Chinchilla Headquarters, Inc.
International Telephone and Telegraph Corp.
Jeffrey-Galion Mfg. Co.
Metallurg, Inc.
Mobil Oil Corporation
National Cash Register Company
Pepsi Co. International
Chas. Pfizer & Co., Inc.
Royal Crown Cola Co.
Scripto, Inc.
Sterling Drug Inc.
St. Regis Paper Co.

3M Corp. (Minnesota Mining &
  Mfg. Co.)
Trans World Airlines, Inc.
Twentieth Century-Fox Film Corp.
Union Carbide Corporation
Union Special Machine Co.
Universal Leaf Tobacco Co.
J. Walter Thompson Co.
F. W. Woolworth Co.
Arthur Young & Co.
Vanadium Corp. of America

C. AMERICAN FIRMS OPERATING IN ANGOLA AND MOZAMBIQUE

Allis-Chalmers
American Cyanamid Company
Caterpillar Tractor Company
Chase Manhattan Corporation
Diamond Distributors Inc.
Diversa, Inc.
California Texas Oil Co.
Clark Oil & Refining Co.
Continental Ore Corp.
Firestone Tire & Rubber Co.
Fort Dodge Laboratory; Division
  of American Home Products Corp.
General Electric Co.
General Tire & Rubber Co.
Gulf Oil Corp.
Halliburton Company
Holiday Inns of America, Inc.
Hunt Intl., Subsidiary of Placid
  Oil, Dallas, Texas
IBM World Trade Corp.
Inter-American Capital Corp.
Intercontinental Marine Drilling
Loffland Brothers, Inc.

Mobil Oil Corp.
National Cash Register Co.
National Marine Service, Inc.
Ocean Drilling & Exploration Co.,
  Subsidiary of Murphy Oil Corp.
Charles Pfizer & Co.
Place Gas Oil Co.
Schlumberger, Ltd.
The Singer Company
Skelly Oil; indirect subsidiary
  of Getty Oil Company
Standard Electric; Subsidiary of
  International Telephone and
  Telegraph
Standard Oil of California
Sunray D.X., Subsidiary of
  Sun Oil Co.
Tenneco Oil Co.
Texaco, Inc.
Tidewater Marine Service, Inc.
Union Carbide Corporation
Universal Tobacco

Sources

Trade List, South Africa, U. S. Department of Commerce, August 1971.

Directory of American Firms Operating in Foreign Countries, 7th Edition,
  Vol. 2, 1969.

American Corporate Investments in South Africa, October 1969, American
  Committee on Africa.

GUIDE TO CHURCH INVESTMENT LISTINGS

Treasurers or representatives of 35 U. S. church boards and agencies were asked to supply information on their agencies' investments in a selected number of corporations with business interests in Southern Africa. Most responded either by completing forms supplied by the Corporate Information Center (CIC) or by furnishing portfolios. Data on 27 agencies of 11 denominations and the National Council of Churches is included in the tables. Except as indicated in the notes below, all information for the tables was taken from either the forms or the portfolios provided.

The information is presented in five tables. Table I is a cross reference indicating whether or not an agency holds securities in each of 53 selected corporations with investments in Southern Africa. Table II lists the number of shares and/or face value of fixed income securities, including annual income, by each agency in 53 corporations. A summary of total investments by agency, including portfolio dates, is provided in Table III, with totals by denominations in Table IV. Finally, total investments held by agencies included in the study in each company are presented by corporation in Table V.

Certain factors apply to all listings. First, the information provided here covers only income from stocks and other securities and is only one measure of determining the significance of investment. In many cases stocks are held for growth potential and not for dividend yield. For any given stock, income shown is dividend income only and does not reflect either growth or depreciation of market value of the shares. Income for fixed-income securities reflects only interest income. Please note that income figures do not include capital gains.

Second, income not reported in portfolios or supplied by agencies was estimated by CIC on the basis of Standard and Poor's projections or quotations for the previous year. Inaccuracies may exist where a stock or bond was bought midyear; figures for stock dividend income and interest on fixed-income securities were computed as if they had been held in the portfolio for the entire year preceding the portfolio date. This method of determining income is also used on most standardized portfolio reports. In cases where a security was bought shortly before the portfolio date, an inflated income figure may result. The discrepancy may be offset, however, by securities sold just prior to the portfolio date; while the securities sold would not appear in the portfolio, income would have been received up to the date of sale.

Finally, holders of fixed income securities and preferred stock are not legally owners of a given corporation in the same way as are holders of common stock. The former therefore cannot participate in the rights and responsibilities of ownership, including such corporate challenges as votes on shareholder resolutions. It should be noted that pension funds, in particular, frequently have large portions of their holdings in the form of bonds or other fixed-income securities. Listings of fixed-income securities and preferred shares have been included in this study only as additional indicators of the extent to which various church agencies have some financial stake in the 53 selected companies with business interests in Southern Africa.

Of agencies and boards invited to participate, those that did not reply or refused to cooperate in the study were:

Christian Church (Disciples): National Benevolent Association
Pension Fund
Presbyterian Church in the U. S.: Board of Christian Education
Board of World Ministries
Protestant Episcopal Church in the U.S.A.: Episcopal Church Foundation
United Methodist Church: Board of Discipleship
Board of Pensions

While market values of portfolios for some of the above agencies are not known, it should be noted, for example, that the United Methodist Pension Fund portfolio had an estimated market value of $401 million on June 30, 1972. The addition of this amount would more than triple the market value represented by the three divisions of the United Methodist Board of Global Ministries, which participated in this study. The denominational totals as listed in Table IV should not be taken as reflections of any denomination's total investments.

Names of denominations and addresses of agencies included in the study are listed below so that readers may contact treasurers regarding any recent changes in portfolios or for further information. Abbreviations used throughout the accompanying tables are given in parentheses, and a summary key to abbreviations follows. Please check the notes for those agencies marked with an asterisk (*) for full explanation of CIC computations.

AMERICAN BAPTIST CHURCHES (ABC)

Board of Education and Publication (BEP)
Valley Forge, Pa. 19481

Home Mission Society (HMS)
Valley Forge, Pa. 19481

Foreign Mission Society (FMS)
Valley Forge, Pa. 19481

Ministers and Missionaries Benefit
Board (MMBB)
475 Riverside Drive, 17th floor
New York, N. Y. 10027

CHRISTIAN CHURCH (Disciples of Christ) (CCD)

United Christian Missionary Society
222 South Downey Avenue
Indianapolis, Ind. 46219

CHURCH OF THE BRETHREN (CTB)

General Board
1451 Dundee Avenue
Elgin, Ill. 60120

LUTHERAN CHURCH IN AMERICA (LCA)

*Board of Pensions (BP)
608 Second Avenue South
Minneapolis, Minn. 55402

*Common Investing Fund (CIF)
Office of Administration and Finance
231 Madison Avenue
New York, N. Y. 10016

174

NATIONAL COUNCIL OF CHURCHES (NCC)

Office of Administration, NCC
475 Riverside Drive
New York, N. Y. 10027

PRESBYTERIAN CHURCH IN THE U. S. (PCUS)

*Board of Annuities and Relief (BAR)
341 Ponce de Leon Avenue, N.E.
Atlanta, Ga. 30308

*The Presbyterian Foundation, Inc. (U.S.)
1402 Wachovia Bank Building   (PF)
Charlotte, N. C. 28202

*Board of National Ministries (BNM)
341 Ponce de Leon Avenue, N.E.
Atlanta, Ga. 30308

PROTESTANT EPISCOPAL CHURCH IN THE U. S. A. (PECUSA)

*The Church Pension Fund (CPF)
800 Second Avenue
New York, N. Y. 10017

*Domestic and Foreign Missionary Society
815 Second Avenue   (DFMS)
New York, N. Y. 10017

REFORMED CHURCH IN AMERICA (RCA)

Office of the Treasurer
475 Riverside Drive, 18th floor
New York, N. Y. 10027

UNITARIAN UNIVERSALIST ASSOCIATION (UUA)

Department of Education and Social Concern
25 Beacon Street
Boston, Mass. 02108

UNITED CHURCH OF CHRIST (UCC)

Board for Homeland Ministries (BHM)
287 Park Avenue South
New York, N. Y. 10010

The Pension Boards (PB)
287 Park Avenue South
New York, N. Y. 10010

Board for World Ministries (BWM)
475 Riverside Drive, 16th floor
New York, N. Y. 10027

United Church Foundation (UCF)
287 Park Avenue South
New York, N. Y. 10010

UNITED METHODIST CHURCH (UMC)

BGM - Board of Global Ministries

Women's Division (Women's)
475 Riverside Drive, 15th floor
New York, N. Y. 10027

National Division (National)
475 Riverside Drive, 3rd floor
New York, N. Y. 10027

World Division (World)
475 Riverside Drive, 15th floor
New York, N. Y. 10027

UNITED PRESBYTERIAN CHURCH IN THE U.S.A. (UPUSA)

Board of Christian Education (BCE)
Witherspoon Building
Philadelphia, Pa. 19107

*Board of National Missions (BNM)
475 Riverside Drive, 11th floor
New York, N. Y. 10027

*Board of Pensions (BP)
Witherspoon Building
Philadelphia, Pa. 19107

Commission on Ecumenical Mission and
                    Relations (COEMAR)
475 Riverside Drive
New York, N. Y. 10027

*United Presbyterian Foundation (UPF)
475 Riverside Drive, Room 1031
New York, N. Y. 10027

* <u>Guide to Church Investment Listings: Notes on Specific Agencies</u>

<u>LCA - Board of Pensions</u>

CIC computed the estimated annual income on bonds and other fixed-income securities from principal and interest rate supplied in the portfolio; figures should be accurate unless these securities were bought midyear.

The portfolio provided only the number of shares of stock; the closing market quotation of the previous month was used to compute the market value. (For the portfolio date of December 1, 1972, market quotations were taken from "November, 1972, last," <u>Standard and Poor's Stock Guide</u>, New York, December, 1972.)

Dividends for 1972 were computed from <u>Standard and Poor's Stock Guide</u>, New York, December, 1972 (Year's End), using the dividends paid in 1972. The annual income figures were computed from dividends paid times the number of shares of stock. Any shares purchased during the year would not have received all of the dividends paid.

It should also be noted that the figure for total market value of the portfolio was based on book (face) value of corporate bonds and other fixed-income securities and market value of stocks in the Variable Income Pension Fund portfolio as of December 31, 1972, and December 29, 1972, respectively. No market value for bonds was given. Further, while figures for the total portfolio were based on the portfolios mentioned above, the figures for investments in specific corporations as listed in Tables II and V were taken from portfolios dated November 30, 1972 (for bonds) and December 1, 1972 (for stocks).

<u>LCA - Common Investing Fund</u>

Portfolio dates of income reported are only for January 1, 1972, to September 30, 1972, and dividend information was not provided in the portfolio. CIC computed dividends based on the full year of 1972, although the portfolio annual income total only covers up to September 30, 1972. Stocks bought during the year will not have received the full dividend, and if shares in a corporation with business in Southern Africa were sold after September 30, the income reported for those shares will be inflated.

<u>PCUS - Board of Annuities and Relief</u>

Bond interest was computed by CIC on the basis of information given in the portfolio (rate times principal). Dividends paid were taken from <u>Standard and Poor's Stock Guide</u> ("Dividend Total Paid 1971"), New York, Year's End, 1972. Stock income was computed from dividend times the number of shares.

<u>PCUS - Board of National Ministries</u>

Only the numbers of shares of stock were given in the portfolio; market value was computed from the <u>Standard and Poor's Stock Guide</u>, December, 1972, using the closing price on the portfolio date, December 31, 1971. Annual income (dividends) from the shares was also computed from the guide.

177

PECUSA - Church Pension Fund

CIC computed annual income for fixed-income securities from rate and principal provided in the portfolio; figures should be accurate except where a security was bought during the year, and the annual income will thus be an inflated amount.

The portfolio provided only the number of shares of stock; market value was computed from Standard and Poor's Stock Guide, July, 1972, using "June OTC Last" quotations because the portfolio was dated June 30, 1972. Note in particular that dividends reported were those paid for the entire year of 1972, as listed in Standard and Poor's Stock Guide, Year End, 1972; annual income was computed from this and may not be totally accurate if there were changes in holdings.

PECUSA - Domestic and Foreign Missionary Society

CIC computed fixed-income security income from rate and principal stated in the portfolio. Stock dividends and annual income were not given. Dividends for 1971 (matching the portfolio date) were taken from Standard and Poor's Stock Guide ("Dividend Total Paid 1971"), Year End, 1972. Annual income for 1971 was computed by CIC with the assumption that shares held on the portfolio date were held for the entire year.

UPUSA - Board of National Missions

Annual income for bonds was computed by CIC from rate and principal provided. Stock dividends and estimated annual income were not provided; CIC computed annual income on the basis of dividends paid for the entire year of 1972, although the portfolio is dated June 30, 1972. Figures for dividends paid were taken from Standard and Poor's Stock Guide ("Dividend Total So Far 1972"), Year End, 1972. Varying purchase dates would affect the accuracy of income as listed.

Note especially that while the portfolio was dated June 30, 1972, total annual income was available only as of December 31, 1971. Figures for total portfolio market value and total portfolio annual income are reported as of December 31, 1971.

UPUSA - Board of Pensions

All information for fixed-income securities (rate and principal) was provided; multiplication to derive the annual income was done by CIC.

The portfolio listed dividends per share and market value for stocks; CIC multiplied the number of shares times the dividend to obtain the income.

UPUSA - United Presbyterian Foundation

All information for fixed-income securities was provided in the portfolio report except for computation of annual income. Stock dividends and annual income were not listed; CIC computed annual income from Standard and Poor's Stock Guide ("Dividend Total Paid 1971"), Year End, 1972.

Since total annual income of the portfolio could not be provided by the foundation, CIC computed it using figures supplied in <u>Building a Better World, United Presbyterian Foundation</u>, Report of the UP Foundation for 1971, p. 22. Given the sample investment of $1,000 in 1947, which would have a market value of $2,247.71 at December 31, 1971, and would have yielded a net income of $99.38 in 1971, the rate of yield (about 4.4 percent) was computed. Based on this rate, the net income of the entire invested security holdings as of December 31, 1971 ($32,913,548 x .044214) was computed to obtain an estimated net income for the entire portfolio for the year.

Key to Denomination and Agency Abbreviations

Where only a single agency is included for a given denomination, the denomination and not the agency name is used throughout the tables. For example, listings for "CTB" refer only to the General Board of the Church of the Brethren. Denominations always appear in alphabetical order, with agency listings indented beneath them. Please check the notes for those agencies marked with an asterisk (*) for full explanation of CIC computations.

<u>ABC</u> - American Baptist Churches

    BEP - Board of Education and Publications
    FMS - Foreign Mission Society
    HMS - Home Mission Society
    MMBB - Ministers and Missionaries Benefit Board

<u>CCD</u> - Christian Church (Disciples of Christ)

<u>CTB</u> - Church of the Brethren

<u>LCA</u> - Lutheran Church in America

    *BP - Board of Pensions
    *CIF - Common Investing Fund

<u>NCC</u> - National Council of Churches

<u>PCUS</u> - Presbyterian Church in the U. S.

    *BAR - Board of Annuities and Relief
    *BNM - Board of National Ministries
    *PF - The Presbyterian Foundation

<u>PECUSA</u> - Protestant Episcopal Church in the U. S. A.

    *CPF - Church Pension Fund
    *DFMS - Domestic and Foreign Missionary Society

<u>RCA</u> - Reformed Church in America

<u>UUA</u> - Unitarian Universalist Association

<u>UCC</u> - United Church of Christ

  BHM - Board for Homeland Ministries
  BWM - Board for World Ministries
  PB - Pension Boards
  UCF - The United Church Foundation

<u>UMC</u> - United Methodist Church

  BGM - Board of Global Ministries
  National - National Division
  Women's - Women's Division
  World - World Division

<u>UPUSA</u> - United Presbyterian Church in the U.S.A.

  BCE - Board of Christian Education
  *BNM - Board of National Missions
  *BP - Board of Pensions
  COEMAR - Commission on Ecumenical Mission and Relations
  *UPF - United Presbyterian Foundation

CHECKLIST OF CHURCH AGENCY HOLDINGS

```
                     ABC____     CTB CCD LCA NCC PCUS      PECUSA RCA UUA UCC      UMC-BGM  UPUSA
                          M                                                                  C
                     B F H M           C      B B    C F         B B  U N W W    B B   O U     Total
                     E M M B           B I    A N P  P M         H W P C A O O   C N B M P     Number
                     P S S B           P F    R M F  F S         M M B F T M R   E M P R F     Agencies

Addressograph-Multigraph   x      x                                                              2
American Metal Climax                               x                    x          x x x        5
ARMCO Steel                        x      x              x x x x            x                     7
Bethlehem Steel       x            x               x       x             x   x                    7
Bristol-Myers         x   x      x x         x          x       x                                 7
Burlington Industries x              x       x x         x                     x                  6
Burroughs              x x     x x x         x          x       x          x x                    9
Caterpillar Tractor   x x     x x x              x x     x x     x           x x     x x         12
Chase Manhattan Bank  x            x             x x  x x x x  x   x         x x                 13
Chrysler                     x x                                           x   x                  4
Colgate-Palmolive                        x                                                        1
Control Data                     x              x   x      x   x                                  5
Deere and Co.                    x       x          x      x     x           x     x x            8
Dow Chemical          x       x x               x                x           x x                  7
Engelhard Minerals & Chemicals                     x                                              1
Exxon               x x x x  x     x     x x x   x x   x  x x x x  x        x x       x           20
Firestone Tire & Rubber          x     x                  x x   x                                5
First National City Bank  x x    x       x    x           x x x x    x       x x x x             14
Ford Motor            x   x x  x         x        x x   x  x                                      9
General Electric      x   x        x     x x x x  x x    x x x x            x x     x x x x        19
General Foods         x       x          x x                                           x          5
General Motors      x x  x x  x  x x x    x x     x x   x x x x  x x x     x x x x x x            25
Gillette                x                 x                        x                              3
Goodyear Tire & Rubber x                  x               x   x            x       x              4
Gulf Oil              x              x    x             x   x                                     5
Holiday Inns                     x   x                                                            2
Honeywell             x                   x               x x   x            x     x              7
Ingersoll-Rand                                                   x             x                  2
International Business Machines x x x x  x   x x  x x x x  x x   x  x x x x   x x     x x x x x    27
International Harvester x  x x    x       x x            x   x x           x x                    11
Internatl. Tel. & Tel. x x  x      x x         x     x x              x      x   x x              12
Johnson & Johnson     x   x               x             x          x        x       x            6
Eastman Kodak         x x x x    x       x x     x   x x  x x x x  x x       x x       x          20
Eli Lilly             x                                          x         x                      3
Minnesota Mining & Manufacturing x    x   x x          x x   x             x     x               9
Mobil Oil           x x x  x    x   x x   x x     x   x x x x x  x x        x x x x               21
Monsanto              x           x                        x               x   x                 5
Motorola                         x                                                               1
National Cash Register       x                     x                          x                  3
Owens-Illinois               x   x x               x      x   x x  x                              8
Pfizer                x       x             x   x         x                   x x x               8
Phelps-Dodge          x                                 x                                         2
Phillips Petroleum    x     x x  x    x       x        x  x                   x x                 10
Polaroid                         x   x       x            x       x x         x x                 7
Singer                x          x        x x             x                   x x       x         7
Sperry Rand                      x                 x      x                x         x            5
Standard Oil of California       x           x       x        x x  x x  x x          x            8
Tenneco               x   x x    x x         x x    x     x x x x    x                x           9
Texaco                x   x   x  x x         x x    x   x  x x x x    x          x     x           15
Union Carbide                x   x           x     x       x                  x   x x             7
U. S. Steel           x            x             x   x x   x x  x x        x   x x x   x          11
Weyerhaeuser                                 x     x              x x       x         x x x x x   9
Xerox                   x x x x   x x  x x x x   x x                        x x     x x x x        18
```

II. INVESTMENTS OF CHURCH AGENCIES (BY COMPANY) IN FIFTY-THREE SELECTED CORPORATIONS WHICH CONDUCT BUSINESS ACTIVITIES IN SOUTHERN AFRICA

Company	Stocks (Common & Preferred)			Fixed Income Securities	
	# shares	$ market value	$ annual income	principal	$ annual income
Addressograph-Multigraph					
ABC					
HMS	26,000	1,056,250	15,600		
CTB	400	17,600	240		
	26,400	1,073,850	15,840		
American Metal Climax					
RCA				100,000	7,500
UMC					
BGM-Women's	300	8,250	420		
UPUSA					
BNM	67	2,010	94		
UPUSA					
BP				80,000	3,600
UPUSA					
COEMAR	3,000P	276,000P	15,750P		
	367	10,260	514	180,000	11,100
	3,000P	276,000P	15,750P		
Armco Steel					
CTB	2,300	48,975	2,300		
LCA					
BP				100,000	4,500
UCC					
BHM	19,500	409,500	19,500		
BWM	5,000	101,250	5,000	98,000	4,263
PB	129,200	2,713,200	129,200	49,000	2,132
UCF	3,800	79,800	3,800		
UPUSA					
BNM				200,000	9,000
	159,800	3,352,725	159,800	447,000	19,895
Bethlehem Steel					
ABC					
FMS				100,000	9,000
LCA					
BP				250,000	13,500
	30,000	948,750	36,000	600,000	54,000
PECUSA					
DFMS				400,000	18,000
UCC					
BWM				100,000	5,400
UMC					
BGM-Women's	1,400	36,225	1,680		
UPUSA					
BCE				5,000	225
BP				2,000,000	108,000
	31,400	984,975	37,680	3,455,000	208,125

Company	Stocks (Common & Preferred)			Fixed Income Securities	
	# shares	$ market value	$ annual income	principal	$ annual income
Bristol Meyers					
ABC					
FMS	6,200	403,000	7,440		
MMBB	30,000	2,032,500	36,000		
LCA					
BP				325,000	28,031
CIF	5,000	324,375	6,000		
PCUS					
PF	2,000	135,500	2,400		
UCC					
BWM	1,510	98,150	1,812		
UMC					
BGM-National	2,400	150,000	2,880		
	47,110	3,143,525	56,532	325,000	28,031
Burlington Industries					
ABC					
FMS	300	9,000	420		
NCC	900	33,075	1,260		
PCUS					
PF	3,400	104,975	4,760		
PECUSA					
CPF	4,880	175,070	6,832		
UCC					
PB				100,000	4,750
UPUSA					
BP	6,500	230,750	9,100		
	15,980	552,870	22,372	100,000	4,750
Burroughs					
ABC					
HMS	7,600	1,683,400	4,864		
MMBB	6,000	1,332,000	3,840		
CCD	300	65,100	192		
LCA					
BP	4,000	860,000	2,480		
NCC				60,000	3,600
UCC					
PB				60,000	2,700
UMC					
BGM-Women's				100,000	9,000
UPUSA					
BP	3,400	731,000	2,176		
UPUSA					
COEMAR	4,400	976,800	2,728		
	25,700	5,648,300	16,280	220,000	15,300

Company	Stocks (Common & Preferred)			Fixed Income Securities	
	# shares	$ market value	$ annual income	principal	$ annual income
Caterpillar Tractor					
ABC					
FMS	135	8,505	189		
HMS	26,100	1,683,450	36,540		
CCD	858	56,600	1,201		
LCA					
BP				1,000,000	53,000
NCC	1,100	73,150	1,540		
PECUSA					
CPF	37,000	2,183,000	51,800		
UCC					
BWM	7,122	459,369	9,971		
PB				34,000	1,700
UMC					
BGM-Women's	7,000	418,250	9,450		
UPUSA					
COEMAR				100,000	5,125
UPF				300,000	15,900
	87,315	5,258,324	121,491	1,434,000	75,725
Chase Manhattan					
ABC					
BEP	3,033	197,145	6,066		
CTB	595	38,708	1,190		
PCUS					
BNM	602	34,841	1,204		
PF	2,000	131,000	8,000		
PECUSA					
DFMS				250,000	11,500
UCC					
BHM	17,225	999,050	34,450	1,089,000	70,785
BWM	3,263	212,095	6,526	200,000	9,200
PB	12,447	721,926	24,894	326,000	21,190
UCF	2,851	165,358	5,702	220,000	14,300
UMC					
BGM-National	1,800	99,225	3,600		
BGM-World	130	7,394	260		
UPUSA					
BNM				500,000	32,500
				500,000	32,500
BP				1,000,000	52,500
				1,700,000	86,700
	43,946	2,596,742	91,892	5,785,000	331,175
Chrysler					
CCD	1,000	3,800	1,000		
LCA					
BP	30,000	1,027,500	27,000		
UPUSA					
BNM	31,845	983,214	28,661		
COEMAR	18,500	591,250	16,650		
	81,345	2,605,764	73,311		

Company	Stock (Common & Preferred)			Fixed Income Securities	
	# shares	$ market value	$ annual income	principal	$ annual income
Colgate-Palmolive					
PCUS					
PF	3,000	255,000	4,368		
	3,000	255,000	4,368		
Control Data					
LCA					
BP	10,000	615,000		250,000	13,750
PECUSA					
DFMS	3,000	135,000			
UCC					
PB				100,000	5,000
UMC					
BGM-National	1,500	112,125			
UUA				250,000	9,375
	14,500	862,125		600,000	28,125
Deere and Co.					
LCA					
BP	15,000	712,500	15,600		
PCUS					
BAR				82,000	3,690
				39,500	1,777
PECUSA					
DFMS				100,000	4,500
UCC					
PB				145,000	5,494
UMC					
BGM-Women's	9,400	368,950	10,900		
UPUSA					
BNM				103,500	4,658
COEMAR	15,000	615,000	15,600		
UPF	12,000	615,000	12,000	300,000	16,200
	51,400	2,311,450	54,100	770,000	36,319
Dow Chemical					
ABC					
FMS	5,550	532,800	9,990	100,000	8,900
CCD	500	50,500	900		
LCA					
CIF	3,000	287,625	5,400		
BP				264,000	11,880
UMC					
BGM-World	13,010	1,317,263	198		
UPUSA					
COEMAR	5,000	480,000	9,000		
	37,575	3,497,559	44,057	364,000	20,780
Engelhard Minerals and Chemicals					
RCA	33,000	891,000	13,200		
	33,000	891,000	13,200		

Company	Stock (Common & Preferred)			Fixed Income Securities	
	# shares	$ market value	$ annual income	principal	$ annual income
Exxon					
ABC					
BEP	3,565	288,765	13,369		
FMS	4,811	389,691	18,282		
HMS	26,000	2,109,250	101,400		
MMBB	18,600	1,553,100	70,680		
CTB	2,329	188,940	9,083	50,000	3,000
LCA					
BP				1,500,000	90,000
PCUS					
BAR	15,040	986,411	57,152		
BNM	2,412	177,885	9,166		
PF	1,639	137,880	6,228		
PECUSA					
CPF	1,997	148,028	7,589	500,000	15,000
DFMS	12,602	919,946	47,888		
UCC					
BHM	13,699	1,150,716	52,056		
BWM	5,788	468,828	21,956		
PB	40,862	3,432,408	155,275		
UCF	1,981	166,404	7,528		
UMC					
BGM-Women's	6,292	514,371	23,657	400,000	25,000
UPUSA					
BCE	308	24,948	1,201	35,000	963
BNM	15,861	1,175,697	60,272		
UPF	8,160	601,800	31,008		
UUA	6,000	486,750	23,400		
	187,946	14,921,817	717,190	2,485,000	133,963
Firestone Tire and Rubber					
CTB	1,400	31,500	1,165		
LCA					
BP				1,000,000	73,000
UCC					
PB				75,000	3,188
BWM	7,082	161,110	5,892	210,000	6,825
UMC					
BGM-Women's	2,000	43,500	1,600		
	10,482	236,116	8,657	1,285,000	83,013
First National City Bank					
ABC					
FMS				900,000	59,625
BEP	3,428	246,816	4,525		
CTB	1,320	95,040	1,742		
LCA					
CIF	6,000	432,000	7,920		
PCUS					
BAR	21,600	1,004,400	28,512		

Company	Stock (Common & Preferred)			Fixed Income Securities	
	# shares	$ market value	$ annual income	principal	$ annual income
F. N. C. B. (Cont'd)					
UCC					
BHM	18,217	1,348,058	24,046	400,300	16,012
BWM	7,111	511,992	9,387		
PB	3,720	275,280	7,366	405,000	16,200
UCF				205,000	8,200
UMC					
BGM-World	18,954	1,300,720	25,020		
UPUSA					
BNM	44,000	2,645,500	58,080	20,000	1,324
BP	5,212	357,674	6,880		
BP (CV Cap Note)	660,000	1,346,400	26,400		
BP (CV Cap Note)	340,500	694,620	13,620		
COEMAR	9,500	703,000	12,540	400,000	25,000
UPF	14,000	651,000	18,480		
	153,062	9,571,480	204,498	2,330,300	126,361
CV Cap Note	1,000,500	2,041,020	40,020		
Ford Motor					
ABC					
FMS	6,000	402,000	16,200	400,000	26,000
MMBB	26,800	1,775,500	72,360		
CCD	2,000	148,000	5,400		
CTB	200	13,475	540		
NCC	750	59,719	2,025		
PCUS					
PF	2,000	132,500	5,400		
PECUSA					
CPF				195,000	7,800
UCC					
BWM	2,000	133,000	5,400		
UUA	5,000	336,875	13,500		
	44,750	3,001,069	120,825	595,000	33,800
General Electric					
ABC					
FMS	8,320	549,120	11,648	200,000	12,500
MMBB	55,000	3,513,125	77,000		
LCA					
BP	25,200	1,710,450	35,280		
NCC	1,900	138,463	2,660		
PCUS					
BAR	30,400	1,903,952	41,040		
BNM	4,140	259,268	5,589		
PF	3,000	191,625	4,800		
PECUSA					
CPF	56,636	3,723,817	79,290		
DFMS	10,600	657,200	14,310		
UCC					
BHM	13,000	832,000	18,200		
BWM	8,390	557,935	11,746	200,000	7,000
PB	11,506	736,384	23,012	60,000	2,100
UCF	9,572	612,608	19,144		

Company	Stock (Common & Preferred)			Fixed Income Securities	
	# shares	$ market value	$ annual income	principal	$ annual income
General Electric (cont'd)					
UMC					
BGM-Women's	10,900	203,608	14,715		
BGM-World	13,790	939,996	19,306		
UPUSA					
BCE	400	26,400	560	20,000	700
BNM	11,106	730,220	15,548	217,000	not listed
				1,101,000	
BP	93,500	6,346,313	130,900		
COEMAR	3,000	192,000	4,200		
	370,360	23,824,484	528,948	1,798,000	22,300
General Foods					
ABC					
FMS	500	12,500	700		
CTB	4,000	102,000	5,600		
PCUS					
BAR	32,500	1,166,100	45,500		
BNM	2,060	73,903	2,884		
UPUSA					
UPF	10,000	358,750	14,000		
	49,060	1,713,253	68,684		
General Motors					
ABC					
BEP	2,633	208,007	9,610		
FMS	6,300	497,500	23,045		
MMBB	14,000	1,046,500	62,300		
CCD	2,832	226,500	12,600		
CTB	1,660	130,568	6,640		
LCA					
BP	10,000	811,250	44,500		
CIF	5,000	393,125	22,250		
NCC	700	56,787	3,115		
PCUS					
BAR	18,907	1,388,308	64,284	65,000	2,113
BNM	1,847	148,684	6,280		
PF	2,113	157,418	7,184	50,000	3,562
PECUSA					
CPF	34,292	2,567,614	152,599		
DFMS	12,574	944,000	42,752		
UCC					
BHM	3,006	225,450	10,220		
BWM	3,438	270,742	12,549	105,000	4,200
				25,000	1,219
PB	10,951	821,325	37,233	35,000	1,138
UCF	2,462	184,650	8,371		
UMC					
BGM-National	10	745	37		
BGM-Women's	7,947	588,078	27,096		
BGM-World	18,001	1,460,332	80,105		

Company	Stock (Common & Preferred)			Fixed Income Securities	
	# shares	$ market value	$ annual income	principal	$ annual income
General Motors (cont'd)					
UPUSA					
BCE	200	15,800	894		
BNM	19,014	1,423,673	84,612		
BP				10,000	325
COEMAR	3,800	281,200	16,910		
UPF	10,000	805,000	34,000		
	191,687	14,653,256	769,186	290,000	12,557
Gillette					
ABC					
HMS	24,000	1,284,000	33,600		
NCC	2,150	137,331	3,010		
UMC					
BGM-National	2,600	125,450	3,640		
	28,750	1,546,781	40,250		
Goodyear Tire and Rubber					
ABC					
BEP	3,000	87,000	2,640		
NCC	900	28,350	796		
UMC					
BGM-Women's	8,000	220,000	6,800		
UPUSA					
BP	20,000	640,000	17,600	30,000	2,580
	31,900	975,350	27,836	30,000	2,580
Gulf Oil					
ABC					
FMS				100,000	8,500
LCA					
BP	10,000	268,750	15,000	1,000,000	66,250
PCUS					
BAR	21,500	536,123	32,250		
UCC					
PB				100,000	5,350
UUA				300,000	25,500
	31,500	804,873	47,250	1,500,000	105,600
Holiday Inns of America					
CCD	4,300	182,700	1,160		
LCA					
CIF	5,300	225,250	1,420		
	9,600	407,950	2,580		
Honeywell					
ABC					
FMS				25,000	1,000
PCUS					
BAR	13,200	1,760,616	17,160		
UCC					
BWM	3,083	412,351	4,316		
PB				200,000	9,250

Company	Stock (Common & Preferred)			Fixed Income Securities	
	# shares	$ market value	$ annual income	principal	$ annual income
Honeywell (cont'd)					
UMC					
BGM-Women's	100	13,000	130		
UPUSA					
BP				1,500,000	84,000
UPF				30,338	2,199
	16,383	2,185,967	21,606	1,755,338	96,449
Ingersoll-Rand					
UMC					
BGM-Women's	2,000	129,500	4,000		
UPUSA					
UPF	10,000	562,500	20,000		
	12,000	692,000	24,000		
International Bus. Machines					
ABC					
BEP	275	111,650	1,485		
FMS	1,240	504,680	6,696		
HMS	6,000	2,439,000	32,400		
MMBB	32,280	12,443,940	174,312		
CCD	650	253,500	3,510		
CTB	452	184,846	2,441		
LCA					
BP	5,600	2,189,600	30,240		
CIF	2,300	934,950	12,420		
NCC	280	112,560	1,512		
PCUS					
BAR	6,400	2,153,600	33,280		
BNM	20	6,730	104		
PF	798	307,629	4,309		
PECUSA					
CPF	35,838	14,048,496	193,525		
DFMS	8,512	2,860,032	44,262		
RCA	4,233	1,720,714	22,858		
UCC					
BHM	6,400	2,470,400	34,560		
BWM	503	204,469	2,716		
PB	9,710	3,748,060	50,492		
UCF	1,242	479,412	6,458		
UMC					
BGM-Women's	9,532	3,474,414	54,472		
BGM-World	10,040	3,905,640	54,216		
UPUSA					
BCE	1,084	441,188	5,854		
BNM	12,386	4,855,312	66,884		
BP	51,801	20,254,191	279,725		
COEMAR	3,000	1,155,000	16,200		
UPF	2,362	794,813	12,282		
UUA	1,534	626,639	8,283		
	214,472	82,681,465	1,155,496		

Company	Stock (Common & Preferred)			Fixed Income Securities	
	# shares	$ market value	$ annual income	principal	$ annual income
International Harvester					
ABC					
FMS	11,000	407,000	15,400		
MMBB	17,500	647,500	24,500		
CTB	1,200	43,800	1,680	15,000	713
LCA					
BP				200,000	9,250
				500,000	38,125
NCC	1,550	59,481	2,325		
PCUS					
BAR				550,000	47,438
UCC					
BHM				190,000	9,120
PB				432,300	20,750
UCF				175,000	8,400
UPUSA					
BNM				53,100	2,549
BP				73,800	3,542
	31,250	1,157,781	43,905	2,189,200	139,887
International Telephone and Telegraph					
ABC					
BEP				25,000	1,225
FMS	800P	73,600P	4,000P		
	3,125	168,750	3,719		
MMBB	10,000P	915,000P	50,000P		
	30,000	1,608,750	35,700		
CCD	500P	35,000P	2,500P		
	1,125	65,250	1,395		
LCA					
BP	10,000	592,500	11,900		
PCUS					
BAR	23,000	1,342,740	26,450		
PF	3,500	187,687	4,175		
PECUSA					
CPF	41,200	2,147,550	49,280		
UMC					
BGM-National	1,000P	92,000P	4,000P		
UPUSA					
BCE	4,200	226,800	4,998		
BP	19,000P	1,396,500P	42,750P		
	8,500	503,625	10,540		
COEMAR	8,000	428,000	9,520		
	31,300P	2,512,100P	103,250P	25,000P	1,225P
	132,650	7,271,652	157,677		

Company	Stock (Common & Preffered)			Fixed Income Securities	
	# shares	$ market value	$ annual income	principal	$ annual income
Johnson and Johnson					
ABC					
FMS	3,800	475,000	1,700		
MMBB	15,000	1,940,625	6,750		
PCUS					
BAR	171	9,904	74		
RCA	4,800	567,720	2,064		
UMC					
BGM-Women's	1,000	(purchase approved)			
UPUSA					
BP	80,500	9,961,875	35,619		
	104,271	12,955,124	46,207		
Eastman Kodak					
ABC					
FMS	3,600	289,800	4,825		
HMS	7,000	960,750	9,590		
MMBB	5,400	792,625	7,398		
CTB	1,000	128,250	1,370		
LCA					
CIF	5,750	789,187	7,877		
NCC	650	96,444	923		
PCUS					
BAR	13,000	1,264,250	17,160		
PF	2,000	278,750	1,600		
PECUSA					
CPF	43,010	5,704,201	58,924		
DFMS	11,228	1,089,116	14,821		
RCA	1,800	247,050	2,448		
UCC					
BHM	4,100	569,900	4,264		
BWM	2,354	323,086	3,225		
PB	20,835	2,896,065	21,668		
UCF	11,987	1,666,193	15,823		
UMC					
BGM-Women's	5,500	725,312	6,832		
BGM-World	19,496	2,700,196	26,710		
UPUSA					
BNM	20,000	2,652,500	27,400		
BP	61,200	8,476,200	85,612		
UPF	6,000	583,500	7,920		
	245,910	32,193,375	326,390		
Eli Lilly and Company					
ABC					
FMS	6,400	460,800	4,672		
UMC					
BGM-World	16,250	1,232,970	11,830		
UPUSA					
BP	57,600	4,370,400	41,970		
	80,250	6,064,170	58,472		

Company	Stock (Common & Preferred)			Fixed Income Securities	
	# shares	$ market value	$ annual income	principal	$ annual income
Minnesota Mining and Manufacturing					
CCD	500	42,000	480		
LCA					
CIF	4,300	343,463	4,132		
NCC	1,000	85,625	962		
PCUS					
BAR	13,000	1,755,000	12,025		
PECUSA					
CPF	18,500	1,410,625	17,779		
DFMS	2,000	270,000	1,850		
RCA	10,600	846,675	10,197		
UPUSA					
BP	78,000	6,620,250	74,985		
UPF	3,000	405,000	2,775		
	130,900	11,778,638	125,185		
Mobil Oil					
ABC					
BEP	1,300	88,400	3,120		
FMS	3,800	258,400	9,880		
HMS	20,000	1,367,500	52,000		
CCD	1,000	70,000	2,800		
CTB	400	26,900	1,040		
LCA					
BP	15,000	1,100,625	39,750		
CIF	6,500	444,437	17,225		
NCC	2,100	155,400	5,880		
PCUS					
BAR	13,000	710,190	33,150		
PECUSA					
CPF	45,449	2,556,506	120,440		
UCC					
BHM	13,468	929,292	35,017		
BWM	5,527	378,599	14,370		
PB	61,734	4,259,546	157,422		
UCF	4,550	313,950	11,603		
UMC					
BGM-Women's	14,600	981,850	37,207		
BGM-World	19,200	1,408,801	53,760		
UPUSA					
BNM	550	30,937	1,458		
BP	41,700	3,059,738	116,760		
COEMAR	3,000	207,000	7,950		
UPF	7,000	382,375	17,850		
UUA	6,850	460,662	17,810		
	286,728	19,191,108	756,492		

Company	Stock (Common & Preferred)			Fixed Income Securities	
	# shares	$ market value	$ annual income	principal	$ annual income
Monsanto					
ABC					
FMS	6,000	318,000	10,800		
LCA					
BP				400,000	36,500
UCC					
BWM	3,446	181,776	6,203		
UPUSA					
BCE	157	8,321	283		
BP				2,500,000	228,125
				600,000	54,750
	9,603	508,097	17,286	3,500,000	319,375
Motorola					
LCA					
BP	13,000	1,599,000	8,112		
	13,000	1,599,000	8,112		
National Cash Register					
CTB	990	36,011	396		
PCUS					
BNM	500	14,687	360		
UPUSA					
BNM				23,000	1,005
	1,490	50,698	756	23,000	1,005
Owens-Illinois					
CCD	400P	32,800P	1,900P		
CTB	600	26,850	840		
LCA					
BP				100,000	3,750
PECUSA					
CPF				970,000	48,500
UCC					
BHM	3,600	147,600	5,040		
PB	32,500	1,332,500	43,875		
UCF	2,200	90,200	2,970		
UMC					
BGM-Women's	3,200	130,800	4,320		
	400P	32,800P	1,900P		
	42,100	1,727,950	57,045	1,070,000	52,250
Pfizer and Company					
ABC					
BEP	1,200	51,600	828		
CTB	4,800	205,363	3,312		
PCUS					
BAR	37,500	1,570,500	24,375		
PF	3,000	123,000	1,920		
UCC					
BWM	9,000	387,000	5,940		

Company	Stock (Common & Preferred)			Fixed Income Securities	
	# shares	$ market value	$ annual income	principal	$ annual income
Pfizer & Co. (cont'd)					
UPUSA					
BP	31,400	1,373,750	21,666		
COEMAR	14,000	574,000	9,380		
UPF	11,000	460,625	7,150		
	111,900	4,745,838	74,571		
Phelps Dodge					
ABC					
BEP	1,600	60,800	3,360		
PECUSA					
CPF	30,000	1,113,750	63,000		
	31,600	1,174,550	66,360		
Phillips Petroleum					
ABC					
BEP	6,400	22,400	8,320		
MMBB	40,000	1,430,000	52,000		
CTB				50,000	3,813
LCA					
BP				400,000	30,700
				500,000	38,125
PCUS - BNM	30	919	39		
PECUSA					
DFMS	15,600	468,000	20,280		
RCA	39,000	1,365,000	50,700		
UCC					
BWM	4,140	144,900	5,382		
UPUSA					
BNM	676	19,097	879		
BP				1,500,000	114,375
	105,846	3,450,316	137,600	2,450,000	187,013
Polaroid					
LCA					
BP	5,000	606,250	1,600		
NCC	880	110,990	282		
PECUSA					
CPF	38,400	4,896,000	12,288		
UMC					
BGM-National	900	115,988	288		
BGM-World	225	27,281	72		
UPUSA					
BP	40,700	4,934,875	13,024		
COEMAR	5,600	714,000	1,792		
	91,705	11,405,384	29,346		
Singer					
ABC					
FMS				100,000	8,250
LCA					
BP	20,000	1,445,000	48,000		

Company	Stock (Common & Preferred)			Fixed Income Securities	
	# shares	$ market value	$ annual income	principal	$ annual income
Singer (cont'd)					
PCUS					
BAR	18,200	1,405,950	43,680		
BNM				50,000	4,125
UCC					
BWM	2,500	203,125	6,000		
UPUSA					
BP	10,000	722,500	24,000		
COEMAR				500,000	41,250
	50,700	3,776,575	121,680	650,000	53,625
Sperry Rand					
LCA					
BP	35,000	1,658,125	21,000	90,000	4,950
PECUSA					
CPF				280,000	15,400
RCA				300,000	24,600
UMC					
BGM-Women's				89,000	4,895
UPUSA					
COEMAR	20,000	940,000	12,000		
	55,000	2,598,125	33,000	759,000	49,845
Standard Oil of California					
LCA					
BP	20,600	1,601,650	59,740		
PCUS					
BNM	28	1,607	78		
PECUSA					
DFMS				200,000	8,750
UCC					
BWM	3,235	223,215	9,382		
PB				75,000	3,281
UMC					
BGM-Women's	1,120	79,660	3,136		
BGM-World	400	31,100	1,160		
UPUSA					
BP	350	27,213	1,015		
	25,733	1,964,445	74,511	275,000	12,031
Tenneco					
ABC					
BEP	2,500	65,000	3,300	40,000	2,700
HMS	40,000	1,025,000	52,800		
MMBB	40,000	1,130,000	54,400		
PCUS					
PF				25,000	1,562
PECUSA					
DFMS				50,000	3,375

Company	Stock (Common & Preferred)			Fixed Income Securities	
	# shares	$ market value	$ annual income	principal	$ annual income
Tenneco (cont'd)					
UCC					
BWM	6,797	173,323	8,972		
PB				442,000	23,953
UMC					
BGM-Women's	5,500	139,562	9,636		
UPUSA					
UPF				400,000	24,000
				300,000	28,125
	94,797	2,532,885	129,108	1,257,000	83,715
Texaco					
ABC					
BEP	2,000	74,000	3,320		
MMBB	30,500	1,128,500	50,630		
CCD	5,100	183,600	8,460		
CTB	6,342	230,651	22,375		
LCA					
BP				840,000	65,100
PCUS					
BAR	30,000	1,031,400	48,000		
BNM	1,770	60,844	2,832		
PECUSA					
DFMS	19,000	646,000	30,400		
RCA	4,600	168,475	7,636		
UCC					
BHM	50,500	1,868,500	83,830		
BWM	14,903	543,959	24,739		
PB	79,750	2,950,750	127,600	100,000	3,625
UCF	15,960	590,520	25,536		
UMC					
BGM-World	24,574	933,812	40,793		
UPUSA					
UPF	6,426	220,894	10,281		
	291,425	10,631,905	486,432	940,000	68,725
Union Carbide					
CTB	2,300	108,600	4,600		
LCA					
BP				1,125,000	59,625
PCUS					
BNM	1,020	43,095	2,040		
PECUSA					
CPF				684,932	30,821
UCC					
PB				150,000	7,950
UPUSA					
BNM	200	9,175	400		
UPF	11,000	464,750	22,000		
	14,520	625,620	29,040	1,959,932	98,396

Company	Stock (Common & Preferred)			Fixed Income Securities	
	# shares	$ market value	$ annual income	principal	$ annual income
U. S. Steel					
ABC					
BEP				40,000	1,600
CTB				40,000	1,700
PCUS					
BAR				1,411,000	65,259
				100,000	4,625
PECUSA					
CPF				50,000	2,312
DFMS				150,000	6,750
				426,200	19,712
RCA				100,000	7,750
UCC					
BWM				206,000	8,240
				200,000	9,250
PB				300,000	13,125
UPUSA					
BCE				17,000	786
BNM				5,200	240
				5,000	225
COEMAR				350,000	16,187
				3,400,400	157,761
Weyerhaeuser					
PCUS					
BNM	30	1,388	24		
PECUSA					
CPF				1,000,000	86,250
UCC					
BWM	4,000	140,000	3,200		
PB				100,000	5,200
UMC					
BGM-Women's	4,000	197,000	3,200		
UPUSA					
BCE	80,000	4,000,000	64,000		
BNM	12,000	562,500	9,960		
BP				1,000,000	86,250
UPF	7,200	333,000	5,760	250,000	13,000
	107,230	5,233,888	86,144	2,350,000	190,700
Xerox					
ABC					
FMS	3,200	508,800	2,688		
HMS	14,000	2,219,000	11,760		
MMBB	22,400	3,575,600	18,816		
CCD	500	73,500	420		
CTB	2,300	361,738	1,932		
LCA					
BP	2,000	299,500	1,660		
CIF	2,800	443,800	2,234		
NCC	750	111,937	630		

Company	Stock (Common & Preferred)			Fixed Income Securities	
	# shares	$ market value	$ annual income	principal	$ annual income
Xerox (cont'd)					
PCUS					
BAR	13,000	1,628,250	10,400		
PF	1,500	239,437	1,220		
PECUSA					
CPF	26,037	3,925,078	21,611	1,820,000	97,825
RCA	8,350	1,323,475	7,014		
UMC					
BGM-Women's	2,200	325,000	1,760		
BGM-World	13,650	2,044,088	11,466		
UPUSA					
BCE	2,250	357,750	1,890		
BNM	1,500	226,125	1,245		
BP	37,000	5,540,750	31,080	91,000	4,891
COEMAR	1,000	159,500	830	260,000	15,600
	154,437	23,363,328	128,656	2,171,000	118,316

III. 53 CORPORATIONS

TOTALS BY DENOMINATIONAL AGENCIES
INCLUDING PORTFOLIO DATE, TOTAL MARKET
VALUE, AND ANNUAL INCOME

Church Agency		Portfolio Date	Total Market Value of Portfolio	Estimated Total Annual Income of Portfolio	Market Value of Stocks Com. and Pfd.	Dividend Income from Stocks	Principal of Fixed Income Securities	Interest Income from Fixed Securities
ABC	BEP	9/30/72	8,279,428	436,836	1,501,583	59,943	105,000	5,525
	FMS	9/30/72	31,700,686	1,225,000	6,268,946	152,294	1,925,000	133,775
	HMS	9/30/72	40,506,830	1,037,944	15,827,600	350,554	0	0
	MMBB	10/31/72	188,177,250	4,872,000	36,825,265	796,686	0	0
CTB		9/30/72	19,000,000	1,235,000	2,019,815	68,486	155,000	9,226
CCD		12/21/72	10,500,000	500,000	1,488,850	43,918	0	0
LCA	BP*	11/30/72	132,455,193	6,024,284	18,046,450	397,862	10,444,000	694,036
	CIF	9/30/72	17,983,967	515,706	4,618,212	86,878	0	0
NCC		12/31/72	3,375,203	81,460	1,259,311	26,920	60,000	3,600
PCUS	BAR	12/31/71	103,223,305	3,875,432	21,617,694	534,492	2,247,500	124,901
	BNM	12/31/71	3,981,242	270,941	823,851	30,600	50,000	4,125
	PF	11/1/72	9,249,175	401,000	2,372,401	56,364	75,000	5,124
PECUSA	CPF	6/30/72	274,469,041	8,272,227	44,599,733	834,957	5,499,932	303,909
	DFMS	12/31/71	38,863,208	1,811,391	8,365,294	227,363	1,576,200	72,587
RCA		8/30/72	29,806,977	925,640	7,130,110	116,117	500,000	39,850
UUA		8/31/72	22,160,125	1,152,010	1,910,926	62,993	550,000	34,875
UCC	BHM	10/31/72	60,632,250	3,134,035	10,950,466	321,183	1,679,300	95,917
	BWM	9/30/72	30,850,371	1,051,456	6,290,283	184,684	1,344,000	55,597
	PB	10/31/72	176,770,982	7,245,000	23,887,444	778,037	3,288,300	158,076
	UCF	10/31/72	22,511,264	817,520	4,349,095	106,935	600,000	30,900
UMC	BGM-National	7/10/72	7,330,723	230,610	695,533	14,445	0	0
	BGM-Women's	10/16/72	35,401,577	1,247,049	8,597,330	221,011	589,000	38,895
	BGM-World	11/30/72	118,463,572	3,090,966	17,309,593	324,896	0	0
UPUSA	BP	11/30/72	398,897,140	12,788,286	77,588,623	985,422	12,084,800	829,638
	BNM	6/30/72	94,337,350	3,532,016	15,315,959	355,493	2,727,800	84,001
	BCE	9/29/72	14,675,595	466,389	5,101,207	79,680	77,000	2,674
	COEMAR	11/1/72	58,000,000	2,300,000	8,292,750	151,050	1,610,000	103,162
	UPF	12/31/71	33,873,858	1,455,240**	8,068,378	234,075	1,580,338	99,424
Total			1,985,476,312	69,995,438	361,122,702	7,603,338	48,768,170	2,929,817

* See LCA notes on p.177.
** See UPUSA notes on p. 178.

200

IV. 53 CORPORATIONS
TOTALS BY DENOMINATION

Denomination	Number of Agencies and Boards Included	Total Market Value of Portfolios	Total Estimated Annual Income of Portfolios	For 53 Corporations			
				Total Market Value of Stocks	Total Estimated Annual Dividend Income from Stocks	Principal Value of Fixed Income Securities	Interest Income from Fixed Income Securities
ABC	4	268,664,194	7,571,780	60,423,394	1,359,477	2,030,000	139,300
CTB	1	19,000,000	1,235,000	2,019,815	68,486	155,000	9,226
CCD	1	10,500,000	500,000	1,488,850	43,918	0	0
LCA	2	150,439,160*	6,539,990*	22,664,662	484,740	10,444,000	694,036
NCC	1	3,375,203	81,460	1,259,311	26,920	60,000	3,600
PCUS	3	116,453,722	4,547,373	24,813,946	621,456	2,372,500	134,150
PECUSA	2	313,332,249	10,083,618	52,965,027	1,062,320	7,076,132	376,496
RCA	1	29,806,977	925,640	7,130,110	116,117	500,000	39,850
UUA	1	22,160,125	1,152,010	1,910,926	62,993	550,000	34,875
UCC	4	290,764,867	12,248,011	45,477,288	1,390,839	6,911,600	340,490
UMC	3	161,195,872	4,568,625	26,602,456	560,352	589,000	38,895
UPUSA	5	599,783,943	20,541,931	114,366,917	1,805,720	18,079,938	1,118,899
Total	28	1,985,476,312	69,995,438	361,122,702	7,603,338	48,768,170	2,929,817

* See LCA notes on p. 177.

V. 53 CORPORATIONS

TOTAL CHURCH INVESTMENTS BY CORPORATION

Corporation	Stock (Common and Preferred)			Principal Value of Fixed Income Securities	Annual Interest Income
	Number Shares	$ Market Value	$ Annual Income from Dividends		
Addressograph-Multigraph	26,400	$ 1,073,850	$ 15,840		
American Metal Climax	367	10,260	514		
	3,000P	276,000P	15,750P	180,000P	11,100
Armco Steel	159,800	3,352,725	159,800	447,000	19,895
Bethlehem Steel	31,400	984,975	37,680	3,455,000	208,125
Bristol-Myers	47,110	3,143,525	56,532	325,000	28,031
Burlington Industries	15,980	552,870	22,372	100,000	4,750
Burroughs	25,700	5,648,300	16,280	220,000	15,300
Caterpillar Tractor	87,315	5,258,324	121,491	1,434,000	75,725
Chase Manhattan Bank	43,946	2,596,742	91,892	5,785,000	331,175
Chrysler	81,345	2,605,764	73,311		
Colgate-Palmolive	3,000	255,000	4,368		
Control Data	14,500	862,125		600,000	28,125
Deere and Co.	51,400	2,311,450	54,100	770,000	36,319
Dow Chemical	37,575	3,497,559	44,057	364,000	20,780
Engelhard Minerals	33,000	891,000	13,200		
Exxon	187,946	14,921,817	717,190	2,485,000	133,963
Firestone Tire & Rubber	10,482	236,116	8,657	1,285,000	83,013
First National City Bank	153,062	9,571,480	204,498		
Cv. Cap. Note	1,000,500	2,041,020	40,020	2,330,300	126,361
Ford Motor	44,750	3,001,069	120,825	595,000	33,800
General Electric	370,360	23,824,484	528,948	1,798,000	22,300
General Foods	49,060	1,713,253	68,684		
General Motors	191,687	14,653,256	769,186	290,000	12,557
Gillette	28,750	1,546,781	40,250		
Goodyear Tire & Rubber	31,900	975,350	27,836	30,000	2,580
Gulf Oil	31,500	804,873	47,250	1,500,000	105,600
Holiday Inns	9,600	407,950	2,580		
Honeywell	16,383	2,185,967	21,606	1,755,338	96,449
Ingersoll-Rand	12,000	692,000	24,000		
IBM	214,472	82,681,465	1,155,496		
International Harvester	31,250	1,157,781	43,905	2,189,200	139,887
ITT	31,300P	2,512,100P	103,250P		
	132,650	7,271,652	157,677	25,000	1,225
Johnson & Johnson	104,271	12,955,124	46,207		
Eastman Kodak	245,910	32,193,375	326,390		
Eli Lilly	80,250	6,064,170	58,472		
3M	130,900	11,778,638	125,185		
Mobil Oil	286,728	19,191,108	756,492		
Monsanto	9,603	508,097	17,286	3,500,000	319,375
Motorola	13,000	1,599,000	8,112		

V. 53 Corporations (concluded)

Total Church Investments by Corporation

| | Stock (Common and Preferred) | | | Principal | Annual |
	Number Shares	$ Market Value	$ Annual Income from Dividends	Value of Fixed Income Securities	Annual Interest Income
National Cash Register	1,490	50,698	756	23,000	1,005
Owens-Illinois	400P	32,800P	1,900P		
	42,100	1,727,950	57,045	1,070,000	52,250
Pfizer	111,900	4,745,838	74,571		
Phelps-Dodge	31,600	1,174,550	66,360		
Phillips Petroleum	105,846	3,450,316	137,600	2,450,000	187,013
Polaroid	91,705	11,405,384	29,346		
Singer	50,700	3,776,575	121,680	650,000	53,625
Sperry Rand	55,000	2,598,125	33,000	759,000	49,845
Standard Oil of Calif.	25,733	1,964,445	74,511	275,000	12,031
Tenneco	94,797	2,532,885	129,108	1,257,000	83,715
Texaco	291,425	10,631,905	486,432	940,000	68,725
Union Carbide	14,520	625,620	29,040	1,959,932	98,396
U. S. Steel				3,400,400	157,761
Weyerhaeuser	107,230	5,233,888	86,144	2,350,000	190,700
Xerox	154,437	23,363,328	128,656	2,171,000	118,316
Total		$361,122,702	$7,603,338	$48,768,170	$2,929,817

203

Albert Park, Durban.

Children playing out-
side shanty homes for
Coloured families
near Capetown.

V. ACTIONS: INVESTMENTS IN SOUTHERN AFRICA

For nearly a decade Protestant churches in the United States have been engaged in analysis, interpretation, and action campaigns around the question of American corporate investment in Southern African countries. Their assessment of ways in which they could influence meaningful social change has led to various actions: pressure on U.S. corporations conducting business in Southern Africa; legal and Congressional actions; relief work and support for humanitarian programs of liberation movements; support of economic sanctions; and research and education projects concerning the issues.

During the early 1960's many Protestant denominations passed resolutions concerning the situation in Southern Africa (see p. 210), but by the mid-1960's attention was focused on a floating credit arrangement of $40 million by ten U.S. banks to the South African government. A "Bank Campaign" was launched against the bank consortium demanding withdrawal of the credit arrangement, and several churches were active in bringing pressure to bear against this loan, which was eventually withdrawn. This campaign strengthened the view that social concerns and investment policies could not be separated. Further stockholder actions were taken by churches regarding Gulf Oil's role in Angola and General Motors' investments in the South African auto industry in the early 1970's.

In 1972 a coalition of six major Protestant denominations was formed for the purpose of filing disclosure resolutions asking corporations to reveal the full facts of their involvements in Southern Africa. Disclosure resolutions were filed with eight companies: General Motors, General Electric, Gulf, Goodyear, IBM, American Metal Climax, Newmont Mining, and Mobil Oil.

In continuing and expanding corporate social responsibility challenges in 1973 participants in the Church Project on U.S. Investments in Southern Africa-1973 (Room 845, 475 Riverside Drive, New York, New York 10027) filed resolutions with eighteen companies concerning their current activities or proposed engagement in Southern Africa. The Church Project is a coalition of boards and agencies of six Protestant denominations, the Episcopal Churchmen for South Africa, and the National Council of Churches, which have stock in the companies with whom resolutions were filed. Contact the Church Project for current information on the actions described here. The resolutions filed with IBM, First National City Corporation, General Electric Co., and Caterpillar Tractor Co. asked them to disclose to shareholders noncompetitive information about the history of their operations in South Africa. Items requested in the disclosure included a description of the annual profits, annual capital investment broken down by source, legal form of ownership, relations with the South African government, a description of relations with workers, a break-down of work force and job description by race, and plans to invest in the Bantustan areas or areas bordering on the Bantustans. Burroughs Corp., Minnesota Mining & Manufacturing Corp., Eastman Kodak Co., Ford Motor Co., ITT Corp., Texaco Inc., and Xerox Corp. agreed to supply this information to all shareholders, so the Church Project withdrew the resolution filed with those companies.

As Exxon has applied for a license to explore for oil off the shore of Angola, the Church Project resolution called for "a broad-based committee to fully examine the implications for both the company and for Angola of its proposed new investment in this Portuguese colony." This committee would report publicly(including recommendations) within six months of the 1973 stockholders' meeting on the contribution of investment to the maintenance of Portuguese control, the effect the investment would have on stockholder investment, customer goodwill, and international reputation, the possibility of future losses if oil operations were nationalized upon independence, and the amount of monetary payments expected by and military protection provided by the Portuguese government.

The resolutions filed with Continental Oil Corp. and Phillips Petroleum Co. proposed an amendment of the Certificate of Incorporation of the corporations to read that the companies would "not conduct exploration, mining or drilling activities in Namibia (South-West Africa), either directly or through affiliates and shall wind up any operations currently underway in that country as expeditiously as possible." The proposal was based on a decision of the International Court of Justice that South Africa's continued occupation of Namibia is illegal and on official U.S. policy prohibiting American corporations from investing in Namibia.

Episcopal Churchmen for South Africa (14 West 11 Street, New York, New York 10011), an independent group of Episcopal churchmen, filed identical resolutions with American Metal Climax Corp. and Newmont Mining Corp. It asked them to amend their Composite Certificates of Incorporation to read that they will not conduct exploration, mining, or drilling activities in Namibia.

The Gulf Boycott Coalition (Box 123, D.V. Station, Dayton, Ohio 45406) planned either to attend or have its regional chapters plan activities centered around the Gulf annual meeting.

A separate resolution filed with Newmont Mining Corp. and Mobil Oil Corp. requested that their by-laws be amended to read, "In its operations abroad, the Corporation will practice principles of fair employment.... In any country where local laws involve racial discrimination in employment, the Corporation will initiate affirmative action programs to achieve meaningful equality of job opportunity." In the end Newmont left the resolution off its proxy statement (with the approval of the SEC), arguing that adoption would force Newmont to break local law.

Recent actions other than the proxy resolutions described above may be found in other sections of this report: religious institutions' policy statements and investment policies (p. 210); United Nations actions and resolutions (p.224); recent Congressional action (p. 223). In addition, many actions have taken place in European countries and in other nations throughout the world. An important part of current actions include the World Council of Churches' divestment and selective investment policy (p.221).

There are many action possibilities for local and regional churches and individuals concerned about issues of U.S. investment in Southern Africa in addition to support of the proxy resolutions outlined above. The first step in the process of responsible action is education. One should be <u>as fully educated as</u> possible in the issues of U.S. corporate involvement in Southern Africa. Further information is available in the publications listed on pages 229-35. Research/action groups (pp.225-28) concerned with Southern African issues are also good sources of information and are helpful in providing strategies for local action and involvement.

Some specific action options for the interested church or individual include:

A. At the Corporate Level

1) Research and Publication: Accurate fact finding and research on specific problems and issues is always a precondition for an effective
campaign against a questionable policy of a corporation. While 15
companies are covered in depth in this study (company profiles, pp.33-141)
and 53 are included in the entire study, there are over 300 American
companies with investments in Southern Africa, and little is known about
many of their activities there.

2) Meetings with Management: Stockholders or concerned citizens can attempt
to meet with corporate managements to discuss an area of corporate responsibility pertinent to the Southern African situation. This provides an
opportunity to gain information and to raise questions with management
concerning corporate policies.

3) Fact-finding trips: Although this is an expensive option in the case of
Southern Africa, 16 church persons went to South Africa in 1971 to look
at the role of U.S. business there. Facts discovered while there and
impressions of the situation are helpful in continuing to put pressure on
companies involved in Southern Africa.

4) Hearings: Hearings may be held to discuss a U.S. company's response to a
specific Southern African issue. These can be useful in gaining publicity
for the particular problem and also serve an educational function.

5) Resolutions of Concern: Churches and other local groups may press for
resolutions such as those passed by the national denominations and the
National and World Councils of Churches with regard to U.S. corporate
involvement in Southern Africa. These resolutions serve an educational
function and inform a wide public.

6) Direct Action Confrontation Tactics: A variety of direct action tactics
are available for use in a specific campaign. These include boycotts,
demonstrations, picketing, leafleting, and guerrilla theater, etc.

7) Class Action Suits: Stockholders may bring legal suits against a company
which participates in socially harmful or irresponsible activities. This
presents the company with a specific challenge and calls the public's attention to the issue. While this can sometimes be an effective tool, it is
extremely expensive and needs to be used only in selected cases.

8) Stockholder Resolutions: Church denominations and other institutional
investors may file stockholder resolutions with a company such as the
ones described above. These resolutions serve to decentralize an issue
because it provides the potential for debate in universities, foundations,
churches, unions, or individual households of stockholders who may vote
on the resolution.

9) Stockholders' Meetings: Any individual or institutional stockholder
may attend the annual stockholders' meeting of a corporation. Various
forms of direct actions have been tried at these meetings with very
limited success. However, they are a source of information about the
company and its activities, although it goes without saying that any
information that may in the least way be controversial is generally restricted.

10) Letters: Individuals may write to the chairman of the board or president of a corporation expressing their opinions about that company's involvement in Southern Africa or requesting information about a company policy exercised in that country.

11) Meetings and Forums: A local church or group may arrange for company representatives to speak about their activities in Southern Africa.

12) Individuals and groups may write or meet with major institutional investors in one of the companies and encourage them to address the corporation about concerns which they share. There are many large institutional investors with which individuals have some contact: churches, unions, pension funds, mutual funds, insurance corporations, banks, universities, and others.

B. At the Government Level

1) Mobilize people to demand changes in American governmental policy toward South Africa, Rhodesia, Namibia, and Portugal.

2) Support the work of Congressman Diggs as his committee continues to probe African issues through the hearing process in Congress. (See "Recent Congressional Action," p. 223 .)

3) Express interest in the Senate Foreign Relations Committee's (Senator Frank Church,Dem., Idaho) probe of multinational corporations and emphasize the importance of exposing the effects of U.S. corporations on the countries of Southern Africa.

4) Write letters to Senators and Representatives resisting passage of the sugar quota bill, which gives a quota to South Africa.

5) Contact the Washington Office on Africa, 110 Maryland Avenue, Washington, D.C. 20002, to cooperate and lend support to its lobbying activities for various Congressional actions concerning Southern African issues. It is a vital source of information on upcoming legislative issues.

C. At the University Level

1) Hold seminars on U.S. corporate involvement in Southern African countries in participation with African students and African studies specialists.

2) Utilize the campus press as a forum for opinion and as a means of disseminating information about Southern African issues and U.S. corporate involvement in those countries.

3) Join or form committees to investigate university portfolios or to establish criteria for socially responsible investment. Press for appropriate action by the investment committee on proxy resolutions and other investment decisions relating to Southern African issues.

D. On the International Level

  1) Support the work of the United Nations Unit on Apartheid, Department
     of Political and Security Council Affairs, in its efforts to put an
     end to apartheid and to aid the victims of the repressive aspects of
     this inhuman social system.

  2) Support and encourage aid for the various liberation movements, both
     to end colonial oppression by Portugal and to resist the system of
     apartheid (see pp. 225-28 for a list of these groups).

VI. RESOURCES AND APPENDICES

A. CHURCH POLICY STATEMENTS

American Baptist Convention

In 1967 the American Baptist Convention passed a resolution concerning Africa asking in part that U.S. policy toward Africa: "3) Support national and international policies and programs aimed to bring about the equal rights and opportunities and responsibilities of all people now living on the continent of Africa - (a) in South Africa with the ending of the policy of apartheid; (b) in Southwest Africa through UN action to end the control by South Africa of the mandate territory. . ." (Resolution passed by the American Baptist Convention, 1967, pp. 8-9.)

At the May, 1972, American Baptist Convention meeting in Denver, Colorado, the Resolutions Committee reported on several issues that were not voted on by the delegates because the time allotted for debate and action on the resolutions had come to an end. However, they recommended that the Convention "protest: 1) the continued refusal of the United States government to support UN resolutions which seek to put economic, political, and moral pressure on South Africa. 2) The willingness of some American corporations and their investors to operate in South Africa in a manner largely uncritical of the apartheid system and in fact profiting from the low wages paid to Black workers. 3) The extension of the apartheid system to Namibia by South Africa in defiance of the UN which is now legally responsible for Namibia. 4) The U.S. government action which undercut the United Nations Security Council sanctions against the illegal, racist regime in Rhodesia (Zimbabwe) by importing chromium, one of the items on the embargo list. 5) The assignment of more than 400 million dollars in credit to Portugal by the U.S. government, thus enabling that country to continue its repression of majority Black populations of Mozambique, Angola, and Guinesa Bissau. . . Therefore, we urge all American Baptist Convention agencies, churches, and individual investors holding stock in companies doing business in the Republic of South Africa to support stockholder resolutions and other efforts to influence American business management to work for the following: 1. Equal pay for equal work among all races; 2. Recognition of Black unions for purposes of collective bargaining in good faith; 3. Genuine efforts to expand vocational and technical training for Black employees and to accelerate their participation in skilled trades and management; 4. Scholarship programs for Black employees and their families; 5. Retirement programs for all employees. We recognize that we all benefit economically from apartheid through high rates of income on investments in these companies and through lower prices of consumer goods in this country. We urge deeper commitment to both the Christian conviction and the American ideal of the intrinsic worth of every human being and willingness to accept the lower standard of living which these recommendations may necessitate. We urge the U.S. government to reverse its stand by supporting UN resolutions which seek to put economic, political, and moral pressure on South Africa. . . ." (Report of the Resolutions Committee to the American Baptist Convention," Denver, Colorado, May 10-14, 1972, pp. 9-10.)

In the "Guidelines Relating to Social Criteria for Investments" adopted by the Board of Managers of the Society* on November 1, 1972, it is stated that "in exercising its rights . . . as a shareholder, the Society may take action in exceptional circumstances if a finding has been made that a company's activities may cause serious social injury." After specifying the types of action that may be taken, it continues: "For the purpose of these Guidelines social

---

* American Baptist Home Mission Society and the Women's American Baptist Home Mission Society

injury will include: (v) foreign investments which have the effect of contributing to the economic support of governments whose policies seriously inhibit the political and economic rights of any substantial social group."

In May, 1972, the Board of Education and Publications initiated a shareholder resolution with Goodyear Tire and Rubber Company asking that the corporation provide a "full written report to the shareholders within four months of the date of the 1972 annual meeting on the involvement of the Corporation in the Republic of South Africa." (Letter from Horace Gale, Treasurer, American Baptist Convention, November 21, 1972, p. 1.)

Currently, the Board of Education and the Home Mission Society are "considering initiating shareholder resolutions with Goodyear and Xerox respectively asking for fuller disclosure of each corporation's activity in the Republic of South Africa," dealing with its history, relations with workers, and relations with the government. (Letter from Horace Gale, Treasurer, American Baptist Convention, November 21, 1972, p. 2.)

Church of the Brethren

The Church of the Brethren has no general policy statement concerning South Africa, but one of the General Investment Guidelines of the Brethren General Board does refer to the practice of apartheid: "6. Investments will not knowingly be made in companies which do not have fair and equal opportunity employment practices. Except as indicated under Guideline No. 3 (referring to stockholder action against companies with unacceptable policies), the Board shall invest in no company or bank that carries out business transactions with governments which practice apartheid." ("Investments: Church of the Brethren General Board, A Summary of Guidelines/Portfolios," Offices of the General Secretary/Treasurer, June, 1972, p. 4.)

In the past year the General Board has sold stock in eleven corporations over the military issue, but many of these corporations also have operations in South Africa. (Phone conversation with Mr. Robert Greiner, Treasurer, Church of the Brethren, November, 1972.)

The General Brotherhood Board of the Church of the Brethren has stated:

"THE PROBLEM - The nations of western Europe and the United States carry some of the responsibility for conditions in South Africa because the status quo is supported through the high level of trade and investment controlled by these nations. Economic assistance and long-range credit further implicated the United States and western Europe. Around 250 major American firms conduct about 700 million dollars' worth of trade each year with South Africa, and individual American investment there continues to rise. A consortium of American banks headed by Chase Manhattan and First National City Bank of New York extend liberal credit arrangements to the South African government. Trade, investment, and loans all help stabilize the white government and bolster the internal social and political system.

"WE URGE THAT -- the United States Government contribute generously to the United Nations Trust Fund for South Africa to provide legal aid to those charged under apartheid laws, relief for dependents of persons persecuted by the laws, education of prisoners, their children and dependents, and relief for refugees from South Africa.

"-the United States Government support and join other nations in applying economic sanctions against South Africa as one means by which South Africa might be induced to modify its racial policies.

"-the National Council of Churches and member denominations make significant withdrawals of their funds from any banks which do not cease providing such a revolving credit arrangement."

Interreligious Foundation for Community Organization

Press statement issued by the Interreligious Foundation for Community Organization, 475 Riverside Drive, Room 560, New York, New York - June 22, 1971.

"The Interreligious Foundation for Community Organization, Inc., being clear in principle and firmly committed to the self-determination and total liberation of African people wherever we may be, has convened this press conference:
   1. to urge public examination and rejection of dialogue with South Africa until apartheid is ended and majority rule instituted.
   2. to announce our rejection of a United States - South African Leadership Exchange Program invitation to participate in a symposium to be held in Johannesburg, South Africa, in July.
   3. to place on the record our call to all brothers and sisters to refrain from support of this and similar programs so long as apartheid and the illegal government of South Africa continues.
   4. to declare publicly our solidarity, advocacy and full support for those African majorities who seek self-determination and liberation from oppressive and racist regimes.
   5. to call upon the churches of America: a) first, to develop a program of study and action to combat the evils of apartheid, b) secondly, to develop a program of Christian witness and assistance to bring about self-determination for the oppressed people of Southern Africa, c) thirdly, to withhold participation in programs such as US-SALEP until apartheid is ended and South Africa is restored to majority rule."

In October, 1972, a 25-member Task Force on African Affairs was formed, which will become increasingly active on South African issues in 1973. (Interview with Ms. Karen Whitmore, IFCO, December, 1972.)

Lutheran Church in America

In July, 1972, the Board of Social Ministry submitted a report on the "Social Criteria for Investments" to the biennial convention of the Lutheran Church in America. This report was not passed by the convention but the convention did authorize its distribution and approve it as a report.

The report states that one of the major issues focusing attention on investments is: "3. Racism, at home and abroad. Ugly practices of discrimination persist, even though some changes are discernible. Some American and Canadian corporations and their stockholders and also trade union members may profit from a system that exploits peoples at home and abroad. For example, current concerns focus on South Africa and Latin America, where the church's investments offer it an opportunity, but not its only opportunity, to influence the economic policy and practice of such corporations in the direction of justice." ("Social Criteria for Investments," a Report to the Lutheran Church in America from the Board of Social Ministry, July, 1972, p. 3.)

National Council of Churches

On December 6, 1972, the General Assembly of the NCC adopted a resolution stating, in part, "we seek continuously to be true to Christ's mission to 'proclaim release to the captives and to set at liberty those who are oppressed. . . . In concert with Christ's mission in the world and the church's mission to the disinherited of this world, we express our commitment to, and support for, the oppressed black peoples of Southern Africa. We affirm the courageous acts of the black majorities in Southern Africa as they seek to remove the yokes of oppression to achieve human dignity and self-determination.

I. The National Council of Churches of Christ in U.S.A. Therefore Condemns:
 1. The policy of Portuguese colonialism and the refusal of Portugal to grant independence to its African colonies, even while legitimate movements for independence fight for self-determination.
 2. The illegal Rhodesian regime of Ian Smith which has maintained white minority control and has ignored the overwhelming wish of the people for black majority rule.
 3. The South African Government for continuing its racist apartheid practices in the face of almost unanimous international opposition, for its repressive acts of torture, imprisonment and detention without trial, for denying the black majority their right to vote or own land and for their illegal occupation of Namibia.
 4. The policies of the United States and other Western countries which assist the white minority governments of Southern Africa.
 5. The acts of those multinational corporations which through their investments have strengthened and supported white minority governments; which pay huge taxes to white governments and strengthen their military capabilities; and which pay dividends to their shareholders, taking advantage of racist laws which permit them to pay 'slave' wages to black employees.

II. The NCC therefore calls upon the U.S. Government to end all forms of support for the unjust minority regimes of Southern Africa by:
 (i) immediately halting the purchase of chrome from Rhodesia and by observing full sanctions against it
 (ii) cancelling the sugar quota from the Republic of South Africa
 (iii) revoking the Azores Pact and terminating loans to Portugal
 (iv) cancelling the NASA contract with the South African government and transferring the tracking station in South Africa to an independent African country
 (v) refusing tax credits to corporations doing business in Namibia as long as it is illegally occupied by South Africa

(vi) discouraging future economic investment in Southern Africa until there is majority rule.

III. We Also Propose That the National Council of Churches:

(i) support actions already being taken in the above areas by concerned denominations

(ii) endorse the call of the United Nations, the Organization of African Unity, and the World Council of Churches Central Committee to foreign economic investors to withdraw from white-ruled Southern Africa

(iii) use its stock ownership powers and other strategies to press companies investing in Southern Africa to cease operations and gradually withdraw

(iv) call upon all member denominations in keeping with the commitment of the World Council of Churches expressed in the Programme to Combat Racism to increase significantly their financial contributions to the liberation movements of Southern Africa, preferably channeled through the Programme to Combat Racism

(v) urge the churches of the U.S.A. involved in mission in non-liberated areas of Southern Africa and Guinea-Bissau seriously to re-examine their roles in relation to justice, liberation and human development

(vi) give serious consideration to Southern Africa as a program priority for the next triennium setting up procedures to implement the above proposals."
("Resolution on the Churches Policy Toward Southern Africa," National Council of Churches of Christ in the U.S.A., adopted by the General Assembly, December 6, 1972. The policy basis for this resolution is found in the policy statement on Southern Africa adopted by the General Board, February 23, 1966, and in the policy statement on Consumer Rights and Corporation Responsibility adopted by the General Board, February 14, 1972.)

Presbyterian Church in the U.S.

In a resolution on Southern Africa taken from the 1972 General Assembly Minutes the racial situations and foreign investment contributions to the continuation of apartheid were assessed. The General Assembly then recommended "that individual Christians, sessions, churches, presbyteries, synods, boards and agencies be urged: (a) to study the total Southern African situation, lifting in prayer the hope that some equitable resolution of the injustices perpetrated by white against black will be found before bloody violence erupts, with unimaginable suffering borne by both blacks and whites; (b) to examine their personal investment portfolios to see what is the most responsible use of the shares they may hold in companies whose Southern African investments help maintain oppressive systems in radical contradiction to the gospel of brotherhood; (c) that as churchmen seek facts about these companies with investments in Southern Africa, they inquire specifically about pay inequities between black and white workers, lack of job mobility for blacks and other unjust employment practices; (d) that American Churchmen devise strategies to influence American investments in Southern Africa, with the intention of bringing economic justice to the black majorities in these countries."
(Minutes of the 1972 General Assembly, Presbyterian Church in the U.S., pp. 183, 184, supplied by letter from Dr. Joseph L. Roberts.)

The PCUS national office has also been in communication with IBM over its investment policies in South Africa.

Protestant Episcopal Church

In June, 1966, the Executive Council "Resolved, that the Executive Council, all diocesan councils, and all parish vestries be asked to consider the moral dilemma in which we are placed by our present investment policies whereby we profit from investments in South Africa; and to this end we ask members of our Church, including those who hold responsible positions in the financial and industrial world, to consider what steps can be taken to deal with this complex situation." (Resolution of the Executive Council, June, 1966.)

In 1967 the General Convention recognized "the moral dilemma we face by virtue of our investments in South Africa" and called upon the officials of this church "to exercise responsible stewardship over the funds entrusted to their care." (Report of the Committee on Social Criteria for Investments, submitted to the Executive Council of the Episcopal Church, Fall, 1971, p. 1.)

A special committee of twelve members was appointed by the Presiding Bishop at the direction of the Executive Council in 1968 to study and report on "the question of the responsible stewardship and use by the Church of its financial resources and investments in banks and industries doing business with and in southern African nations. . . ." (Resolution of the Executive Council concerning financial relations with Southern Africa, May, 1968.)

Also in 1968 the Executive Council directed the Executive and Finance Committee to apply certain criteria in relation to the investments of the Executive Council in companies and banks doing business in Southern Africa. Generally, the criteria (1) establish the presence of the business or bank in Southern Africa; (2) determine how significant the involvement is; (3) if significant involvement, "what is the effect in promoting such things as: Education of Africans; Development of family life; Labor-management relations and the collective bargaining process; Increased skills of the Africa labor force and integration into higher levels of leadership; Equalization of wage scales, pension provisions, and social security; Hospitalization and other benefits; Breaking down of the pass-law system and other restrictions." Further, the council resolved to consider investments in companies and banks that would promote the welfare or education of all the people of Southern Africa without regard to race. (Resolution of the Executive Council concerning investments in Southern Africa, December, 1968.)

In May, 1969, the Executive Council directed that council funds be withdrawn from banks participating in the Consortium Credit to the Government of South Africa if that loan were renewed, but the request for renewal was never made. (Report of the Committee on Social Criteria for Investments, submitted to the Executive Council of the Episcopal Church, Fall, 1971, p. 1.)

The Ad Hoc Committee on Companies Doing Business in Southern Africa made its final report to the Executive Council on October 5, 1970, listing the companies essential to the economy of the Republic of South Africa in which church funds were most heavily invested, but advising against divestment "at this time." (p. 2.)

The Committee on Social Criteria was organized in September, 1970, to replace and expand upon the duties of the ad hoc committee. If first discussed

South Africa proposed stockholder actions in January, 1971, and on January 29, Bishop Hines, acting for the committee, filed a stockholder resolution with General Motors concerning its involvement in South Africa. (pp. 2-3.)

In 1971 the Committee on Social Criteria recommended that for its second year (1971-1972) it, in concert with other denominations and concerned groups: "A) Continue talks with General Motors and other companies; B) Continue talks with the Sate Department; C) Prepare and submit resolutions and one proxy statement for companies which practice discrimination; D) Convene southern Africa consultation; E) Assess the Polaroid experiment; F) Develop an international strategy; G) Participate in a joint investigative trip in southern Africa; H) Purchase polaroid stock; I) Consider filing stockholder proposals with AMAX over its activities in South West Africa." (pp. 10-11.)

The Reformed Church in America

The Reformed Church in America published a statement in 1967 attacking the Dutch Reformed Church in South Africa for its support of the government policy of apartheid. The South African Church then responded with "A Plea for Understanding," which was rebutted by the American body.

A South African Committee has been established as part of the Christian Action Commission of the Reformed Church and it has endorsed corporate responsibility proposals but as yet has not succeeded in getting them passed by the General Synod. However, the General Synod has approved: "That the Treasurer of General Synod, under the direction of the General Secretary, be responsible for reviewing all proxies and recommending any action he deems warranted to the appropriate officers of the corporations holding title to the investments." ("Corporations" are understood to mean the boards and agencies of the denomination holding stock.) (Information obtained from a phone conversation with a letter from Herman Harmelink III, Minister, The Reformed Church, Poughkeepsie, New York.)

Unitarian Universalist Association of Churches and Fellowships

In action taken at the UUA General Assembly in Hollywood, Florida, in May, 1966, the following statement was issued concerning apartheid:

"The Unitarian Universalist Association:

Deplores the refusal of the Government of South Africa to comply with the resolutions of the United Nations Security Council and the General Assembly and its continued implementation of the policies of apartheid,
Urges the Governments of the United States and Canada to continue to comply fully with all the resolutions of the Security Council on this question and continue to halt the sale and delivery to South Africa of arms and ammunition of all types,
Suggests that the Governments of the United States and Canada vote for increased diplomatic and economic sanctions against South Africa by member nations of the United Nations and subsequently enforce these sanctions."

In action taken at the UUA General Assembly in Dallas in June, 1972, the General Assembly recommended that the Board of Trustees cooperate in the development of programs to foster social responsibility in the investment of endowment funds and in the corporate management of companies in whose securities they invest and "designate as a principal priority the development of a program concerned with the role of American industry in the continuing exploitation and oppression of Blacks in Southern Africa, by means of an intensive program of education conducted by the UUA through the Department of Education and Social Concern and affiliated members."

In cooperation with the Westchester Clergy and Laymen Concerned, the Unitarian Fellowship of Northern Westchester (Rev. Rudolf Gelsey, R.F.D. 2, South Bedford Road, Mt. Kisco, New York) has approached IBM in hopes of discussion on a series of concerns. One of these is as follows:

". . . we propose a reexamination of the I.B.M.'s involvement in South Africa. . . . It is well established that the South African regime totally oppresses the majority black population and that American capital is one of the mainstays of that oppressive regime. We propose that I.B.M. assume leadership in the American business community in withdrawing the vital support of American business from the South African regime. In this area, we support the efforts of the Corporate Information Center of the National Council of Churches and the World Council of Churches." (Letter of September 29, 1972, from Westchester Clergy and Laymen Concerned to Mr. Thomas Watson, I.B.M., Armonk, New York, p. 1.)

United Church of Christ

In a resolution adopted by the Eighth General Synod on June 28, 1971, the General Synod "reaffirms its deepest concern for all human beings in the quest for Whole People in a Whole World. It urges upon the constituency of the United Church of Christ, personal and corporate, a sense of outrage in the continuation and reinforcement of any and all institutions that divest any people of their God-given right to peace, security, and liberty.

"In 1965 the General Synod stated that the United States should actively support United Nations recommendations for economic sanctions as a remedial action pending changes in apartheid, and that U.S. corporations should be encouraged to make known their opposition to apartheid in as effective a manner as possible. The General Synod further urged the church membership to provide wider discussion of this problem in local churches and communities, and otherwise to express concern to their representatives in government.

"In 1969 the Gerneral Synod passed a specific resolution urging withdrawal of funds from banks 'doing business with South Africa.'"

The 1971 resolution further urged members, local churches, associations, conferences, instrumentalities, and boards of the United Church of Christ: "1. To urge the U.S. Government and her NATO allies (a) to refrain from any sales of arms to South Africa and Portugal; (b) to end those military, diplomatic, and economic practices and policies which support minority rule and colonialism, especially the preferential sugar quota; (c) to seek new ways to press for racial justice in Southern Africa. 2. To discourage United States tourism to Portugal and to the Republic of South Africa. 3. To examine the role which U.S. Corporations play in Southern Africa in maintaining the status quo; furthermore, to use their various resources, including the leverage of their investment and stock ownership powers, to press these companies to develop vigorous policies and practices in employment, compensation, public relations attitudes, and business operations which will challenge repressive and unjust conditions. If their activities appear to strengthen colonial or racist oppression rather than change it, they should be pressed to withdraw. 4. To support the humanitarian programs of Southern African liberation organizations through the World Council of Churches. 5. (a) To educate themselves about the situation in Southern Africa, the serious implications of this situation, and the extent to which the United States is involved; (b) to hold seminars, conferences, and educational workshops on this issue." (All the above quotes are taken from "A Resolution Adopted By the Eighth General Synod on Southern Africa," June 28, 1971.)

United Methodist Church

"In early 1965 the Board of Missions came to the following decisions: As a step toward the implementation of section eleven of the Methodist Charter of Racial Policies - 'We will . . . support world-wide movements for basis human rights and fundamental freedom for peoples everywhere' that the Board of Missions will join . . .efforts to reinforce and publicize the struggle of responsible individuals and organizations in South Africa: to provide relief and assistance to persons persecuted by the Government of South Africa and their families. "They also urged businesses with operations in South Africa and the U.S. government to register opposition to the policy of apartheid." (Statement by the Board of Missions, United Methodist Church, to the Special Committee on the Policies of Apartheid, UN General Assembly, A/AC/15/L. 248, May 6, 1969, p. 4.)

In January, 1968, the Board of Missions in its annual meeting reaffirmed the use of its resources in a positive manner to "assist in the improvement of the conditions of human life, particularly among those who have been oppressed for racial reasons." Further: "While recognizing the ambiguity and complexity of judgements in this area such stewardship of resources may involve the withdrawal of support from institutions, corporations, and programs which by their economic or other actions support governments in power which uphold the principle of apartheid or otherwise exert suppression of black Africans." Later in 1968 the Board withdrew a $10 million investment portfolio from the First National City Bank, protesting the bank's financial support of the government of South Africa. ("Actions Related to the Southern Africa Concern of the Board of Missions," p. 1., available from the Board of Missions, United Methodist Church, 475 Riverside Drive, New York, New York.)

In 1971 the World Division of the United Methodist Board of Missions strongly endorsed H.R. 600, the bill introduced by Rep. Bingham in the House of Representatives to amend the Sugar Act of 1948 to terminate the quota for South Africa. Although this bill was unsuccessful, the sugar quota will come up for renewal again in 1973. ("South Africa Sugar Quotation Resolution," World Division of the United Methodist Church Board of Missions, February 13, 1971.)

The General Conference of the United Methodist Church Board of Missions issued a "Statement on Southern Africa" in April, 1972. In it it reaffirmed the official position of the United Methodist Church relative to the brotherhood of man adopted in May, 1968, which stated: "Our Lord Jesus Christ teaches us that all men are brothers. His gospel makes no room for the arbitrary distinctions and expressions of racial or group prejudice. . . . 'In Christ Jesus . . . there is neither Jew nor Greek, there is neither slave nor free, there is neither male nor female.'" It further recommended that the General Conference affirm the intent of the 1968 and 1969 statements on Southern Africa:

> . . . We are convinced that the struggle for freedom by the majority population in Southern Africa will be won. As a church, we support these signs of freedom and those groups and individuals in the countries that recognize and act on the claims of the Gospel. . . .
>
> . . . We see, as Christians, a strategic mission issue. We see mission in terms of assisting forces that are likely to bring changes leading to justice and peace. . . .
>
> . . . We urge that our church be mobilized with all our energies, that our government and industry be sensitized to our inescapable involvement and obligations in Southern Africa. . . . (Excerpted and paraphrased from 1968 and 1969 statements of the Board of Missions, the United Methodist Church.)

and

> "We recommend that the United Methodist Church continue the support of liberation movements, in the non-military aspects of their program, including education, medical assistance and special assistance to women and children." ("Statement on Southern Africa," April, 1972, pp. 1-2.)

Noting also the United Nations resolutions concerning the persecution of persons in South Africa for their opposition to apartheid, the involvement of the U.S. corporate system in helping to maintain the status quo, and the exploitation of these territories by foreign interests:

> "We, therefore, discourage the United Methodist Church from investing in those U.S. companies which invest in Southern Africa and urge the United Methodist Church to continually assess the role of the companies in Southern Africa, and if it is ascertained that they support minority rule, press those companies to cease doing business in those areas." (p. 3.)

Minimally:

We urge that income from investments in businesses operating in South Africa be used to enlarge the Board of Missions' Southern Africa Fund. (paraphrased, p. 3.)

We urge the UMC to seek from all U.S. corporations doing business in Southern Africa, the facts of their involvement in Southern Africa including the history of such involvement, relations with workers and with the governments and ask that these facts be public. (p. 3.)

We urge that all U.S. corporations in Southern Africa adopt affirmative action policies for equal employment as they are required to do in the U.S. (paraphrased, p. 3.)

We recommend that the United Methodist Church urge all U.S. corporations doing business in Southern Africa to contribute a sum equal to a substantial portion of the amount which they are required to pay yearly to the governments of the area in taxes:

- to the educational, medical and welfare programs of liberation movements,
- to those organizations supportive of racial justice and basic social change,
- to the UN Trust Fund for Southern Africa for the victims of racism and colonialism. (p. 3.)

United Presbyterian Church

The 177th General Assembly (1965) of the United Presbyterian Church called upon South Africa to "abandon its dangerous Apartheid policy and took certain actions appealing to both the church and the United States government for a review of American involvement in South Africa. The 179th General Assembly (1967) adopted a pronouncement on Southern Africa which again urged gradual disengagement by American firms and the United States government from direct and indirect participation in the blatant injustices south of the Zambesi River." ("The Task Force on Southern Africa," COCAR reports to the 181st and 182nd General Assembly, Journal, Part I, p. 1.) The 181st General Assembly (1969) directed the Council on Church and Race to form an inter-agency Task Force on Southern Africa. Among its duties was the responsibility to "examine the corporations and banks from which Boards, Agencies and Institutions now purchase goods and services or in which they have investments to ascertain what if any connections these firms and banks have in Southern Africa; to inquire of such firms what their present policies and practices are with regard to racial discrimination in Southern Africa; and upon finding racial discrimination to apply effective pressure for change. Firms refusing to make changes will be reported to the proper Boards, Agencies and Institutions who shall immediately initiate action to withdraw from business dealings and to divest themselves of investments in these firms." (p. 3.)

The 182nd General Assembly (1970) passed the recommendations of the Standing Committee on Church and Race that:
1. the 182nd General Assembly affirm that the Church of Jesus Christ is called upon to arouse herself and espouse the cause of black people who are the majority in Southern Africa and who seek justice, freedom and the right of self-determination. . . . .
2. the 182nd General Assembly affirm that the Christian community in this nation must analyze the implications of the U.S. Government's policy for this region, and the implications of the U.S. corporate economic power as it is involved in this region;
3. the 182nd General Assembly affirm that we must determine what tools, what leverage or influence for good we have to hand, such as our own corporate investments and our legitimate access to government and world opinion, and we must unrelentingly advocate self-determination, justice and human development for all Africans and oppose colonialism, racism, and repression wherever these occur.

In furtherance of these goals:
1. the 182nd General Assembly directed the Southern Africa Task Force to review continually United Presbyterian involvement in and financial support of programs in Southern Africa;

2. the 182nd General Assembly directed that the United Presbyterian Church take appropriate steps to reduce financial and personnel support by the Church and others of programs in Rhodesia to an absolute minimum in the light of the fact that Rhodesia is a country internationally condemned as racist;

3. the 182nd General Assembly directed the Task Force to continue to examine corporations and banks with which United Presbyterian boards, agencies and institutions now invest or trade to ascertain what, if any, connections these corporations and banks have in Southern Africa and to make appropriate recommendations to the boards, agencies, and institutions as to what actions are necessary to make their investment or purchasing policies consistent with the positions of the General Assembly against apartheid, racism and colonialism in Southern Africa;

4. the 182nd General Assembly reaffirmed the 181st General Assembly mandate that the Task Force on Southern Africa "seek practical ways in which the churches can give immediate material and moral support to those engaged in the struggle to secure justice and freedom for the people of Southern Africa." Such support could include medical services, support for families of detainees, education for children, housing and scholarships which are related to Southern Africa liberation movements. (Excerpted and paraphrased from "The Task Force on Southern Africa", COCAR reports to the 181st and 182nd General Assembly, Journal, Part I, pp. 675-689(1969) and 649-655(1970) respectively.)

Now in its fourth year, the Task Force on Southern Africa has been involved in a wide-ranging variety of responsibilities in coordinating the United Presbyterian response to racism, apartheid, and colonialism in Southern Africa. It monitors ecumenical programs that operate in Southern Africa, it helped organize the Ecumenical Commission of Southern Africa (ECOSA), it has been involved with legislative issues in Washington, it encourages study of United Nations materials, it encourages exchange visits by black South African clergy, and has been very active on the question of U.S. corporate involvement in Southern Africa. ("Report of the Southern Africa Task Force," 184th General Assembly, 1972.)

World Council of Churches

The situation of racial oppression in Southern Africa has been a major concern for the WCC since its inception. Throughout the years various policy statements have emanated from the Assembly, the Central Committee, and other constituent parts of the Council. The following are some of the statements directly related to the subject of foreign investments in Southern Africa:

"Racism is linked with economic and political exploitation. The churches must be actively concerned for the economic and political well-being of exploited groups so that their statements and actions may be relevant. In order that victims of racism may regain a sense of their own worth and be enabled to determine their own future, the churches must make economic and educational resources available to under-privileged groups for their development to full participation in the social and economic life of their communities. They should also withdraw investments from institutions that perpetuate racism." (Fourth Assembly of the WCC at Uppsala, Sweden, 1968.)

In February, 1969, the Finance Committee of the WCC approved the following directive to its investment managers: "The desire of the WCC is that the portfolio shall be built of investments in concerns engaged in socially constructive activities and it is therefore required that <u>no resources be invested in concerns which are</u> primarily or wholly engaged in: a) production or handling of armaments; or b) activities in or trade with South Africa or Rhodesia."

The Commission of the Programme to Combat Racism (PCR) in its policy statement of April, 1972, under the caption of "The role of International Finance" stated: "A special feature of the Southern Africa conflict is the extent of external support given to the racist system by international corporations and banks (through investment, loan, etc.). <u>Recommended</u> that PCR should publicize the extent and nature of this involvement and select targets for appropriate action by the WCC, its member churches and related bodies."

In August, 1972, the 120-member Central Committee passed a resolution instructing "its Finance Committee and its Director of Finance: i) to sell forthwith existing holdings and to make no investments after this date in corporations which, according to information available to the Finance Committee and the Director of Finance, are directly involved in investment in or trade with any of the following countries: South Africa, Namibia, Zimbabwe, Angola, Mozambique and Guiné-Bissao; and ii) to deposit none of its funds in banks which maintain direct banking operations in these countries." (World Council of Churches, Central Committee Meeting, August 13-23, 1972, Utrecht, Netherlands.)

B. U.S. CONGRESSIONAL ACTIONS

<u>Sugar Act of 1971</u> - To ensure that American consumers have a cheap and stable supply of sugar, Congress since 1961 has assigned quotas to domestic and foreign sugar-producing areas. South Africa was assigned a quota of 57,745 short tons out of the total foreign quota of approximately 5,000,000 short tons in 1971. Of the South African sugar imported by the U.S., 92.4 percent of the profits go to white growers and millers, while only 7.9 percent benefit Africans and Indians (<u>Congressional Record</u>, July 27, 1971). Therefore, our expendable assignment of a quota to South Africa amounts to a subsidy to white South Africans and an act of complicity with the economic and political system of the minority government.

HOUSE - Last year Representative Diggs was prepared to offer an amendment to strike the quota to South Africa from the Sugar Act, but the Rules Committee recommended a "closed rule" to prohibit amendments from being made on the floor. On June 10, 1971, after a debate focusing on the desirability of the South African sugar quota, the House adopted a closed rule by a vote of 213 to 166. Representatives Diggs, Dow, Bingham, Howard, Reid, Anderson, Morse, Madden, and Gonzalez spoke in opposition to the closed rule and in favor of striking the quota for South Africa.

SENATE - Senator Harris made a motion in the Senate Finance Committee to delete the quota for South Africa from the committee bill, which was defeated 9 to 6. Senator Kennedy offered two amendments on the floor of the Senate on July 27 and July 28, first that the South African quota should be eliminated entirely, and second that the quota be suspended until the President determined that (1) the government of South Africa does not discriminate against any American officials or private citizens with respect to their freedom of movement into and within South Africa; (2) substantial benefits from the quota will be received by field and mill workers; and (3) substantial progress is being made toward recognition of fundamental basic human rights, and that the South African quota be reallocated to American domestic producing areas. Both of these amendments were defeated, the first by a vote of 45 to 47 and the second by 42 to 55. In favor of striking South Africa's quota were Kennedy, Brooke, Cooper, Cranston, Harris, Javits, Ribicoff, Stevenson, Tunney, Bayh, Case, Hart, McGovern, Mondale, Muskie, Pell, and Williams. The leaders of the opposition were Long, Bennett, Inouye, and Fong.

<u>What Lies Ahead</u> - On the House side, Congressman Diggs will continue to probe on the African issues through the hearing process. These will probably focus on Namibia, American aid to development in Africa, trade and monetary patterns, and possible leaks in the arms embargo against South Africa and Portugal. The Diggs bill on fair employment practices by American corporations that are investors in South Africa should be heard by one of the subcommittees of the Judiciary Committee, which will now be headed by Congressman Rodino. The sugar quota bill will come up again for renewal in September, 1973.

On the Senate side, the Senate Foreign Relations Committee will begin its probe of multinational corporations. Staff has been hired for the $200,000 study, and the director has expressed an interest in the views of those concerned about the effect of U.S. corporations on Third World economies and in South Africa.

Contact the Washington Office on Africa (see section on Research/Action Groups) for further information on the legislative scene.

C. UNITED NATIONS ACTIONS

The Security Council of the United Nations first seriously considered the question of apartheid in the aftermath of the March 21, 1960, shooting of peaceful African demonstrators in Sharpeville and adopted a resolution on April 1, 1960, recognizing that the situation in South Africa had led to international friction and if continued might endanger international peace and security. It called upon the South African government "to initiate measures aimed at bringing about racial harmony based on equality. . . and to abandon its policies of apartheid and racial discrimination."

The council considered the situation again in 1963 and 1964 and adopted four resolutions. It recognized that the situation in South Africa was seriously disturbing international peace and security and solemnly called on all states to cease supply of arms to South Africa. It also provided for the establishment of an educational and training program for South Africa.

In July, 1970, the council adopted a further resolution condemning violations of the arms embargo and calling upon all states to strengthen the arms embargo and observe it strictly.

In December, 1970, the General Assembly adopted a resolution at the recommendation of the Special Committee on Apartheid condemning apartheid and all its repressive restrictions and criticizing the continued cooperation by certain states and foreign economic interests with South Africa in military, economic, political, and other fields. All states were urged to terminate diplomatic relations, military, economic, technical, and other cooperation, and cultural, educational, sporting, and other exchanges. They were also asked to ensure that companies registered in their countries and their nationals comply with the United Nations resolutions on this question.

On the recommendation of the Special Committee, the General Assembly, in November, 1971, appealed to all national and international trade union organizations to intensify their action against apartheid by: a) discouraging the emigration of skilled workers to South Africa; b) taking appropriate action in connection with the infringements of trade union rights and the persecution of trade unionists in South Africa; c) exerting maximum pressure on foreign economic and financial interests which are profiting from racial discrimination against non-white workers in South Africa; and d) cooperating with other organizations engaged in the international campaign against apartheid.

On November 15, 1972, the General Assembly adopted resolution 2923 A-E (XXVII), which called on the government of South Africa immediately to put an end to all forms of physical and mental torture and other acts of terror against opponents of apartheid under detention and imprisonment and requested the Special Committee on Apartheid to take appropriate steps to promote an international campaign against repression, maltreatment, and torture. The maltreatment and torture resolution, 2923 A (XXVII), was adopted with 121 member states in favor, one against (South Africa), and one abstention (Portugal). The other resolutions, 2923 B-E (XXVII), to intensify the international campaign against apartheid in South Africa and to assist the victims of apartheid, also passed by overwhelming majorities.

D. RESOURCES

Research/Action Groups

Africa Information Service
112 West 120 Street
New York, N. Y. 10027
212/850-4070

Since the Africa Research Group has disbanded, the Africa Information Service will be taking over some of its functions. Although it is doing no research specifically on Southern Africa now, it plans to do some in the future. AIS actively works on educating Americans about Southern Africa.

Africa Research Group

The A.R.G. published research on Africa from a radical perspective, but as it has recently disbanded, its material must now be obtained from the Africa Information Service or from the New World Resource Center, 2546 North Halsted Chicago, Illinois 60614.

The African American Institute
866 United Nations Plaza
New York, N. Y. 10017
212/421-2500

The African American Institute is the wealthiest and largest U.S. private organization working to further African development and to increase American understanding of African economics, culture, and politics and of such issues as human rights and racial equality. Informing Americans about Southern African issues has been of increasing importance even though the institute does not take positions on policy issues. Africa Report regularly carries articles and commentary about developments in and U.S. relations with Southern Africa. AAI's African Policy Information Center has focused on Southern African issues for foundations, universities, and other major institutional investors whose portfolios include stock in U.S. companies working in Southern Africa.

The African Studies Association
218 Shiffman Center
Brandeis University
Waltham, Mass. 02154

A nonprofit membership organization open to all with scholarly or professional interest in Africa, its members receive African Studies Review (tri-annually), the ASA Newsletter (bimonthly), and Issue: A Quarterly Journal of African Opinion.

America Committee on Africa
164 Madison Avenue
New York, N. Y. 10016
212/532-3700

ACOA is the largest U.S. organization that has worked consistently for the longest period on the questions of apartheid and colonialism in Southern Africa. A wide variety of literature and films is available from them.

American corporations that have published or will soon publish brief papers concerning their Southern African operations:

Caterpillar Tractor Co., Peoria, Ill. 61602
Gulf Oil Corp., Gulf Oil Building, Pittsburg, Pa. 15230
General Motors Corp., 3044 West Grand Boulevard, Detroit, Mich. 48202
International Business Machines, Old Orchard Road, Armonk, N.Y. 10504
International Telephone and Telegraph, 320 Park Ave., New York, N.Y. 10022
Minnesota Mining and Manufacturing Co., 3M Center, Maplewood, St. Paul, Minn. 55101
Mobil Oil Corp., 150 West 42 Street, New York, N. Y. 10017
Newmont Mining Corp., 300 Park Avenue, New York, N. Y. 10022
Polaroid Corp., Cambridge, Mass. 02138
Texaco, Inc., 135 East 42 Street, New York, N. Y. 10017
Xerox Corp., Stamford, Conn. 06904

California Legislature
Sacramento, Calif. 95814

Legislation will be introduced into the 1973 legislative session by Assemblyman John L. Burton, Chairman of the Rules Committee, concerning the State of California's economic involvement with firms operating in Southern Africa.

Center on International Race Relations
Graduate School of International Studies
University of Denver
Denver, Col. 80210

The center was founded in 1969 to undertake systematic studies of international race relations, which exert increasing internal and external pressures on U.S. foreign policy.

Church Project on U.S. Investments in
        Southern Africa - 1973
475 Riverside Drive, Room 845
New York, N. Y. 10027
212/870-2282

The church project is a joint effort of seven denominations: United Church of Christ, Protestant Episcopal, United Presbyterian, American Baptist Convention, United Methodists, Unitarian Universalist Association, and the National Council of Churches. The separate agencies within each denomination and the church project itself publish and distribute material on various Southern African concerns.

Corporate Information Center
475 Riverside Drive, Room 846
New York, N. Y. 10027
212/870-2295

CIC is a research and interpretative office within the National Council of Churches concerned primarily with church investments and issues of corporate responsibility. The center has published extensive "briefs" of targeted companies as background to the Church Project on U.S. Investments in Southern Africa.

Council for Christian Social Action
United Church of Christ
289 Park Avenue
New York, N. Y. 10011
212/GR5-2121

The council has prepared a packet, "U.S. Business in Southern Africa" ($1.50), as background for churches, other organizations, and individuals studying the role of U.S. business in South Africa.

Episcopal Churchmen for South Africa
14 West 11 Street
New York, N. Y. 10011
212/477-0066

ECSA publishes a number of papers, studies, and occasional magazines on recent and relevant issues on the U.S. and Southern Africa with action suggestions particularly geared toward church people and organizations.

Gulf Boycott Coalition
Box 123
D.V. Station
Dayton, Ohio 45406
513/276-4077

Founded in July, 1971, the GBC turns out literature and coordinates campaigns to boycott Gulf products because of its investment in Angola and its support of Portuguese colonialism there.

Information Service of South Africa
655 Madison Avenue
New York, N. Y. 10021

This official agency of the Republic of South Africa offers free materials with background information and issue discussion from the government's point of view.

Interreligious Foundation for Community
    Organization (IFCO)
475 Riverside Drive, Room 560
New York, N. Y. 10027
212/870-3151

IFCO is a church foundation through which 13 national denominations provide direct grants and technical and organizational assistance to community groups servicing minority and low-income people. Recently IFCO has begun working specifically on Southern Africa.

New World Resource Center
2546 North Halsted
Chicago, Ill. 60614
213/348-3370

The NWRC provides a literature distribution center on Southern African information for the Midwest. Many of its members are also involved in action campaigns on Southern Africa.

Polaroid Revolutionary Workers' Movement
Box 8487
Boston, Mass. 02114

Black workers who challenged Polaroid's involvement in South Africa.

Social Criteria Committee
Episcopal Church
815 Second Avenue
New York, N. Y. 10017

The committee coordinates actions for the Episcopal Church on corporate responsibility and Southern Africa.

Southern Africa Committee
244 West 27 Street, 5th Floor
New York, N. Y. 10010

The Southern Africa Committee has a variety of information and literature available and in addition produces Southern Africa, the only monthly magazine in North America focusing on this subject. It is available at an annual subscription rate of $5.00. The committee is open to volunteer membership and also engages in study, education, and action aimed at changing U.S. involvements and broadening support for the liberation movements.

Southern Africa Task Force
United Presbyterian Church
475 Riverside Drive, Room 918
New York, N. Y. 10027
Attn: Don Wilson

The task force coordinates efforts on Southern Africa for the UPUSA, including corporate campaigns.

United Nations Association
833 United Nations Plaza
New York, N. Y. 10017

The UNA has published a booklet called "Southern Africa: Proposals for Americans" ($1.00).

Unit on Apartheid
Department of Political and Security
                    Council Affairs
United Nations
New York, N. Y. 10017
212/754-1234

The Unit on Apartheid was established in the Secretariat of the U.N. in pursuance of General Assembly Resolution 2114 A (XXI) of October 26, 1966, "to deal exclusively with the policies of apartheid in consultation with the Special Committee on Apartheid in order that maximum publicity may be given to the evils of those policies." It produces a series of occasional papers called "Notes and Documents" for more advanced readers. The United Nations Office of Public Information carries lengthier studies and publishes a quarterly magazine, Objective Justice.

U.S. House of Representatives
Committee on Foreign Affairs
Subcommittee on Africa
Washington, D. C. 20515

Transcripts of hearings of this committee and special reports of study missions to Southern Africa are available from the Government Printing Office, Washington, D. C. 20402.

Washington Office on Africa
110 Maryland Avenue
Washington, D. C. 20002
202/546-7961

This organization is sponsored by four churches and the American Committee on Africa, producing information concerning U.S. Congressional legislation about Southern Africa and organizing lobbying actions for these Congressional actions. It should be contacted to help organize or unify lobbying actions.

Washington Task Force on African Affairs
P. O. Box 13033
Washington, D. C. 20009

This task force is a nonprofit membership organization functioning as an information, education, monitoring, research, and action group to collect data and furnish analyses relevant to U. S. African relations.

World Council of Churches Programme
                to Combat Racism
475 Riverside Drive, Room 439
New York, N. Y. 10027

This office produces a number of "Profiles" dealing with South African issues and interpretative material on World Council of Churches decisions.

Youth Organization for Black Unity
P. O. Box 20826
Greensboro, N. C. 27420

Originally called the Student Organization for Black Unity, YOBU has chapters throughout the U. S. organizing Black College students to engage in community and school actions and raising the issues of U.S. Black struggles and African liberation struggles. It issues the newsletter African World.

Publications	Available from
"Apartheid and Imperialism: A study of U.S. Corporate Involvement in South Africa," in Africa Today, September-October, 1970	American Committee on Africa 164 Madison Avenue New York, N. Y. 10016
"Apartheid in Practice" - presents 200 statements - on the home, family, residence, work, religion, race, and color - intended to provide a clear and accurate description of apartheid - $ .75 Sales No. OPI/404	United Nations Sales Section Room LX-2322 New York, N. Y. 10017
"A Principle in Torment," - a series designed to record the violations of the human rights of millions in Southern Africa today and UN efforts to help them; in the series are "The U.N. and Southern Rhodesia" ($.75, Sales No. E.69.1.26), "The U.N. and Portuguese Administered Territories" ($.75, Sales No. E.70.1.7), and "The U.N. and Namibia" ($.60, Sales No. E.71.1.4)	United Nations Sales Section Room LX-2322 New York, N. Y. 10017
"Background Information: Re Gulf and the Ohio Conference, United Churches of Christ" $1.00	Ohio Conference United Church of Christ 41 Croswell Road Columbus, Ohio 43214
"Background Readings for Institutional Investors," vols. I and II, 1972 - $35.	African American Institute 866 UN Plaza New York, N. Y. 10017
"Chrysler, Ford, and General Motors in Africa," 1970 - $1.	Council on Economic Priorities 456 Greenwich Street New York, N. Y. 10013 or Corporate Information Center 475 Riverside Drive, Room 846 New York, N. Y. 10027
"Conflict in Southern Africa" - five position papers arguing for black independence in white-controlled South Africa; and "Africa Speaks" - documents on South African issues from African leaders - $1.25 ea.	Oxfam-America, Inc. 1028 Connecticut Avenue,N.W.,Suite 922 Washington, D. C. 20036 202/659-1791
"Foreign Investment in Apartheid in South Africa" - a paper written by Ruth First (a South African now in exile in London) covering the extent of American and European investment in South Africa, the role of foreign capital, the nature of investment, and how investment strengthens implementation of the government's apartheid policy - (No. 21/72, October, 1972)	Unit on Apartheid Dept. of Political and Security Council Affairs United Nations New York, N. Y. 10017

"Inhuman Conditions in South Africa's Gold Mines," Charles C. Diggs, Jr. (member U.S. House of Representatives and Chairman of its Subcommittee on Africa) - this paper takes the position that the South Africa gold-mining industry is based on a system of exploitation and oppression and as such should not be encouraged; it also stresses the idea that the whole white-supremacy system in South Africa has been backed up by gold (Sales No. 19/72, September, 1972)

Unit on Apartheid
Department of Political and
    Security Council Affairs
United Nations
New York, N. Y. 10017

"Intercom: # 70; Southern Africa: Problems and U. S. Alternatives," September, 1972, published by the Center for War/Peace Studies of the New York Friends Group - $1.50

Intercom
218 East 18 Street
New York, N. Y. 10003

"Is Southern Africa Wisconsin's Business" - $.45

Madison Area Committee on Southern
    Africa
309 North Brooks Street
Madison, Wis. 43715

"Mobil in South Africa" - a report on specific information in various categories requested by the United Church Board of World Ministries in January, 1972, concerning employee makeup by racial categories and employee salaries and benefits, etc.

Mobil Oil Corporation
150 East 42 Street
New York, N. Y. 10017

"Namibia: U. S. Corporate Involvement" - a report by company of U. S. corporate involvement in Namibia (largely mining and oil interests) - $.50

The African Fund
164 Madison Avenue
New York, N. Y. 10016

"Objective: Justice" - each issue of this quarterly UN publication contains a series of articles on the crucial implications of the problems of apartheid, racial discrimination and colonialism - $3.

UN Sales Section
United Nations
New York, N. Y. 10017

"Poverty, Apartheid, & Economic Growth" - Free

Unit on Apartheid
United Nations
New York, N. Y. 10017

"Profits, Politics, & Apartheid," Tim Smith, in American Report - $.25

Corporate Information Center
475 Riverside Drive, Room 846
New York, N. Y. 10027

"Progress Through Separate Development: South Africa in Peaceful Transition" - a compilation of views of members of the South Africa government on the policy of "separate development"

Information Service of South Africa
655 Madison Avenue
New York, N. Y. 10021

"Proxy Resolutions Filed with Newmont Mining Corp. and American Metal Climax" - Free	Episcopal Churchmen for South Africa 14 West 11 Street New York, N. Y. 10011
"Race for Power," prepared by the former African Research Group of Cambridge, Mass. - concerns power relationships in South Africa and is critical of U. S. business and government policy there - $2.	American Committee on Africa 164 Madison Avenue New York, N. Y. 10016
"South Africa and Apartheid" and "Resistance to Apartheid: South Africa and Namibia," Robert Adam DeBaugh ' $.20 ea.	Center for the Study of Power and Peace 110 Maryland Avenue, N.E. Washington, D. C. 20002
"Southern Africa - A Time for Change" - $1.95	Friendship Press 475 Riverside Drive, Room 753 New York, N. Y. 10027
"Southern Africa Issues" - a packet of materials on Southern Africa - $5.	IFCO 475 Riverside Drive, Room 560 New York, N. Y. 10027
Southern Africa magazine - $5. yearly subscription	Southern Africa Committee 244 West 27 Street, 5th floor New York, N. Y. 10010
"Southern Africa: Proposals for Americans" - $1.	UN Association of the U.S.A. 833 UN Plaza New York, N. Y. 10017
"Southern Africa Task Force Proxy Statement on Gulf Oil Corporation" - Free	South African Task Force United Presbyterian Church 110 Maryland Avenue, N.E. Washington, D. C. 20002
"Special Southern Africa Package" - $1.	American Committee on Africa 164 Madison Avenue New York, N. Y. 10016
"The American Corporation in South Africa: an Analysis," Tim Smith - $.50	Council for Christian Social Action United Church of Christ 289 Park Avenue South New York, N. Y. 10016
"The Standard of Living of Africans in South Africa" - Free	Unit on Apartheid United Nations New York, N. Y. 10016 or American Committee on Africa 164 Madison Avenue New York, N. Y. 10016

"The State of California and Southern African Racism: California's Economic Involvement with Firms Operating in Southern Africa" - a report by the California Assembly's Office of Research on the role of the American corporation in South Africa, the extent of California's involvement with corporations that do business in South Africa, and actions that could be taken by California to influence these corporations to discontinue investing and doing business in South Africa

Assembly Office of Research
Library and Courts Building,
  Room 500
Sacramento, Calif. 95814

"Trends, A Journal of Resources," "The Liberation of Southern Africa," Vol. 4, No. 1, September, 1971, and "Big Brother to the World," Vol. 4, No. 7, March, 1972 - $.75 ea.

The Geneva Press
391 Steel Way
Lancaster, Pa. 19107

"Update" - a bi-monthly publication providing background readings and articles of current interest on U. S. corporate investments in Southern Africa - $60./Yr. for non-profit institutions, $90./Yr. for profit institutions

African-American Institute
866 UN Plaza
New York, N. Y. 10017

"U. S. Business in Southern Africa" - a kit providing background materials on the question of the role of U. S. business in Southern Africa - $1.80

Corporate Information Center
475 Riverside Drive, Room 846
New York, N. Y. 10027

"U. S. Business Involvement in Southern Africa" - Hearings before the Subcommittee on Africa of the Committee on Foreign Affairs, House of Representatives, 92nd Congress, 1st session, Parts 1 & 2; also "Faces of Africa: Diversity & Progress; Repression and Struggle" - these are the transcripts of the hearings conducted by Representative Diggs - $3.75 ea. Parts 1 & 2; $1.75 - "Faces of Africa"

Superintendent of Documents
U. S. Government Printing Office
Washington, D. C. 20402

"White Rule in Black Africa: What U. S. Policies in Southern Africa?" - this will provide background information and a presentation of U. S. policy options - $3.

Foreign Policy Association
345 East 46 Street
New York, N. Y. 10017

"Wisconsin Companies in South Africa"

American Committee on Africa
164 Madison Avenue
New York, N. Y. 10016

"Work, Wages, & Apartheid" - Free

Unit on Apartheid
United Nations
New York, N. Y. 10016
  or
American Committee on Africa
164 Madison Avenue
New York, N. Y. 10016

"Workers Under Apartheid" - a document
prepared by the International Defence
& Aid - $1.20

American Committee on Africa
164 Madison Avenue
New York, N. Y. 10016

The following series of briefs concerning specific U. S. corporations actively
engaged in Southern African operations have been prepared by the Corporate
Information Center. They are available at a price of $1.35 each (the Mobil Oil
brief is $.60) from:

> The Corporate Information Center
> 475 Riverside Drive, Room 846
> New York, N. Y. 10027
> 212/870-2295

"General Electric - Apartheid and Business in South Africa"

"General Motors - Apartheid and Business in South Africa"

"Gulf Oil: Portuguese Ally in Angola"

"I.B.M. in South Africa," by Reed Kramer and Tami Hultman

"I. T. & T. - Apartheid and Business in Southern Africa"

"Mobil in the Republic of South Africa: An Analysis of Mobil's Report on
    Operations in South Africa"

"Rhodesian Chrome: A Profile of Union Carbide and Foote Mineral"

"Tsumeb - Mining in Southwest Africa (American Metal Climax - Newmont)"

"The Withdrawal Debate: U.S. Corporations and Southern Africa," June 1973, $ .60

"The Frankfurt Documents: Secret Bank Loans to the South African Government,"
    July 1973, $ .60

Books

Apartheid, Paris, UNESCO, 1972, 256pp., $4. This report is officially titled
"Effects of the Policy of Apartheid in the Fields of Education, Science,
Culture, and the Dissemination of Information in South Africa." The report
explicitly and sharply charges the Republic of South Africa with violation,
in principle and practice, of the Charter of the United Nations. A summary
of the report is available from United Nations Sales Section, Room LX 2322,
New York, N. Y. 10017 (Sales No. 67.I.6, 40¢ prepaid).

Apartheid Axis: The United States and South Africa, William J. Pomeroy, N. Y.,
International Publishers, 1971, 95pp., $1.25. A Marxist survey of U.S.-
South African interaction in Southern Africa.

The Autobiography of an Unknown South African, Naboth Mokgatle, Berkeley, University
of California Press, 1971, 350pp., $7.95. Mokgatle tells of his personal
involvement in trade union activities in the 1930's and 1940's and the
failure to change the relation of the black man to the South African economic
system - a failure attributed to the close link between economic issues and
political power in South Africa.

Cry the Beloved Country, Alan Paton, N. Y., Scribner, 1948, 280pp., $1.95. This
beautiful novel, by an outspoken white South African opponent of apartheid,
is a vivid portrayal of the devastating effects of the transition from
tribal village to urban slum. (See also Paton's later novel Too Late the
Phalarope, as well as Tales from a Troubled Land.)

Down Second Avenue, Ezekiel Mphahlele, London, Faber & Faber, 1959. A first-hand
account of life under apartheid.

Let My People Go, Albert Luthuli, N. Y., World Publishing Co., 1969, 256pp., $3.45.
An illuminating autobiography and description of the lifelong nonviolent
struggle against racial discrimination in South Africa, by ex-chief Luthuli,
winner of the 1960 Nobel Peace Prize.

Mine Boy, Peter Abrahams, London, Heinemann Educational Books, 1946, 252pp., $1.50
This novel deals with the impact of "baasskap" and industrialization on a
simple man from a rural area. It provides a sharp look at the life of a
black South African under white rule.

No Easy Walk to Freedom, Nelson Mandela, London, Heinemann, 1965. Speeches,
articles, and trial addresses of African National Congress leader who is
now serving a life imprisonment term on Robben Island in South Africa.

Oxford History of South Africa, Leonard Thompson and Monica Wilson, eds., London,
Oxford University Press, 1970. An up-to-date history of South Africa, which
is interesting to read, thorough, and well-documented.

The Peoples and Policies of South Africa, Leo Marquard, rev. ed., N. Y., Oxford
University Press, 1969, 266pp., $1.95. A good standard description of
contemporary South Africa, with a unified historical summary. Although
Marquard is opposed to apartheid, the book has been critized as written
from the white point of view, lacking insight into African society and
attitudes.

The Rise of the South African Reich, Brian Bunting, London, Penguin African Series,
1969 (revised). Good account of twentieth-century South Africa, emphasizing
the cycle of resistance and repression.

South Africa and the World: The Foreign Policy of Apartheid, Amry Vandenbosch, Lexington, University of Kentucky Press, 1971, 303pp., $8.50. Focuses on the historical development of South African foreign relations. The author feels the ultimate choice will be between national security and apartheid, that the two are incompatible.

South Africa: Crisis for the West, Colin and Margaret Legum, N. Y., Praeger, 1964, 333pp. $7.50. Although somewhat dated, this book stresses what many still conceive as the central dilemma: the whites can rule but cannot be secure in that rule. The South African crisis cannot be resolved without international intervention.

South Africa: The Peasants Revolt, Govan Mbeki, London, Penguin Books (Africa Library), 1964, 159pp., 95¢. Mbeki argues that either apartheid will be destroyed if the Bantustans are allowed to develop and become urbanized and industrialized or the peasants will revolt.

Southern Africa: A Time for Change, N. Y., Friendship Press, 1969, 94pp., $1.95. An effort to drive home the deepening plight of Southern Africa. It makes no attempt to be unbiased or balanced, presenting instead an urgent message of concern for those forced to live under white domination.

Southern Africa and the United States, William A. Hance, ed., N. Y., Columbia University Press, 1968, 171pp., $7. Four analytical essays dealing with U.S. relations with the Republic of South Africa, Rhodesia, Angola, and Mozambique. The writers disagree somewhat on the possible impact of economic factors, but there is consensus on the meager immediate prospect for rapid improvement in the position of South African blacks.

South West Africa, Ruth First, London, Penguin Books, 1963, 269pp. Although now out of print, it is in many libraries. While it is essentially anti-South Africa in viewpoint, it is essential reading for those especially interested in South-West Africa.

The Struggle for a Birthright, Mary Benson, London, Penguin African Series, 1969 (revised). A valuable history of the African National Congress of South Africa.

Tradition and Change in the Republic of South Africa, Richard B. Ford, N. Y., Holt, Rinehart & Winston, 1968, 86pp., $1.96. An introduction to apartheid, the historical development of South African society, and contemporary conditions.

Films

"Apartheid: Twentieth Century Slavery," 27 min., b&w, 1971, $8. A film charging
        that denial of basic human rights within a country will almost certainly
        lead to massive violence and intervention from outside, threatening world
        peace. Contemporary/McGraw-Hill Films, Princeton Road, Hightstown,
        N.J., 08520.

"Come Back, Africa," 83 min., b&w, 1959, $50. A moving drama of black humiliation
        in South African society, filmed in secret by Lionel Rogosin in Johannesburg.
        The film is bitter and frustrating but also captures the vitality and
        strength of the Africans and the seeds of revolt in the small ghetto meeting
        places beyond the reach of the state. Contemporary/McGraw-Hill Films,
        Princeton Road, Hightstown, N.J., 08521.

"Cry, the Beloved Country," 105 min., 1952, $25 to $50. Alan Paton's memorable
        story of the tragedies of apartheid. Audio Film Classics, 10 Fiske Place,
        Mount Vernon, N.Y.

"The Dumping Grounds," 27 min., b&w, 1970, $50 (20% discount to high schools).
        A documentary on the appalling conditions in the South African "relocation
        centers" set up by the white South African government as part of its "repa-
        triation" scheme. American Documentary Films, 336 West 84 Street, New York,
        N.Y. 10024.

"End of the Dialogue," 45 min., color, 1970, $20. A powerful documentray of
        apartheid in South Africa made secretly by members of the banned Pan-
        Africanist Congress. Some viewers think this film is heavy-handed, over-
        stated, oversimplified, and repetitious, but it engages the viewer and
        leads to intensive discussion. Harold Mayer Productions, 155 West
        72 Street, New York, N.Y. 10023

"Lobola," 26 min., b&w, 1954, $6.75. Depicts personal and social problems confronted
        by millions of South African blacks, showing cultural differences between
        neighboring tribes and the psychological and social adjustments facing a
        village dweller moving to live and work in the city. University of Indiana,
        Audio Visual Center, Bloomington, Ind. 47401.

"South Africa," 27 min., color, 1967, $40 (20% discount for high schools). A look
        at the most industrialized and Europeanized country on the African continent
        and ways in which it has achieved this, largely through the exploitation of
        its black people. Because of the threat of political reprisal, virtually
        no blacks speak, but they are evident as a great silent population.
        American Documentary Films, 336 West 84 Street, New York, N.Y. 10024.

"South African Essay, Part I: Fruit of Fear," 59 min., b&w, 1964, $12. Documents
        the contrast between the conditions of the black majority and the ruling
        white minority in South Africa today.
        "Part II: One Nation, Two Nationalisms," 59 min., b&w, 1964, $12. Takes
        a frank look at apartheid as revealed through the conflicting views of its
        supporters and its enemies. The emphasis is on the relations between blacks
        and the government of South Africa. University of Indiana, Audio Visual
        Center, Bloomington, Ind. 47401.

"White Africa," 40 min., b&w, 1968, $30. Interviews, recordings, and images of white
        South Africa - a striking study. Time Life Films, 43 West 16 Street, New
        York, N.Y. 10003.

"Witnesses," 30 min., color, 1971, $25. Among the new films dealing with South Africa
        it shows the effects of apartheid on the dispossessed majority of blacks.
        American Committee on Africa, 164 Madison Avenue, New York, N.Y. 10016.

E. LIBERATION MOVEMENTS

The liberation movements listed below are recognized by the Organization of
African Unity and are operating in South Africa, Zimbabwe, Namibia, Angola,
Mozambique, and Guinea (Bissau).

The information was taken in part from a list compiled by Sanford Berman,
Makerere Institute of Social Research Library, Kampala, Uganda.

<u>African National Congress of South Africa</u> (ANC)
>   Founded 1912. Banned March 31, 1960, by South African government. Military
>   alliance with ZAPU announced August 13, 1967. <u>Temporary headquarters</u>:
>   P. O. Box 2239, Dar Es Salaam, Tanzania. <u>U.S. address</u>: 28 East 35 Street,
>   New York, N. Y. 10016.

<u>Frente de Libertacao de Mocambique</u> (FRELIMO)
>   Founded June 25, 1962. Armed revolt begun September 25, 1964. First President,
>   Eduardo C. Mondlane, assassinated February 3, 1969. On July 25, 1972, announced
>   the opening of a new military front; operations now cover three provinces.
>   <u>Information department</u>: 201 Nkrumah Street, P. O. Box 15274, Dar Es Salaam,
>   Tanzania. <u>U.S. address</u>: 1133 Broadway, Room 341, New York, N. Y. 10018.

<u>Frente Nacional de Libertacao de Angola</u> (FNLA)
>   Founded 1962 by merger of Uniao dos Populacoes de Angola (UPA) and Partido
>   Democratico Angolano (PDA). November 13, 1972, signed an agreement fully inte-
>   grating its armed forces with those of the MPLA. A Supreme Council for the
>   Liberation of Angola was also agreed upon, with representatives from both MPLA
>   and FNLA. <u>Information department</u>: B.P. 1541, Kinshasa, Zaire.

<u>Movimento Popular de Libertação de Angola</u> (MPLA)
>   Founded December 10, 1956. "Revolutionary action" begun at Luanda, February 4,
>   1961. First Regional Conference held inside Angola August 23, 1968. Agreed to
>   integrate its armed forces with those of the FNLA, November 13, 1972 (see above).
>   <u>Department de l'Information et Propagande</u>: B.P. 2353, Brazzaville, People's
>   Republic of the Congo.

<u>Pan-Africanist Congress of Azania</u> (PAC)
>   Founded April, 1959. Formerly Pan Africanist Congress of South Africa. Banned
>   April, 1960, by South African government. <u>Office</u>: P.O. Box 2412, Dar Es Salaam,
>   Tanzania.

<u>Partido Africano da Independencia da Guine e Cabo Verde</u> (PAIGC)
>   Founded September 9, 1956. Military action launched June 30, 1963. First
>   Congress held inside Guine, February 13, 1964. First Secretary-General,
>   Amilcar Cabral, assassinated January 20, 1973. Controls the country with the
>   exception of the city of Bissau and several fortified towns. <u>Secretariat
>   General</u>, B.P. 298, Conakry, Republic of Guinea.

<u>South-West Africa Peoples' Organization of Namibia</u> (SWAPO)
>   Founded 1958. Armed struggle begun August 26, 1966. <u>Provisional Headquarters</u>:
>   P. O. Box 2603, Dar Es Salaam, Tanzania. <u>U.S. address</u>: 657 West 161 Street,
>   Apt. 3F, New York, N. Y. 10032; telephone: 212/481-0946.

<u>Zimbabwe African National Union</u> (ZANU)
>   Founded 1963. Banned by Rhodesian government. Military activity in the north
>   of the country has increased in 1973. <u>Address</u>: P. O. Box 2331, Lusaka, Zambia.

F. SUPPORT FOR ECONOMIC DISENGAGEMENT FROM SOUTHERN AFRICA

As the pressure of public exposure has grown against the complicity of
U.S. corporations deeply involved in the white-minority ruled countries of
Southern Africa, a fair number of companies have seen the need to develop some
form of rationale in order to justify their initial investment, continued presence
and on-going expansion under the respective systems of apartheid and Portuguese
colonialism, or in violation of United Nations sanctions against Rhodesia.

The corporate response to the public has been a near-universal argument which
seeks to invert the obvious, contending that U.S. companies are really acting
as catalysts for peaceful and constructive change of the racist systems in
Southern Africa. Some have even gone out of their way to quote various persons
purporting to support their position. Yet many persons close to the issue are
hardly convinced by this claim.

What follows is an attempt to set forth significant quotes on the question
of U.S. business in Southern Africa by prominent Americans, black and white, and
by scholars, churchmen and the African peoples themselves. These persons represent
a wide range and diversity of backgrounds; however they are united in their
remarks around a common theme which rejects the delusion that corporate expansion
might lead to significant change in the systematic oppression of the peoples of
Southern Africa. For a host of reasons, most are convinced that the logical
response in support of self-determination should be the immediate disengagement
by U.S. business from the white minority regimes.

***

"The apartheid government grows stronger by the day because of its solvency,
which it gets from foreign investors. If the government had an economic shock,
things might begin to change...." -Mrs. Fatima Meer, an Indian sociologist expressing
the position adopted by the Indian Congress of South Africa, January,1973.

"Our call for disengagement of foreign investment is supported by a large
number of organizations and movements who are against those who advocate violence
as the only solution to gain political and social freedom for the millions of
oppressed and underprivileged people in South Africa." -Sonny Leon, leader of
the Coloured Labour Party, December, 1972.

"The events of the past week have shown how necessary it is to eradicate
apartheid before apartheid eradicates South Africa. We ask for your support in
campaigning for an end to discriminatory practices by foreign firms in South
Africa, or withdraw from the South African economy if they are not prepared to
cease these." -Mr. Paul Pretorius, President, National Union of South African
Students following the massive demonstrations of over 10,000 South African students
and clergy in June, 1972.

"SASO sees foreign investments as giving stability to South Africa's exploitative regime and committing South Africa's trading partners to supporting this regime. For this reason SASO rejects foreign investments.

Further SASO sees the ameliorative experiments like those of Polaroid as at worst, conscience salving and at best, resulting in the creation of a change-resistant middle class amongst the few blacks employed by foreign firms." -1972 statement of policy of the South African Student Organization.

"The economic boycott of South Africa will entail undoubted hardship for Africans. We do not doubt that. But if it is a method which shortens the day of blood, the suffering to us will be a price we are willing to pay. In any case, we suffer already, our children are often undernourished, and, on a small scale (so far), we die at the whim of a policeman." -The late Chief Albert J. Luthuli, Nobel Prize winner and president of the African National Congress.

"The Africans accept sanctions as a price for their freedom and declare as our enemy any person who claims on our behalf that sanctions should be withdrawn to alleviate African suffering through lack of employment. The African National Council calls upon the Security Council and all States which support the cause of human freedom to intensify sanctions." -Methodist Bishop Abel Muzorewa, President, the African National Council of Zimbabwe (Rhodesia), speaking before the Security Council, January, 1972.

"The students and the people of Angola feel that Gulf's exploitation of oil in a colonized and oppressed Angola, is a contribution to the Portuguese colonialism in Angola. Gulf's actions in Angola are a clear indication that its relationship with a future Republic of Angola is in complete jeopardy. The students and the people of Angola request that Gulf removes all its investments from Angola, so as to facilitate the decolonization process and finally, the establishment of good and genuine trade relations between free Angolans and the Corporation." -Mr. Abel Guimares, Representative of the Angolan Student Union in the U.S.A. speaking before the Gulf annual stockholders meeting, 1971.

"Disengagement from these territories (Angola and Mozambique) will no doubt mean financial loss to Gulf, but it will at least provide it with moral leaderhip and set a valuable precedent for social responsibility among other corporations. This leadership will put Gulf in a position of strength especially at this time when African States are beginning to pose incompatible alternatives: either investment in Southern Africa or in independent Africa or in other progressive States, NOT IN BOTH." -Statement of the Executive Secretariat of the Organization of African Unity at the United Nations on Gulf.

"All investments are a direct contribution to the colonial war. I understand how Gulf can say that investment brings progress. Some even say that after independence Africans will have the fruits of this investment. But this progress is not real for the African population. The increased economic interests of Western countries will bring about a need to defend these interests.

To invest in Angola, Mozambique, and Guinea-Bissau is to delay our independence. We are against it.

At the United Nations we stated that we will consider any agreement between Portugal and these companies invalid. These investments are immoral acts against our people." -Marcelino dos Santos, Vice President of FRELIMO, speaking in N.Y., October, 1972.

"...I must report that the idea of doing business in South Africa is <u>totally</u> <u>unacceptable</u>; we could not be true to the basic principles on which we run our business and we should lose our integrity in the process. We should have to operate within a social climate where the colour of a man's skin is his most important attribute and where there is virtually no communication between the races; we should be locked into this system. We should have to operate within an economic climate which is deliberately designed to demoralize and to maintain an industrial helotry; we should in turn profit from such exploitation and ultimately end up with a vested interest in its maintenance." -Mr. Neil Wates, managing director of Wates, Ltd. after visiting South Africa in 1970 and rejecting an invitation to invest in that country.

"I believe that apartheid has to come to an end. I believe that America itself, with its industries and business can no longer underwrite apartheid, whether it be General Motors, Chrysler, Ford, or 300 other companies that are there. The tide is moving in the direction of freedom and opportunity in the world, not in the direction of apartheid, and I am saying that the United States government ought to declare an economic embargo against the Union of South Africa...." -Rev. Dr. Leon Sullivan, Director of General Motors Corporation speaking before "Meet the Press," March 7, 1971.

"We may not be far off from the time when Afro-Americans may respond to companies doing extensive business within southern Africa by declining to buy their products, such as Cadillacs and Chevrolets." -Dr. Karl Gregory, Economics Professor at Oakland University, speaking before the annual meeting of GM, Detroit, May, 1972.

"The basic fallacy in the argument of those who hold out any hope of political change through economic expansionism is that they fail to understand a single fact of history: in authoritarian societies economic forces are controlled by political forces, not the other way about.
It is naive to suppose that South Africa's white society would give up its power, its privileges and its present system of more rapid economic expansion. The change-through-expansion argument should be seen for what it is- a rationalization to justify what is in the best economic interests of those who employ it. Hard-headed political analysis shows that it is almost certain to be a dangerous delusion." -Colin Legum, born and raised in South Africa and widely respected authority on African affairs.

"...one must recognize that apartheid refers properly to the whole system of laws and regulations required to control the nonwhite population. And on this definition, the argument from (economic) growth is simply wrong. Apartheid in this sense has clearly become more harsh and oppressive. The idea that it is somehow "breaking down" is not merely nonsense, but an inversion of the truth. The failure to understand this fact arises from the use of a narrow and misleading definition of the system in the first place. For both these reasons, the case against the argument from growth is strong even before one attempts to analyze its validity in respect to those Africans whom one might expect to benefit from rising wages and incomes." -Sean Gervasi, Research Officer in Economics, Oxford University, England in his paper "Poverty, Apartheid and Economic Growth."

"American business as it increases its economic involvement in South Africa becomes a partner of the South African state as it maintains its control over the great mass of non-white people living within its boundaries. This economic aid has helped South Africa on its way to a self-sufficient economy, has and continues to provide important political and psychological support to the racist system, and now helps the South African economy in its process of economic, military and political expansion into the rest of Africa...To think that a few remedial changes made by U.S. corporations allowing a few more Africans to get skilled positions and to allow some increase in wages (even as the cost of living goes up) will challenge the pattern of apartheid and minority control is naivete of the worst order...Some of us oppose this...Thus we take the view that all sorts of pressure must be brought to bear on U.S. companies to get out of South Africa, and urge truly concerned people to look toward the struggle of the liberation movements and the mass of oppressed peoples for fundamental change in South Africa." -George M. Houser, Executive Director of the American Committee on Africa in "An Open Letter to Ulric Haynes, Jr."

"In sum, a profit motivated initiative by one giant American corporation has seriously diminished the chances of 5.5 million Angolans (or by extension 7 million Mozambicans) for attaining political independence. It has reinforced colonial rule and thus prolonged colonial war in Angola; it has reduced financial pressures that might have pushed Portugal in the direction of granting political rights to Africans...For Gulf then to ignore or dissimulate the enormous political-- and therefore human-- consequences of its entry into Cabinda is for it to compound its moral culpability." -Prof. John Marcum, African expert on Portuguese Africa, from his statement to the Ohio Conference of the United Church of Christ, 1970.

"Each American company operating in South Africa should assess the use to which its products are employed in terms of the government's apartheid policy. Any products used directly in support of apartheid or racial discrimination- particularly those used by the police or military- should be withheld from the South African market." -from a report "Southern Africa: Proposals for Americans" by a National Policy Panel, United Nations Association-USA.

"To the extent that U.S. corporations are agents which support and strengthen the South African economy they are also responsible for the strength of apartheid. A healthy economy strengthens white control, white imperviousness to economic sanctions, white ability to keep blacks oppressed...If indeed U.S. investment in South Africa assists in maintaining the overall system of white control then the only legitimate demand possible by those wishing to challenge that control is that U.S. companies must withdraw from South Africa." -Timothy H. Smith, Executive Secretary, the Interfaith Committee on Social Responsibility in Investments in "The American Corporation in South Africa: An Analysis; A Foundation for Action."

"Most of us believe that American corporations should totally disengage from southern Africa; that the presence of American corporations in which we are shareholders undergirds the system of racism, colonialism and apartheid which prevails in southern Africa...even progressive employment on the part of American companies will not bring the basic changes in society that we support because of our Christian commitment to freedom, justice and self-determination." -from the report by an ecumenical church team of 14 persons who visited South Africa in October- November 1971.

"The basic change sought is majority rule. Accordingly, the Chairman(of the House Foreign Affairs Subcommittee on Africa, Congressman Charles Diggs) supports the principle that U.S. business should disengage from South Africa...External pressure reenforced by the tinderbox nature of South African society may ultimately force withdrawal." -Hon. Charles Diggs, Jr. in "The Faces of Africa: Diversity and Progress; Repression and Struggle" report of Special Study Missions to Africa, February 1971-January 1972.

Africans in downtown Johannesburg board an African bus to take them to a train station on their way home. All travel services in South Africa are segregated, and those for Africans are inadequate and badly crowded.